PAKISTAN

Democracy, Terrorism, and the Building of a Nation

PAKISTAN

Democracy, Terrorism, and the Building of a Nation

IFTIKHAR MALIK

OLIVE
BRANCH
PRESS

First published in 2010 by

OLIVE BRANCH PRESS
An imprint of Interlink Publishing Group, Inc.
46 Crosby Street
Northampton, Massachusetts 01060
www.interlinkbooks.com

Text copyright © 2010 Iftikhar Malik

Published simultaneously in 2010 by New Holland Publishers (UK) Ltd

Library of Congress Cataloging-in-Publication Data
Malik, Iftikhar Haider, 1949–
Pakistan : democracy, terrorism, and the building of a nation / by Iftikhar Malik.
1st American ed.
   p. cm.
Includes bibliographical references and index.
ISBN 978-1-56656-816-6 (pbk.)
1. Pakistan—Politics and government. 2. Civil society—Pakistan.
3. Pakistan—Strategic aspects. 4. Geopolitics—Pakistan. 5. Terrorism—Pakistan.
6. Islamic fundamentalism—Pakistan. I. Title.
DS389.M368 2010
954.9105'3—dc22
                              2010015693

Maps: Stephen Dew

Cover image: A Pakistani displaced man holds his baby next to his tent in Jalozai refugee camp near Peshawar, Pakistan, Monday, June 8, 2009. (AP Photo/ Emilio Morenatti)

Cover design by Juliana Spear

Printed and bound in the United States of America

To request our complete 48-page full-color catalog, please call us toll free at 800-238-LINK, visit our website at www.interlinkbooks.com or write to Interlink Publishing, 46 Crosby Street, Northampton, MA 01060

CONTENTS

PROLOGUE

AS 2009 CAME TO A CLOSE the violence in Pakistan and neighboring Afghanistan seemed to reach unimaginable levels—suicide bombs at security checkpoints, offices, bazaars, and even mosques claimed hundreds of Pakistani lives. The innocent victims of these blasts were ordinary citizens and the perpetrators of these terrible crimes were fellow citizens who followed the same Muslim faith.

On the day that US Secretary of State Hillary Clinton landed in Islamabad for a round of talks with Pakistani authorities, a suicide attack in a busy market in Peshawar, northwestern Pakistan, killed more than a hundred people, including women and children. Exploding next to a mosque in a congested part of the city, the blast on 28 October 2009 destroyed adjacent buildings, burying many people beneath the rubble. The same day, across the border in Kabul, a similar suicide attack on a guesthouse used by UN officials resulted in eight deaths besides the bombers themselves.[1] The Afghani Taliban claimed responsibility for the latter event, whereas the Pakistani Taliban disowned the Peshawar blasts.[2] However, the Taliban remain the main suspects, especially on the heels of the ongoing military operation in South Waziristan, one of the seven semi-autonomous Pushtun tribal agencies on the Pakistani side of the Pak–Afghan border.[3] While Pakistan's relations with India remained stalemated due to disagreements over Kashmir, mutual recriminations, and the sponsorship of terror through proxy elements on each other's soil, the Obama administration is trying to redefine its relationship with its ally in southwestern Asia. President Barack Obama, recently awarded the Nobel Peace Prize but stung by neocon criticism over the continuing loss of NATO and Afghan lives, sent Hillary Clinton to Islamabad to shore up American support for the post-Musharraf civilian administration. Her visit to the country was aimed at redefining this strategic partnership in areas such as energy, agriculture, education, and democratic institutions, rather than just supplying military hardware, as reflected in the recently approved $7.5 billion Kerry Lugar aid bill passed by the US Congress. Primarily aimed at strengthening Pakistan's civic and military areas, the bill sought to help Pakistan balance democratic imperatives with security requirements, with a significant portion of funds earmarked for civic and development purposes conditional on periodic checks on Pakistan's progress towards fully fledged democratization. Although such conditionality is seen by the generals and their supporters as a critique of the military predominance in Pakistan's complex political system, the US Congress sought to prioritize Pakistan's survival as a moderate state strong enough to withstand extremist assaults while simultaneously assisting Washington in fighting al-Qaeda and its sympathizers.

Hillary Clinton denounced the daily attacks on Pakistan's civilian and security personnel; she appreciated Pakistan's sacrifices in human and material terms and acknowledged the role of its armed forces in fighting militants in Swat and South Waziristan. While the Taliban and their anti-Western allies tried to regiment their show of invincibility and ferocity, Clinton toured the country trying to engage the hearts and minds of estranged Muslim allies. Her pronouncements on "standing shoulder to shoulder" against a common threat and pledges to engage in an ongoing dialogue were motivated to allay Pakistani fears of yet another American let down, something frequently experienced since Pakistan's alignment with the West in the early 1950s.[4] Pakistanis were equally distrustful of reports of US covert plans to take over Pakistan's nuclear warheads in case of any coup within the armed forces or any escalation of animosity with India. According to such critics, both George W. Bush and Barack Obama have pushed their faltering war on to Pakistan with the result that Pakistanis are killing fellow citizens, and that earlier secret agreements made by General Pervez Musharraf and his successors had made the country more vulnerable.[5]

A similar upward spiral of violence across Afghanistan claimed the lives of many Afghans and NATO troops in daily skirmishes and suicide attacks. Pakistan, which had often seen ethnic violence in its former eastern wing or lower Indus Valley, now found the violence centered in the upper Indus regions, though occasional urban violence in Balochistan and Karachi also persisted.

Until the recent past the sporadic violence was seen by Pakistanis as the necessary spillover of the Western war on terror that had turned insidiously into a war on Muslims, and the occasional blasts in the cities were often blamed on foreign agents or disgruntled pro-Taliban elements who wanted to wean Musharraf's Pakistan away from Western powers. However, it was the Taliban's ascendance in Swat, with its destruction of hundreds of schools, its beheadings of innocent citizens, its stockpiling of ammunition and establishing of warlords that gradually brought a significant change in public perceptions. Earlier denial gradually gave way to the bitter acceptance of the existence of "enemies within," and the military was given wider support to mount operations against extremists and militants across the Indus regions.

Musharraf's long military rule had seriously affected public perceptions of the armed forces, but the Taliban's encroachments on state authority and public morality soon rehabilitated the military as a formidable bastion against anarchy, wanton violence, and possible external involvement. In fact, the pendulum of support began to swing towards the armed forces out of insecurity and also because of the indolent ruling elite.

The elections of 18 February 2008 returned the Pakistan Peoples' Party (PPP) by a clear majority, with sizeable gains for Nawaz Sharif's Pakistan Muslim League (PML-N), Altaf Hussain's Karachi-based Muhajir/Muttahida Qaumi Movement (MQM) and Asfandyar Wali Khan's Awami National Party (ANP) amidst an atmosphere of hope and goodwill. These elections, on the heels of a populist movement against Pervez Musharraf and his Pakistan Muslim League Quaid group (PML-Q), had put the onus of responsibility on these political forces to restore Pakistan's parliamentary form of government, to reconstruct the economy, and to restore the peace. Asif Ali Zardari, Benazir Bhutto's widower and the de facto PPP head, emerged as the most powerful politician in the country and was catapulted from former prisoner to president in September 2008.

Equipped with unilateral powers imposed by Musharraf, and now supported by Hussain, Sharif, and Khan, along with a vast majority of Pakistanis, Zardari had initially promised a new era of reforms and reconciliation. However, after over a year in power Zardari became an increasingly unpopular head of the state, one high on promises yet dismally low on delivery. The major public demands, including the restoration of senior judges, removal of discretionary constitutional amendments, and more transparent governance, remain stalled. While Pakistanis bled, the president busied himself on foreign visits, and was absent when inspirational leadership could have boosted the country's sagging morale. The PPP Prime Minister Gilani often appeared well-meaning but incapable of undertaking the much-needed systemic overhaul. Pakistan's top political leadership appeared to be either in disarray or dysfunctional, and the daily blasts and heavy death toll as well as the damage to property and morale left the country rudderless.[6]

Although the Kerry Lugar bill, passed by the US Congress, prioritized aid for civil departments within Pakistan, the frequency of Predator drone attacks and the major loss of life in The Federally Administered

Tribal Areas (FATA), along with the stalemated policy on West Asia only added to the pervasive anti-Americanism.[7] The previous US administration had pushed Musharraf for more military campaigns against the tribal Pushtun and al-Qaeda stragglers, yet the fiasco in the Middle East and the policies of detention and rendition targeting Muslims worldwide had made Washington under George W. Bush unpopular in wider Muslim public opinion. Reluctance to support the lawyers and civil society in their struggle for democracy and an independent judiciary in the country, and a preoccupation with waging war against the Taliban, underwrote unwavering Western support for Musharraf's military-led government. Despite altruistic pronouncements on democracy in the Muslim world, the Western powers were, instead, openly shoring up non-democratic regimes over and above the civic imperatives of societies within Pakistan, which only exacerbated its mis-governance.

Now, it appeared that President Obama was attempting to repair the damage through public diplomacy. The appointment of Richard Holbrooke as the special Af-Pak envoy and the visit by Hillary Clinton were meant to win Pakistani hearts and minds. For Pakistanis, however, only short-term and partisan interests had driven American administrations, germinating a significant trust deficit in Pakistan.[8] By late 2009, with militant violence across the Indus Valley unleashed by anti-Western groups, turbulence in Afghanistan and Kashmir, political waywardness amidst Zardari's plummeting opinion polls and the US shoring up Pakistan's morale and economy, the country was back to its three proverbial As—Allah, Army, and America. While the people of Pakistan sought democracy and the primacy of law, desired economic development and modern education, and aspired to regional peace, their leaders lacked the wherewithal to attain these objectives. The conflicts absorbed the public energies and hopes while the nation's meager resources were spent on fighting fellow Pakistanis and their external backers who strove to tear the country apart. The discretionary use of religion, random violence, and serious energy and food crises were pushing the country towards a new polarization between reformism and chaos, peace and disorder, modernity and neo-orthodoxy, and isolation and regional cooperation.

Pakistan needs and desires a breakthrough. Its post-Partition generations seek peace, security, and self-respect, but feel that the world at large and some of their own people have left the country in the lurch.

Looking to the future

Pakistan emerged from a retreating Raj as a predominantly Muslim state, divided into two disparate regions, and its travails with security,

9

democracy and nation-building are a Herculean struggle against great odds. The country's central position in global politics, its conflicts with unfriendly neighbours to the east and west, and ultimately, its struggles to come to terms with its stormy past, underline a unique post-colonial history where demographic, civic, and geopolitical forces have been forced to wrestle. Host to a huge refugee population since its inception, riddled with a complex and often conflicting cultural pluralism, Pakistan defiantly became a nuclear state. However, its struggles with poverty, ethnic and sectarian militancy and military unilateralism have coexisted with heroic attempts by its emerging civil society to achieve an accountable political order, an unfettered judiciary, and an independent media. The inter-weaving of Musharraf's pronouncements on enlightened moderation, Bhutto's reformism, and Political Islam are indicative of resilient party politics that is unique in the developing world.

If allowed to grow, a more stable yet reformist middle ground may yet hold the key to the country's future. Considering the havoc created under the guise of security, alliances with external forces and self-flagellation in the name of Political Islam, Pakistan might finally be ready to usher in a new beginning, although views to the contrary also persist. By mid-2008, the country was being viewed as "on the edge," with whispers of "failing state" bandied around in the Western press.[9] Serious economic problems faced by the vast populace between 2007 and 2009 were further aggravated by the energy crisis and the global financial meltdown, which boded even less well for Pakistan's future. Yet neither the Pakistanis nor the world at large want to see this country slide further into crisis. Pakistan's survival so far—and its progress in several areas—can serve as a beacon of hope and optimism for similar post-colonial states being torn apart by the forces of intolerance, ineptitude, mediocrity, and unrestrained external interventionism.

About this book

Pakistan has attracted a good deal of media attention as well as much academic interest, resulting in an impressive array of historiography. Predictably, many of these works concentrate on state formation, Islam and politics, geopolitical themes involving thorny relations with India, nuclear proliferation and its high-profile role in world affairs since the Cold War. Since treatises on high politics dominate the discourse[10], issues of ideology, intellectual history, civil society, gender, reinterpreting Partition, and class structure are fewer. On the other hand, there is no shortage of alarmist works that focus on negative warnings, including an eventual dissolution of the state and possibly even of its society.[11]

Pakistan: Democracy, Terrorism, and the Building of a Nation focuses largely on more recent developments, where personalities such as Pervez Musharraf, Benazir Bhutto, Asif Zardari, and Nawaz Sharif, and the lawyers, journalists and civil society, signpost significant developments. However, this work is not simply a biographical survey—by reconstructing an early history of this predominantly Muslim region, we discover its various incarnations, especially after 1947. As such, the focus is on the importance of the Indus Valley's geographical and geopolitical location, its historical legacy in South Asian history and the pre-1947 movement for a separate Muslim state. It investigates the role of civil society with reference to class and gender politics, the vexing issues of good governance and some notable, often-missed manifestations of Political Islam within the tradition of party politics.

The Introduction summarizes significant developments as a prelude to understanding the geographical, political, and economic contours of Pakistan. Chapter One focuses on the most current issues and personalities including Zardari's failure to address the crisis situation and Musharraf's exit from the presidency. Chapter Two assesses the personalities and politics of Pervez Musharraf and Benazir Bhutto and the effects of their legacies on the country. Chapter Three explains Pakistan's location as the gateway to South Asia, with all the respective changes and recurring challenges from the northwest, as well as the volatile politics of the post-9/11 military campaigns and their outcomes. Chapter Four evaluates Partition, the importance of the Punjab and refashioning of the legacies of the departing Raj, focusing on how these legacies have added to the country's structural imbalances. Chapter Five looks at the evolution and role of an increasingly vocal middle class, delicately hemmed in between feudal and ideological giants. Chapter Six is an in-depth analysis of the manifestations of Political Islam that often seek electoral and civic recourse and may still offer some hope from jihadi extremism. Chapter Seven returns to the issues of governance and how successive groups of the civil and military elite have continued to falter due to recurring imbalances. And the Epilogue poses questions about Pakistan's future, its prospects and position not just within this volatile region but also within an increasingly uncertain world.

INTRODUCTION

TO UNDERSTAND A COUNTRY as complex and as strategically important as Pakistan, it is vital to take account of the current political situation against the backdrop of the region's geopolitical, historical, religious, and social context.

Pakistan accounts for much of the Indus Valley and is hemmed in by the Himalayas to the north and the Arabian Sea to the south. While mountainous borders with Afghanistan and Iran run to its west, a 2,400 km (1,500 mile) long boundary of plains and deserts is shared with India to the east. Accounting for an estimated population of 175 million people belonging to a variety of ethnicities, this predominantly Muslim country is a historical and geographical bridge between Central and Southern Asia, with a powerful legacy from ancient Indian and Middle Eastern cultures.[1] Pakistan's unique location has been of special interest to archaeologists, historians, strategists, and anthropologists, as Pakistani territories have served as the gateway for endless migrations and invasions into the trans-Indus regions until the recent past, making it both the entry point and the vanguard of defense for the Indian heartland. For geographic, religious, and political reasons, invaders, fortune seekers, and migrants throughout history have found themselves pushed through the five passes of Pakistan's western frontiers on their way into the subcontinent. Lying close to the ancient Silk Route, Pakistan's northern and western regions were even more affected by external influences, due to the waves of traders, missionaries, immigrants, and invaders passing through.

Almost every major religion has made its way across Pakistan's borders, with some leaving more lasting impressions than others. While Zoroastrianism, Judaism, Christianity, and Islam entered South Asia via the ancient Indus Valley, Buddhism traveled from India to East Asia along the same route, establishing itself within the communities along the ancient Silk Route in the valleys and passes of the Karakorams, Hindu Kush, and lower Himalayas.

Geography

Predominantly a hot, dry country with temperate zones in the northwest and arctic conditions in the north, Pakistan's geography combines high mountainous regions with extensive plains, vast sand and gravel deserts, and a coastline that runs along the Arabian Sea and the Persian Gulf. With an area of 796,000 sq km (308,000 sq miles), of which 25,220 sq km (10,000 sq miles) is water, Pakistan is one-twelfth the size of the US.

The Margalla Hills in the Pothowar Plateau divide Pakistan's modern capital Islamabad from its ancient capital of Taxila, at one time home to renowned Buddhist monasteries and universities. By the time Alexander the Great visited Taxila in 326 BCE, it was a bustling city with an advanced intellectual, cultural and commercial society, due to its proximity to the Silk Route and its position at the crossroads of various civilizations. The Margalla Hills join the Murree Hills—which are actually the lower reaches of the Himalayas—and extend into Kashmir. There the 8,126 m (26,660 ft) Nanga Parbat stands sentinel, dividing Kashmir from the Karakoram regions of Kohistan, Baltistan, Gilgit, and Hunza. The second-highest mountain on earth, as well as the most difficult peak to climb, K2 is located within the Karakoram region, which has a dozen of the world's highest peaks.[2] Parallel to these two mountain chains stretches the magnificent Hindu Kush, whose peak Tirichmir demarcates the Pakistani frontier in Chitral that sits between China to the north and 32 km (20 mile) wide Wakhan corridor in Afghanistan's Badakhshan province to the west.

From the northeastern reaches of Chitral to the southwestern end of the Suleiman Mountain in Balochistan, the Pakistan–Afghan frontier traverses mountains inhabited by various Pushtun tribes, one of the oldest and largely intact tribal systems in the world. A shared environment as well as ethno-tribal traits and pastures and the near-autonomous nature of the local tribal population make the modern concept of an international border almost redundant here.

Pakistan shares 523 km (324 miles) of mountainous border with China. Trade and human travel are conducted though the Khunjerab Pass, reached by the Karakoram Highway, which connects the Pakistani Hunza regions with Sinkiang on the other side of the scenic Shimshall Cones. The Karakoram Highway was built by Pakistani and Chinese engineers during the 1970s and 1980s and passes though some of the most scenic and historic regions along the ancient Silk Route.

To the west, Pakistan shares 2,430 km (1,500 miles) of mostly hilly border with Afghanistan, originally demarcated in 1893 by British Indian official Sir Mortimer Durand. Officially known as the Durand Line, it establishes the western boundaries of two Pakistani federated units: the North West Frontier Province (NWFP) and the province of Balochistan. Both of these regions include Pushtun, Baloch, and other ethnic groups, all of whom are predominantly Muslim, though often identified on the basis of their tribal kinship. This border is largely notional since the local Pushtun tribals who straddle a narrow belt on either side of the boundary are governed by their own traditional rules and were guaranteed unhindered movement across the line by both Kabul and Islamabad until post-9/11 geopolitics brought a major change.

Pakistan and Iran share a 909 km (570 mile) common border that mainly passes through the mountainous region of Balochistan in the Iranian plateau. This area is inhabited by the Baloch, a large group of predominantly Muslim people with a distinct cultural identity. Balochistan accounts for 43 percent of Pakistan's total land mass, yet it is sparsely populated, being inhabited by less than 10 million people of Baloch and Pushtun ethnicities.

The Arabian Sea marks the southernmost maritime frontier of Pakistan. The coastline stretches 1,046 km (650 miles) from the Straits of Hormuz to the marshy lands of Kachh. India is the only eastern neighbor, and the two countries share a 2,912 km (1,810 miles) border, passing through marshy lands, the deserts of Sindh and Rajasthan and the fertile plains of Punjab, before finally reaching the disputed mountainous valleys of Kashmir.

The former princely state of Jammu and Kashmir consists of 222,738 sq km (86,000 sq miles) of scenic valleys and towering mountains. The region's rivers feed into the Indus River and its several tributaries, making the area and the issue of water a bone of contention between India and Pakistan. India controls most of the Valley of Kashmir, along with Jammu and Ladakh, while Pakistan administers parts of Poonch and the adjoining regions. A predominantly Muslim region, Kashmir is equal in size to the UK, but with a smaller population; however, owing to its strategic location and wealth of natural resources, it has served as a battleground between the two countries.[3]

At Partition in 1947, Pakistan consisted of two major regions on the western and eastern reaches of the subcontinent respectively. Smaller in size but more populous, East Pakistan on the Gangetic–Burmaputra Delta was formed following the partition of the British provinces of Bengal and Assam. Prone to floods and cyclones, this region suffered a devastating famine in 1943 that cost more than three million lives when rice supplies failed and rural farmers migrated to the cities. Hunger, poverty, and

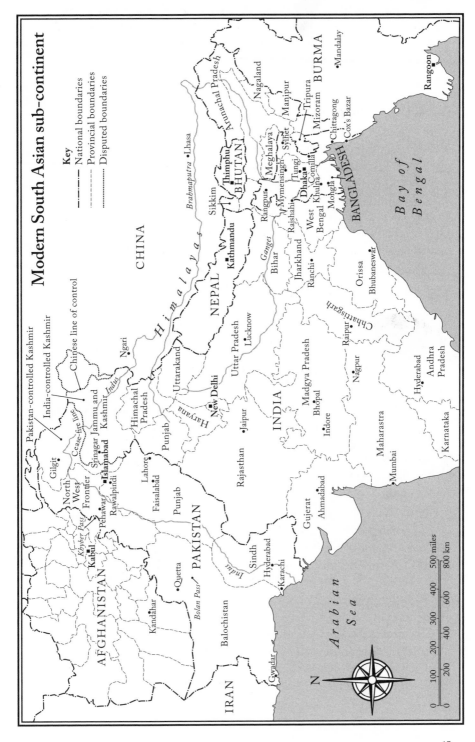

Modern South Asian sub-continent

Key
— National boundaries
--- Provincial boundaries
······ Disputed boundaries

Hindu–Muslim conflict made the idea of a separate Pakistani state a popular ideal for this predominantly Muslim region. Surrounded by India on all three sides, and with the Bay of Bengal to the south, East Pakistan became the sovereign state of Bangladesh in 1971 when its political leaders and populace decided to separate from the post-1947 territorial arrangements.[4]

Society

Throughout its history, Pakistan has received many waves of immigrants and invaders, adding to its demographic diversity—the turbulence of the present-day frontier and the situation in the restive tribal areas may not appear unique if one glimpses at this area's past history. It has always been at the front line of India's defenses against China and is also the conduit for the influx of fresh blood and new ideas. The interaction over the centuries of Turkic, Afghan, Persian, and Arab peoples and cultures with their Indus counterparts has resulted in the evolution of this distinct northwestern Indian society. And today this society still reflects many of these ethnic and linguistic diversities while sharing a common landscape and similar faiths.

The people of Pakistan may be from predominantly Indo-Aryan groups but their family and tribal origins can be traced back to Dravidian and Arab ancestors. The migrations from the north and west, including the most recent arrivals of large numbers of Afghans, may be seen as an ongoing historical process, but the influx of around 10 million people from India in 1947 continues to define the social and political contours of this evolving society.

Pakistanis belong to a number of ethno-linguistic groups and such regional identities, further characterized by tribal and clan-based differences, have attracted various anthropological hypotheses about their commonalities and divergences from the people across their post-1947 borders. The tribal Pushtun and Baloch groups and their steadfast persistence in the face of external invasions and migrations have fascinated observers, while Punjabis and Sindhis have manifested their unique identities within the mainland subcontinent in a similar way.

The Pushtuns Primarily concentrated across the Indus Valley, the Pushtuns are divided into various tribes, which are further subdivided into clans. Along with the religion of Islam as a common identity marker, they share a common mother tongue, and a courageous history further anchors their ethnicity. Tribal honor, hospitality even to former enemies, revenge, and deep commitment to their land, family, and religion feature strongly in the

Pushtun code known as *Pushtunwali*. Pushtu or Pukhtu is one of the oldest languages within the Indo-European group and has a similar script and alphabet to Arabic, Urdu, and Persian. Despite various hypotheses about their origins, including theories about their Semitic genesis, Pushtuns are predominantly Indo-Aryan people. The Pushtun people have traditionally defied foreign encroachments on their territories and, despite a clear majority on the Pakistan side of the Durand Line, maintain common ancestral and cultural linkages with their counterparts in Afghanistan.[5]

The North West Frontier Province (NWFP) holds the largest number of Pushtuns in both countries, although upper Balochistan and some northwestern areas in the Punjab also retain Pushtun communities. Among the Muslim rulers of India, the Pushtun elite held important positions. However, a common decline of Muslim power in India caused more introversion, until the nationalist struggle led by the Muslim League energized an emerging section of Pushtuns to seek better political and economic rights. The creation of Pakistan led to an unprecedented mobility among Pushtuns, and many, especially those from the tribal belt, began moving into cities such as Karachi. Better education and new opportunities in commerce and the military created incentives for many Pushtuns, although in the tribal regions, traditional leaders such as the clerics became apprehensive of losing their hold over their local communities. The landowners and chieftains (*khans*) benefited from the emerging country's urbanization and economic developments and were able to harness the resources put at their disposal during the Afghan war of resistance in the 1980s.

The Afghan war against the Soviet Union had a significant impact on Pushtuns in the tribal belt. In this region, Political Islam began to gain a foothold, until the Taliban and the post-9/11 invasion of Afghanistan by the US and its allies relaunched the clerical sections over and above the *khans*. At this time, a small middle class was also emerging among tribal Pushtuns, especially those who had migrated southwards, including some who were employed in the Gulf States as blue-collar workers. The majority of middle-class Pushtuns, however, now live in urban centers such as Peshawar, Nowshera, Quetta, Mardan, Kohat, Charsada, Bannu, and Hangu. Sizeable towns such as Saidu Sharif, Mingora, Swabi, Timargarha, Thal, and Chaman have experienced significant changes since 1947, including an increased social stratification.

Despite an overwhelming proportion of Pushtuns, the NWFP, like other provinces, has an interesting socio-ethnic mosaic. Since the 1890s the mountainous belt bordering Afghanistan has been divided into seven distinct administrative regions known as agencies, where a mix of traditional norms and more recent official policies govern semi-autonomous groups. In contrast with these seven agencies—Mohmand, Khyber, Tirah, Orakzai, Kurram, North and South Waziristan (or FATA)—the rest of the NWFP is comprised of "settled districts" and here, as elsewhere in Pakistan, the local customary system may not challenge the authority of the state. Within these "settled districts," such as Chitral in the extreme north and Mansehra and Abbotabad in the south, are non-Pushtun regions where the inhabitants trace their origins from a variety of ethnic stocks.

Balochistan This accounts for almost half of Pakistan's landmass and has an impressive, though largely unexplored resource base. Like the NWFP, Sindh, and Punjab, its population comprises a range of ethnic groups: in addition to the Pushtun and Baloch peoples, one comes across sizeable communities speaking Saraiki, Punjabi, Urdu, Brohi, and Sindhi. The coastal regions feature fishing communities alongside Shidi tribes, whose mixed African and Asian ancestries affirm this region's traditional links with Africa and Oman. The Baloch tribal system outside Quetta, Sibi, and Turbat is hierarchical, and land ownership, age and lineage underpin an individual's social status. The Baloch tribal chieftains, known as *sardars*, fiercely defend their influence over the land and local loyalties and can only be superseded by a preeminent *sardar* known as *Tumandar*. The Khan of Qalat has traditionally been at the apex of this system, his primacy assured by a series of moral, political, and matrimonial alliances with other *sardars* from tribes such as the Mazaris, Bugtis, Marris, Lasharis, Magsis, Raisanis, Naushkis, and Gichkis. It is vital to note that the British Raj recruited into its regimental system these tribal hierarchies and used them as local intermediaries. Through political patronage, clannish loyalties operated across the Indus regions, where local landowners defined as *ashraaf* were fixed into a system of loyalty and mutual interdependence. The Pushtun *khans*, Baloch *sardars,* and other landowning castes in the Punjab were knitted into a complex system in which association with the British bureaucracy at a local level guaranteed status as well as security.

The Raj followed a selective policy of defining various communities as "martial races," preferring Sikhs and Muslims, and Punjabis in particular, especially those from the district between the Indus and Jhelum Rivers.[6] Whereas Pushtuns and Baloch were coopted only as local militia to guard posts and communication networks, rural Punjabis made up the bulk of colonial troops fighting for Britain in many local and international wars.

Sindh The province of Sindh sits in the lower Indus Valley and contains Pakistan's largest city and the major port of Karachi. The region derives its name from the Indus River, and this is also the root for familiar terms such as *Hind, Hindustan, Hinduism, Indic,* and *India.* Long after the heyday of the ancient Indus Valley civilization (3300–1300 BCE), this region was frequently integrated into local and India-wide kingdoms, until the arrival of Muslim Arabs in 712 CE, when it became part of the Caliphate located in Damascus. Largely agricultural with increasing maritime interest, Sindh was the hinterland for a huge Bombay presidency under the British. Other than the Sufi dynasties, most land in Sindh was owned by Baloch Muslim clans, though urbanized Hindus made up the moneyed class and loaned funds to their Muslim compatriots.

After a protracted struggle, Muslim Sindh gained the status of a distinct province in its own right in 1935, affording its citizens a unique precedent in political activism. It is not surprising to see this administrative partition as the forerunner of the major Partition in 1947, since Sindh benefited from its own autonomy, as well a series of irrigation schemes, creating better prospects for its landed elite. However, these prospects did not extend to all; in particular, there was a vast majority of landless peasants, known as *haris,* who remained outside the influence of these vital changes. The land belonged to the Muslim dynasties and feudal *waderas*; modern education was monopolized by the Hindu moneyed classes; and the *haris* continued as landless serfs.[7] The historic changes of 1947 raised expectations among Muslim landlords, *haris,* and small entrepreneurs that the Hindu bourgeoisie could be replaced when they migrated to India. However, the arrival of millions of Muslim refugees from India—often with better educational and professional skills—added a new and vital ethnic plurality to Sindh's demography. But critically, it also unraveled the importance of the Sindhi landowning classes (*ashraaf*) as the only vital political force.

Overnight, the new metropolis of Karachi became a city dominated by Urdu-speaking groups (commonly known as Muhajireen), whose superior education and mobility helped them obtain better jobs within central and provincial governments. The creation of Pakistan did consolidate the Sindhi Muslims, allowing the evolution of a middle class, yet Karachi's political, economic, and commercial significance continued to change the demographics of the urban Sindh, much to the chagrin of the largely rural yet ambitious middle class. Their political leaders would often be willing to work with the Punjabi–Muhajir-dominated establishment, yet the younger, educated elements found themselves squeezed from all sides. Karachi may have offered greater opportunities in the young Muslim state for self-confident Muhajireen, yet the influx of Baloch, Sindhi, Pushtun, Kashmiri, and Punjabi migrants, often from rural and tribal backgrounds, created a high level of competition. Conflicts stemming from this competition for jobs, status, and wealth became violent during the 1980s and 1990s.

Karachi is perhaps one of the most pluralistic cities on earth, where layers and layers of South and West Asian ethnicities live cheek by jowl. There are more Baloch living in just one area of Lyari in Karachi than are currently living in the entire province of Balochistan, and the city supersedes Peshawar as the largest Pushtun city in the world.[8] The sizeable numbers of Punjabis and Sindhis, all competing for housing, jobs, and transport, have prompted the emergence of ethnic-based political parties that often overshadow former mainstream national or religio-political parties such as the Muslim League, the Pakistan People's Party, Jamaat-i-Islami, and Jamiat-i-Ulama-i-Islam. Here, the politics of ideology and class often seem to have been replaced by the urban ethnic mix where political patterns remain anchored in tribal/ethnic hierarchical patronage.

Punjab While Sindh may be the second most populous of Pakistan's four provinces, Punjab is its powerhouse, accounting for over 60 percent of the country's population. Most of the civil service, military personnel, and the political leadership hail from the Punjab, and despite its traumatic experiences of Partition in 1947, it gained a dominant role within the new state. From across the post-1947 borders, Punjab received millions of destitute refugees who had experienced brutal violence amidst the large-scale ethnic cleansing, which involved all three major communities of Hindus, Muslims, and Sikhs.[9]

During the 24 years of united Pakistan, Bengalis often complained of West Pakistan's domination of the country's structures and policies, which they attributed to a tactical alliance between Urdu speakers and Punjabis. Criticism of this power axis garnered support from other smaller provinces such as the NWFP, Balochistan, and Sindh, where "Punjabi domination" became a popular recrimination. The lack of a smooth democratic system allowing participatory politics, as well as the uneven nature of power-sharing, highlighted these grievances, which were often exacerbated by political imbalances.

Punjab is seen as the agricultural and industrial heartland of Pakistan and its educational, economic, and political institutions underpin its dominance in the region. Perhaps as a result, there have been demands for devolution within the province. The Pothowar region, hemmed in between the Rawalpindi Hills and the Salt Range, has increasingly become a middle-class enclave due to its inhabitants' small landholdings and greater propensity to join the armed forces. Its profile has been further raised by the location of the army's headquarters in Rawalpindi, the founding of Islamabad and the concentration of several defense establishments and structures in the region.

However, Punjab's preeminence actually revolves around the central Punjab, with Lahore at its heart and other industrial- and canal-based districts surrounding it. The southwestern Punjab or Saraiki tract is populated with landowning families and some Sufi descendants who continue to have local influence. The 1947 Partition has left a permanent imprint on the Punjabi consciousness, as the refugees from India's Punjab and Kashmir arrived with their terrible stories and a keen eagerness to make a success of their new country. The province, owing to its strong economy and close involvement in politics, has found it easy to accept newcomers. With the separation of East Pakistan in 1971, Punjab found itself in a vanguard role steering the country's destiny; its religious conservatism combined with strong patriotism began to underwrite Punjabi attitudes toward its country and its neighbors. Instead of ethnicity as a major political factor, the Punjab's ethos is divided along Sunni–Shia and rural–urban lines, and its vocal middle class is eager to play a mainstream role.

Kashmir and the Northern Areas The Pakistan-administered part of the disputed Jammu and Kashmir region is made up of two administrative areas, known as Azad Kashmir and the Northern Areas. Azad Kashmir has been tightly bound up with Pakistan's political economy since before Partition and a high level of integration following migrations to the UK and elsewhere, which have solidified these mutual linkages. The Northern Areas (consisting of Gilgit, Hunza, and Baltistan) political integration with the rest of the country is slower than its economic and cultural assimilation, owing to the significant connection brought by the Karakoram Highway. In addition, its strategic location and greater social mobility, largely due to educational advances pioneered by official networks and the Aga Khan Foundation, have afforded a better quality of life in some of its areas. The foundation has mainly concentrated on the Ismaili Shia populations in Gilgit and Hunza, though similar work is gradually being undertaken in lower Gilgit and Baltistan as well.[10]

Within some parts of Pakistan, there remain traditional patriarchal networks that are resistant to change, often defying efforts to improve political empowerment, economic enfranchisement, and gender equality. The landholding elite, for instance, generally oppose land reforms as well as the imposition of an agricultural tax, while some of their counterparts in the tribal regions may prohibit the education of women or hamper the work of non-governmental organizations, viewing these "external" elements as cultural intruders.

Linked with the complex post-9/11 geopolitics, FATA and adjoining Swat, Malakand, and Dir districts have recently become battlegrounds between the forces of extremism and reform. While the state and many reformers seek universal education, efficient justice, and economic investments in these areas, the traditional *khans* and the re-energized clerics are using the popular demand for Sharia law (the interpreted law of Islam) and jihad to snub such initiatives. This power struggle has taken root with moderate and civic forces caught in the crossfire between the extremists and the security forces seeking to maintain the authority of the state.

The growth of an indigenous Taliban movement is a post-9/11 development and its recourse to militancy has flourished due to civilian casualties in the war on terror, and the marginalization of moderate elements as a result of the perception that Islamabad is siding with anti-Muslim external forces. As a throwback to the events in Afghanistan, the pervasive anti-Americanism among Pushtuns often converges with anti-reformism. As a consequence, Pakistani officials are seen as serving only the interests of the US and UK, and not those of their own people. Extremism has deepened as more civilian deaths have occurred at the hands of the security forces and as a result of American drone-led missile attacks. The loss of civil authority in Swat in 2008–9 and the primacy of local extremists from the Movement of Pakistani Taliban (Tehreek-i-Taliban Pakistan, TTP) led by Maulana Fazlullah initially succeeded in demoralizing the country, as this scenic valley had always been in the forefront of civic and economic achievements as well as being a favorite destination for Pakistani tourists. The blowback from neighboring FATA and Afghanistan, as well as a demand for the implementation of Sharia law, had allowed this historic region to deteriorate into a hotbed of extremism. By early 2009, the Pakistani Taliban, spawned by Fazlullah through his radio broadcasts and close-knit networks, were able to destroy 190 schools in the valley, as well as implementing severe restrictions on local inhabitants. The "fall" of Swat, despite local disenchantment with this abrasive form of "Talibani-zation," was seen by Pakistani civic groups as an alarming development, and their reaction vacillated between extreme shock and horror.[11]

Eventually, the Pakistan government was compelled to undertake a massive military operation in Swat and the neighboring districts during the summer of 2009. This resulted in the relocation of over two million people but to a great extent, the army was able to flush out the militants. By late 2009, most of the displaced people of Swat had returned to their homes, while the army began a similar operation in South Waziristan. Here the Taliban were led by Baitullah Mehsud, who was killed on 3 August 2009 (see pages 191–199 for biographical details).

Religion and cultural identity

A clear majority of Pakistanis are Muslim, although they are divided among various doctrinal sects based on the diverse interpretations of their faith and practices. Historically, South Asia has accounted for the world's largest number of Muslims; however, given the populous nature of the subcontinent, Hindus have always made up the majority. The Muslim population comes second, with one-third of the population of Hindus. Due to the cross-border migrations in the aftermath of Partition in 1947, radical demographic changes occurred; Pakistan was a predominantly Muslim state with sizeable numbers of Hindus living in its eastern wing and in rural Sindh and Balochistan. Migrations across the new borders continued for quite some time, until the new states eventually implemented strong restrictions. Following the Indo–Pakistani Wars of 1948, 1965, and 1971, even obtaining a visitor's visa for separated family members became almost impossible.

There are around six million Hindus and an equal number of Christians living in Pakistan; both groups are officially categorized as minorities, along with a few thousand Kalasha tribals in the interior of Chitral and a very small number of Zoroastrians/Parsis. In 1974, the Pakistani parliament declared minority status for the the Ahmadis, a religious group who follow Mirza Ghulam Ahmad (1835–1908), a Muslim preacher in 19th-century Punjab, viewing him as a promised Messiah (*Mahdi*). As such, they do not accept the Prophet Muhammad as the last prophet, a pivotal belief that is anathema to most Muslims, causing occasional backlashes against the Ahmadi community, whose hereditary leader is now based in London.

The focus on Islam, both by the state and Pakistani society, has often added to pressures on smaller communities whose practices may vary from the mainstream Sunni and Shia denominations. Whereas Sunnis account for up to 80 percent of the Pakistani Muslim population, Shias make up the rest, though both are further broken down into several more denominational variations.[12]

Shia faith Historically, Sunnis do not dispute the issue of the political succession to the Prophet Muhammad (d. 632 CE), accepting the subsequent mainstream interpretation of religious traditions often called *Sunna* (prophetic traditions). By contract, the Shias view Muhammad's cousin Ali ibn Abi Talib as the only deserving successor, unlike Sunnis, who view him as the final "rightly guided" caliph. Ali was the Prophet's cousin as well as his son-in-law, and eventually rose to the status of caliph. Known for his erudition, courage, and loyalty to the Prophet, Ali is venerated by all Muslims, though Shias view him as superior to all of Muhammad's companions. Ali's assassination by a malcontent in Kufa was quickly followed by the assassination of his son in Karbala (683 CE). This led to the annual mourning tradition among Shias, whose viewpoint and rituals were institutionalized by the Shia monarchy in Persia during the 16th century.[13] Shias in South Asia have a strong connection with Iran and believe in the Twelve Imams (spiritual leaders), all descending from the Prophet's family, with the last Imam having gone into occultation. This belief in the Twelve Imams has led to their more common name, the Twelvers.

A smaller group among the Shias, known as the Ismailis, believe in an uninterrupted Imamate, with the Aga Khan as the contemporary Imam. Ismailis, unlike other Shia and Sunni groups, avoid politicking and mainly tend to business, education, and community-building through mutual assistance. Due to persecution by the Twelvers in Persia since the 16th century, some Ismailis sought refuge in the northern mountains of present-day Pakistan, while many others settled in Bombay and Karachi until the British recognized the Aga Khan as the spiritual head of this community during the 19th century.[14] Long after the Arab decline in the Indus Valley, Ismaili dynasties continued to rule this area until the Turks and Afghans began their assaults on northern India during the early medieval period. Ismailis are also found in Central Asia and East Africa. Their leader, the current Aga Khan, lives in Europe and his grandfather, Sir Sultan Shah Muhammad Khan (1877–1957), was one of the founders of Pakistan.

Sunni faith Sunni Pakistanis are divided into two main doctrinal branches. These branches have always existed, yet they moved into the limelight following the Islamic revivals in British India after 1857. Historically, Muslims in India owed their evolution to the efforts of the sufis (mystics) and ulama (religious scholars), although Muslim monarchs often avoided forcible conversions of Indians to Islam. Thus, sufis, banking on religious coexistence, mingled with other religious communities, while ulama often urged purist separatism. Under British rule, these two major strands were rejuvenated by seminaries at Deoband and Rai Bareilly. The former, committed to anticolonialism, sought a Muslim renaissance by going back to its roots, whereas the seminary at Bareilly sought spiritual solutions, and their successors in present-day Pakistan remain polarized both at the popular level and in party politics.

The global trends toward religious conservatism and purist orthodoxy are certainly manifest in Pakistani practices, where, especially after the violence of the past decade, more and more people are seeking religious solace. As a result, the competition between the purists and traditionalists has become intense. While scholars noticed the importance of purist Islam over its counterpart dating from the 1990s, Sufi traditions are not being helped by their recourse to fatalism and the status quo.[15] The Taliban may be one of several manifestations of purist Islam, but most Pakistanis are still welded to local sufis, *pirs* (sufi mentors), and monasteries that, in several cases, are well endowed and retain political influence, especially in southern Punjab and rural Sindh.

Emerging extremism The Pakistani Pushtun Taliban have largely been driven by an ethno-religious fraternity with the Afghan Taliban. But their aversion to a modernist state system and its educational and reformist agenda also emanates from a feared betrayal of Islamist values that they feel are as relevant today as they were centuries ago.

The shared sense of hurt and humiliation felt by the world's Muslims over Western indifference and their own modernist rulers' subservience to Western interests has converged with local resentments. When Maulana Sufi Muhammad and his son-in-law, Maulana Fazlullah, raised the banner of jihad and the imposition of Sharia law in the settled areas of Dir and Swat from 2007 onward, they were calling on forces that were already deeply aggrieved over official inefficiency and corruption. To these forces, the prevailing system was simply exploitative and corrupt rather than immoral, obediently following its masters in the West regardless of domestic opinion and interests. By invading Afghanistan and Iraq and by co-opting obliging Muslim rulers, Western forces had once again proved that they only cared about their own partisan interests. Musharraf and other rulers, already lacking legitimacy to rule, miserably failed to justify their complicity in a controversial and immensely violent war on terror, which was perceived as a multifaceted assault on the world's Muslims.

Islam's traditional role of resisting the Western hold and championing its own role in influencing domestic and international politics now assumed more visible and extreme dimensions. Some Muslims turned to violence, while others sought solace in introversion, awaiting the time when an exhausted and overstretched West and its allies would give way to new global competitors. Many other Muslims simply felt despondent with the state of their community affairs and, in the process, distanced themselves from their Muslim identity. The three broad responses outlined above are felt across the Muslim world and diaspora, and coincide with a heightened debate on reform, modernity, justice, and empowerment.[16] At one level, amidst this introspection, one may detect more credance being given to clerics, while concurrently, one may also encounter more disenchantment with the violent means adopted by some sections despite the genuine nature of their intense grievances. In other words, it is the means and not the shared consciousness that has created these ideological fault lines among Muslims. Suicide bombings, sectarian violence, attacks on low-paid security officials, and recriminations against girls' schools and polio clinics have certainly deflated the extremist trajectories of Political Islam, although resentment against the West continues to grow as aerial attacks and the resulting innocent deaths continue.[17]

For a partial explanation of Pakistan's current situation, it is instructive to look back to General Zia-ul-Haq's (1977–88) time in office and his drive toward Islamization within the backdrop of his own religiosity, his quest for legitimacy, and the Afghan jihad. Supported by all Western powers and their allies, these factors can be seen as a trigger pushing the country toward fundamentalism. But Islam, as perceived by Muslims in all its manifest-ations, has been a constant reminder of the interdependence between *Deen* (creed) and *Duniya* (worldly life). However, maintaining that balance has been a daunting task for the regimes and the respective communities. Demonizing Political Islam as "Islamofascism,"[18] or a permanent crisis within the creed itself,[19] is problematic for Muslims and others. It is easier for Western powers to pursue Muslim-specific policies, including unlawful invasions, mass profiling, detention and torture, extraordinary rendition and other violations of human rights, as has been evident in Palestine, Iraq, Kashmir, Afghanistan, the Balkans, and Chechnya.

It is true that in countries like Pakistan there has been a sustained tradition of ideological polarization between orthodoxy and reform that has grown in intensity in recent times. Other than its ideological context, the roots for this polarity can be sought in political, economic, and psychological factors, where issues such as economic development, universal empowerment and human rights, irrespective of creed, ethnicity, and gender, are to be taken on board. Development in these areas has taken place, but the pace has been slow and the remit of such policies has been limited to specific areas. Consequently, major sections of the population remain disillusioned. The problems of governance, uncertainty inside and outside the country, along with global indifference if not outright hostility, have fed into this trust deficit, leaving many young people within Pakistan and throughout the Muslim world vulnerable to extremism.

The role of language The majority of Pakistanis understand Urdu, which has become the main medium of conversation and the bedrock of the national identity while remaining the mother tongue of a small section of the population. Competition between the main spoken languages of English, Urdu, and ethnic languages is still unresolved, but this tension has certainly decreased. The languages still provide a bedrock to ethnic politics, but they are not the only determinants, since political, global, and economic issues also bring Pakistanis together from across the ethno-sectarian divides.[20] While ethnic languages have become the storehouse of folk culture, Urdu has equally solidified the common political, romantic, and literary ethos. Significantly, since the 18th century Urdu has been the mainstay of Islamic literature in the subcontinent. Despite the powerful push of Hindi as a populist medium, Urdu is now the lingua franca at the established Muslim seminaries in India, a position it certainly holds in Pakistan.

The role of education Pakistan's growing population has always posed a serious challenge to its infrastructure, and the attempt to bring education to rural and tribal communities, especially those in remote areas, has been an ongoing struggle. While the urban areas are far ahead in terms of English-speaking schools, professional institutions, and private universities, the rural and tribal regions still have literacy as their main challenge. Here, economic and social challenges roadblock the provision of basic education to *haris* in Sindh and to women in Balochistan. Local clerics and elders impart basic religious instruction to younger women, and mosque-based religious seminaries (madrassas) offer a specifically religious education geared toward producing clerics to younger men who may lack other socio-academic alternatives. The reformation of the madrassas, and the move to use them as a tool for universal literacy, has long been overdue. Instead of suspecting them as dens of violent extremism, perhaps a coordinated educational system could help advance literacy and openness at the grassroots.

History and politics: an overview

Though Pakistan was home to the ancient Indus Valley civilization (3300–1200 BCE) long before the evolution of Hinduism and other subsequent religio-political traditions, it has equally been a melting pot for West Asian and Central Asian cultures. The ancient Indian civilization of the Indus Valley—one of the mainsprings of Pakistani culture—remained undiscovered until the 1920s, when archaeologists found the ruins of several ancient cities such as Harrapa and Mohenjodaro that had flourished long before their Mesopotamian and Egyptian counterparts.[21]

Like their counterparts today, the inhabitants of these predominantly urban cultures were subdued by invaders from the north who crossed the mountain passes into the valleys of the Punjab and Sindh in order to establish their own dominance. The ancient Dravidians (ancient Indians) were overcome by nomadic warrior Aryans (who came from Central Asia around 2000–1500 BCE) using chariots to capture the valleys, where brick houses complete with sanitation systems and wide streets existed in relatively prosperous societies. The Aryans gradually settled in these valleys in the two millennia before the birth of Christ, and had expanded into the upper Gangetic Valley. They formed their own socio-religious organizations based on the importance of their priestly Brahmin class. Eventually, these organizations evolved into a new faith, now known as Hinduism. While their cousins in Persia may have converted to Zoroastrianism, the Indian Aryans used Sanskrit for their epics and spiritual literature, and initiated a regimented caste system while establishing their kingdoms.

Buddhism was born in the Indus Valley. Siddhartha Gautama (c.563–483 BCE), subsequently referred to as Buddha, was a Hindu prince from Bihar who became unhappy with the pervasive violence and human misery and sought peace (*nirvana*) through internalizing and even celebrating pain. His followers established monasteries in the Punjab and the trans-Indus regions, with Taxila, Peshawar, and Charsada emerging as educational and spiritual centers of Buddhism.

The rivalry between ancient Greek and Persian cultures brought Alexander the Great (356–323 BCE) to the region in his attempt to obliterate the eastern reaches of the Sassanid Empire led by Darius III (c.380–330 BCE). Alexander entered Chitral through the passes of the Hindu Kush and left some of his soldiers behind in the lush green valleys before reaching Swat and defeating local opponents. Alexander fought his most important battle by the Jhelum River at the foot of the Salt Range. After claiming all of the Punjab, he sailed down the Indus to return to his native Macedonia. After Alexander, the Indus Valley witnessed Greek,

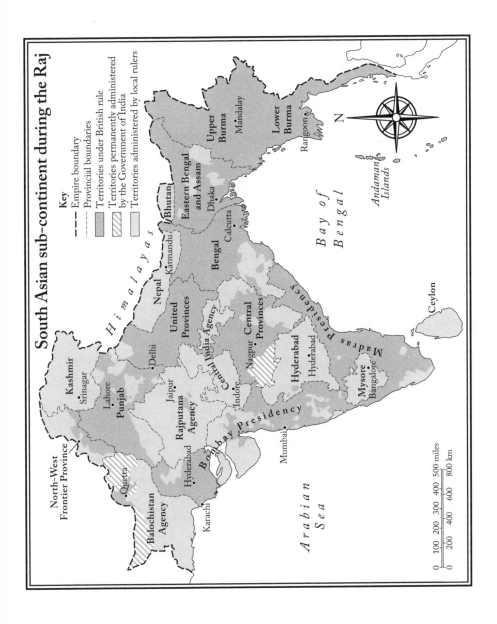

South Asian sub-continent during the Raj

Key
- - - Empire boundary
········ Provincial boundaries
Territories under British rule
Territories permanently administered by the Government of India
Territories administered by local rulers

Mandalay
Upper Burma
Lower Burma
Rangoon
Eastern Bengal and Assam
Dhaka
Bhutan
Calcutta
Nepal
Kathmandu
Bengal
H i m a l a y a s
United Provinces
Central India Agency
Central Provinces
Nagpur
Kashmir
Srinagar
Delhi
Lahore
Punjab
Jaipur
Rajputana Agency
Indore
Hyderabad
Hyderabad
North-West Frontier Province
Quetta
Hyderabad
Karachi
Balochistan Agency
Bombay Presidency
Mumbai
Madras Presidency
Mysore
Bangalore
Ceylon
Bay of Bengal
Andaman Islands
N
Arabian Sea

0 100 200 300 400 500 miles
0 200 400 600 800 km

Persian, and Bactrian control; eventually, Hindu and Buddhist generals were able to establish their own empires, which extended from present-day Afghanistan to Bangladesh. Taxila became even more important under Emperor Ashoka (304–232 BCE), who had converted to Buddhism following a brutal war in Orissa. Ashoka ensured the preservation of Buddhist relics in stupas and monasteries across his empire, spreading his chosen religion through what is now Sri Lanka, Afghanistan, and along the Silk Route. Following his efforts, northern Pakistan, Tibet, and the adjacent Chinese regions turned overwhelmingly to Buddhism. The end of Ashoka's dynastic empire caused a Hindu revival in politics and religion, flourishing under the Maurya dynasty (321–185 BCE), whose rule unified India as a Hindu community.

Northern Pakistan, meanwhile, still embodied a highly sophisticated combination of Greek, Persian, Central Asian, and Indian artistic and religious values, commonly known as the Gandhara culture, which continued to exist until just before the emergence of Christianity. Despite a short-lived experience of Christianity in the 1st century CE, Taxila and the surrounding areas remained a melting pot of religions and cultures, although they largely subscribed to Hinduism, with temples such as Raj Kattas attracting pilgrims from across South Asia.

In the wake of political fragmentation, the Indus Valley suffered further invasions from the north, preventing the emergence of any strong, united political leadership.[22] With this state of affairs, Muslim Arabs were able to penetrate Balochistan and Sindh in the early 8th century and soon their influence reached the Punjab, which was already being visited by Muslim sufis and ulama from Persia and Central Asia. India continued to attract new waves of invasions, which were led by Turkic and Afghan dynasts, but with one difference: these people were primarily Muslim. In addition to seeking economic prospects, they were equally enthused by Islam. Invasions began in the 10th century and continued for 200 years, with Lahore, Multan, and Ghazni becoming metropolitan cities until, in 1206 CE, Delhi was selected as the capital by Sultan Qutub-ud-Din Aibak (1150–1210), a former slave determined to establish a permanent political base in the heart of India.

These Delhi Sultans came from the families of Tughluqs, Khaljis, Syeds, and Lodhis until, in 1526, an Uzbek prince was able to establish a dynasty from which emerged the Great Mughal Empire. This prince Babur (1483–1531) was a grandson of Tamerlaine and traced his ancestry from Genghis Khan. Following his conquest of Kabul, he captured Delhi and Agra from the Lodhis and other Hindu rajas. His descendants raised Indo–Islamic culture to its pinnacle, and through an efficient and tolerant administration, advanced literature and the arts, leading India to new cultural heights. It was during the Mughal era that Europeans began to venture into India and gradually established their presence in coastal towns.[23]

The decline of the Mughal Empire began following the death of Emperor Aurengzeb in 1707; its demise was complete by 1857, by which time the East India Company had already been in the ascendancy across South Asia for an entire century. The Indian Rebellion of 1857—often mistakenly called the Indian Mutiny—involved soldiers, former ruling elites, and peasants in an armed struggle that exposed serious institutional weaknesses on the Indian side. The dismissal and ignoble exile of the last king Bahadur Shah II and the sacking of Delhi and other predominantly Muslim centers of power led directly to the seizing of power by the Raj throughout the subcontinent.[24]

Like other communities, India's Muslims went through a period of introspection and displayed a range of responses to the challenges of European supremacy. Some groups carried on with active resistance in the form of jihad from the mountains of Swat and Dir, whereas others, especially the regional landowners, accepted the colonial writ as junior partners and sought to promote their own local influence. However, a small class of intelligentsia promoted modern education and the reorganization of community rights. Led by Sir Syed Ahmed Khan (1817–98), these reformists prioritized education and the acceptance of scientific aspects of Western civilization. They were modernists, and their institutions such as Aligarh Mohammaden Anglo-Oriental College (later Aligarh Muslim University) were to germinate the idea of a separate Muslim political creed. During the 1940s, this idea was known as the "Movement for Pakistan." However, they were constantly challenged by religio-political groups who saw India as a homeland for all, irrespective of caste and creed, and sought a Muslim future within a free and united India. Opposed to the All-India Muslim League founded in 1906 and led by Muhammad Ali Jinnah (1876–1948), these Muslim nationalists included leading ulama such as Abul Kalam Azad and Husain Ahmad Madani, who were willing to work with the Hindu majority and minorities of a polyglot India, rather than pursue Muslim separatism. The distance between the League and the Indian National Congress—both led by a class of lawyers and professional elite—grew with the introduction of reforms under the British, and competition for safeguards and tangible political rights eventually became a seemingly impossible struggle for the two divergent political programs.[25]

The birth of Pakistan   Pakistan came into existence a few hours earlier than India, on 14 August 1947; however, Pakistan's two major regions in the Indus Valley and the Gangetic Delta were split, with non-Muslim majority areas in Punjab and Bengal added to India. These new borders prompted huge spontaneous migrations, which caused massive sectarian violence and death due to the lack of any official controls, and added to the tense relations between the successor states. The disputes over water resources as well as over princely states such as Kashmir, Junagarh, and Hyderabad hampered the efforts made to accommodate mutual interests. The assassination of Mohandas Gandhi in 1948, followed by the death of Pakistan's founder Muhammad Ali Jinnah later that year, marked the continuation of Indo–Pakistani discord, which eventually resulted in three wars, the separation of East Pakistan into Bangladesh, and the nuclear arming of both states.

Democratic government vs. the generals   Starting from scratch with no industrial base, only two universities, and its difficult geographical problems, the future did not look promising for Pakistan. Drawn into problems of security rooted in regional and global politics, Pakistan attempted to steer a steady course while negotiating a balancing act between the main ideological and ethnic debates. In its early years, Pakistan charted its administrative, economic, educational, and political pathways, and entered into defense alliances with the US and other Western powers. The country's weak political culture fell victim to bureaucratic unilateralism in 1958 when General Ayub Khan led the army to seize power following a decade of ineffectual governments.

A parliamentary constitution had been formulated in 1956, after overcoming several regional and political barriers, but was aborted by General Ayub Khan's military coup two years later. The country's highest judiciary validated this coup through an often-cited "law of necessity," whereby the generals escaped reprimand for subverting civil authorities. Since 1958, the acquisition of power and legitimacy has been a seesaw between political forces and the powerful generals.

Ayub Khan created a political structure that suited his own personal interests while denying universal suffrage. When faced with public protest Khan bequeathed his powers to General Yahya Khan in March 1969. Under the second military regime, Pakistan's problems of governance were aggravated further, and the relationship between its two disparate regions turned sour. The generals refused to transfer power to the elected parties of the Awami League of Sheikh Mujibur Rahman (1920–75) and the Pakistan People's Party of Zulfikar Ali Bhutto (1928–79). As a consequence Pakistan suffered a civil war and, with India's help, East Pakistan became Bangladesh. Pakistan was now left with the major portion of the Indus Valley, hemmed in between the Hindu Kush, the partitioned Punjab plains and the deserts of Sindh-Rajasthan. Zulfikar Bhutto

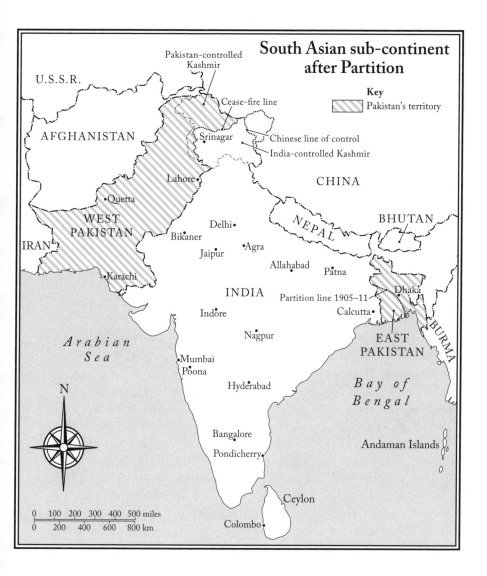

South Asian sub-continent after Partition

Pakistan-controlled Kashmir

Cease-fire line

Key
Pakistan's territory

U.S.S.R.

AFGHANISTAN

Srinagar

Chinese line of control

India-controlled Kashmir

CHINA

Lahore

•Quetta

WEST PAKISTAN

Delhi•

NEPAL

BHUTAN

IRAN

Bikaner

Jaipur

•Agra

Allahabad

Patna

•Karachi

INDIA

Partition line 1905–11

Dhaka

Indore

Calcutta•

EAST PAKISTAN

BURMA

Arabian Sea

Nagpur

N

•Mumbai
Poona

Hyderabad

Bay of Bengal

Bangalore

Andaman Islands

Pondicherry•

Ceylon

0   100   200   300   400   500 miles
0   200   400   600   800 km

Colombo•

took over the leadership of the truncated country, retiring an immensely unpopular Yahya Khan and some of his senior military colleagues who had been responsible for the country's humiliating loss of Bangladesh. The shocked society became acutely aware of the critical juncture their country had reached with regard to governance; its elite had successively failed to put the country on stable political rails. Bhutto's preoccupation with nationalizing major industries, banks, and insurance companies fell in line with his exhortations on Islamic socialism; however, he stopped short of substantive land redistribution because of fear of the dominant landed elite. Crucially, Bhutto's efforts in 1973 to forge a nation through a commonly agreed constitution stipulating a parliamentary form of government won him wide support from even his fiercest opponents.

However, his authoritarian tendencies and obsession with power only succeeded in bringing together his opponents, who disputed the election results of 1977. Bhutto's intolerance of the vocal opposition—now known as the Pakistan National Alliance (PNA)—caused him to vacillate on resolving the political deadlock. This inaction, in turn, rehabilitated the political ambitions of the generals. On 4 July 1977 Bhutto was overthrown by General Zia-ul-Haq, the Chief of Army Staff, ostensibly a non-politicized general who sought his own security by removing Bhutto once and for all. Two years later, following a contentious civil trial, Bhutto was found guilty of ordering the murder of a political opponent and was hanged in his jail cell in Rawalpindi on 4 April 1979.

General Zia-ul-Haq surreptitiously consolidated his power through the use of military courts that dished out quick and repressive punishments to offenders, most of whom happened to be from political and civic groups. Public flogging, solitary confinement, and harassment by various security services became the norm, especially for PPP supporters, some of whom ended up in exile, including the Bhutto family. Zia duly benefited from the Western generosity following the Soviet invasion of Afghanistan in 1979, while simultaneously pursuing his policy of Islamization, which was selectively punitive and compromised the rights of minorities, women, and political dissenters. It was under Zia that intelligence organizations, such as the Inter-Services Intelligence (ISI), otherwise meant to protect Pakistan from external threat, became heavily involved in creating a loyalist and submissive political culture to fortify the military regime. Zia's martial law, the most repressive of its type, muzzled civic forums and mainstream politics, causing a backlash in the form of sectarian and ethnic violence. The Sunni–Shia feuds and violence between Karachi-based, Urdu-speaking Muhajireen and the rest reached horrific proportions. Pakistan's wasted decades under the strong thumb of the army, along with Zia-endorsed clerical groups, have left their legacy. This is why successive governments have often remained vulnerable to the same divided interests.

General Zia's party-less elections of 1985, mostly boycotted by the mainstream parties, were aimed at safeguarding his own hold on the country. He allowed the removal of martial law only after indemnifying all of his earlier measures and policies, and he concentrated his powers in the office of the president. The 1973 constitution was radically amended to suit his personal office, and the parliament and the prime minister became the weakest in the political triumvirate, in which the president and the army chief emerged as the most powerful brokers. Zia's regime only served to exacerbate Pakistan's governance dilemma, which was desperately in need of fresh ideas, dynamic leadership, and a return to civil government. A few months before his death in August 1988, Zia had dismissed parliament and the provincial assemblies, as well as dissolving the regime of Muhammad Khan Junejo, who had earlier been picked by Zia as a docile prime minister.

Despite Zia's radical transformation of the country's political, constitutional, and judicial structures, in 1988 Pakistan found another opening to redress its misgovernance. However, due to the distorting influence of the army generals as the major power brokers in collaboration with the powerful president Ghulam Ishaq Khan, politicians such as Benazir Bhutto and Nawaz Sharif failed to make any headway. Benazir Bhutto had led the Pakistan People's Party (PPP) since the early 1980s, while Nawaz Sharif headed the Pakistan Muslim League (PML), though the party often remained divided into several factions. These two democratically elected prime ministers did not attempt to introduce substantive political reforms that would have guaranteed stability and greater public participation in the system.

Benazir Bhutto, the daughter of charismatic Zulfikar Ali Bhutto, had returned from exile in Britain in 1986 amidst euphoric expectations, gained a slight majority in the parliamentary elections in 1988. However, an unstable Kashmir, a turbulent Karachi, and a violent stalemate in Afghanistan following the Soviet departure narrowed her remit, especially after the president and army chief blocked any return to parliamentary sovereignty. Her own naiveté in negotiating with formidable allies and opponents left her vulnerable, until President Khan dismissed her eighteen months later. Nawaz Sharif, previously the chief minister of the powerful province of Punjab and a diehard Bhutto rival, gained the majority of seats in both the national and provincial assemblies in 1990. However, in addition to the structural imbalances already in place, his continued enmity with Bhutto's PPP did not allow him a smooth tenure. Like his opponent, he was dismissed by President Khan in 1993, allowing the return of Bhutto to head a second PPP term, though her travails in Karachi, Kabul, and Kashmir continued until she faced her second dismissal in 1996.[26]

Sharif's second tenure was similar to Bhutto's, and despite the temporary euphoria over nuclear tests following those of India in May 1998, the structural imbalances continued to haunt the government. Both India and Pakistan were soon fighting a high-altitude war on the Kargil Heights in the disputed region of Kashmir. Sharif disowned this military venture and apportioned part of the blame to General Pervez Musharraf, the impetuous army chief. Their mutual bickering finally led to Sharif's overthrow by Musharraf in October 1999, the fourth time Pakistan was to undergo a military takeover in the 50 years of its existence as a sovereign state.

On his assumption of power, Musharraf, like his military predecessors, had promised accountable and transparent political culture, before eventually coming to rely on familiar groups and divisive tactics. He exiled Nawaz Sharif to Saudi Arabia, while Benazir Bhutto, already facing corruption charges in Pakistan and Europe, decided to live in Dubai. While Sharif's Muslim League (PML-N) suffered official intimidation, it splintered into several groups, while some members of the PPP, known as the PPP Parliamentarians, decided to work with Musharraf's regime.

The constitution and its place in Pakistan's future

Pakistan's constitution of 1973 has remained a consensus document even after several major amendments over successive decades, many of which were introduced during the military regimes of Generals Zia-ul-Haq and Pervez Musharraf. The constitution's original blueprint, similar to those of India and the UK stipulated two chambers in parliament (a bicameral legislature), which was to be elected on the basis of universal adult voting rights. Formulated during the term of Zulfikar Ali Bhutto and commonly agreed by all parties of various ethnic and ideological persuasions, the constitution provided a fair distribution of legislative powers between the Senate and the National Assembly. The Senate was to be formed through indirect elections from the national and provincial assemblies, guaranteeing equal seats to all four provinces of Pakistan, with proper representation of women and minorities. The National Assembly was to be formed of elected representatives from all areas of Pakistan on the basis of universal voting rights available to every adult citizen. These voters would also elect provincial assemblies, representing their respective provinces—Punjab, Sindh, Balochistan, and the NWFP—and would be single-house mini-parliaments. The constitution also devised mechanisms for power-sharing between the center and the four provinces in various areas from administration to revenue and resources.

Highlighting the separation of powers, the constitution allowed sovereignty as well as interdependence to the executive, judiciary, and parliament through a proper system of checks and balances. While the country was to be headed by an indirectly elected president having only ceremonial powers, the central government was to be run by the prime minister, who was the majority party leader in the National Assembly. Here, parliament and prime minister were to create and implement policies, with the president remaining nonpartisan and keeping the federation together. On a local level, each province would be headed by a governor who would not have any major role in day-to-day governance. This would be the prerogative of the respective chief minister, representing the majority party in the provincial assembly.

The judiciary was to be totally neutral and independent of political influences all the way from its highest echelons to its local subdivisions, while the highest court, the Supreme Court, would be empowered to hear and issue judgments on constitutional matters.

This system worked well until Zulfikar Ali Bhutto was overthrown in 1977 in a military coup led by General Zia. Zia introduced constitutional amendments through a pliant parliament in 1985. As a result, the pendulum of power shifted from the prime minister to the president, which made the elected institutions and their representatives somewhat redundant. Nawaz Sharif did away with this amendment during his second tenure as prime minister in 1997, but these changes were reinstated by General Musharraf in 2002. They allow the president to nominate four provincial governors, chiefs of armed forces, judges and, most of all, permit the president to dismiss the national and provincial assemblies at will. These changes have distorted the parliamentary character of the constitution, and despite agreeing to remove this serious anomaly, President Zardari has procrastinated, rendering parliament and the prime minister less effective, with power remaining concentrated in his presidential office.

RETURN TO DEMOCRACY?

ON 18 AUGUST 2008 a crestfallen Pervez Musharraf resigned the presidency of Pakistan during a television address to the nation, although the speech had been pre-recorded at his office in Rawalpindi, where he had been living like a recluse. The world was not shocked—nor was his nation—since the question being asked over the past year was not *why* he would resign, but rather *when*. Musharraf's resignation paved the way for Asif Ali Zardari (widower of Benazir Bhutto) to ease himself into the country's highest office after winning a majority vote from Pakistan's bicameral parliament of the Senate and the National Assembly, and the four provincial assemblies.

Zardari took the oath as twelfth president of Pakistan on 20 September 2008, marking an amazing journey from accused prisoner to the most powerful person in the land. He had earlier assumed the leadership of the Pakistan People's Party (PPP) following the assassination of his wife Benazir Bhutto on 27 December 2007. Bhutto, the charismatic party leader and two-time prime minister of Pakistan, was leaving a rally in Rawalpindi when a suicide bomber claimed her life and those of 20 followers. The attack was presumably carried out by anti-American Islamists based in Pakistan's tribal regions who were wary of Islamabad's support for the US-led war on terror. Bhutto's earlier statements criticizing al-Qaeda, the Taliban, and other militants had not endeared her to a wide range of anti-American groups intent on eliminating her.

Musharraf himself was not fond of her politics, but through American and British efforts, he reluctantly entered into a secret power-sharing deal with her in 2007. Her return to Pakistan in October 2007, from almost a decade-long self-imposed exile, had been preceded by Zardari's release from a Pakistani jail where he had been incarcerated on corruption charges since the late 1990s. As part of this deal, Musharraf's regime withdrew all cases of financial misdemeanor against the couple both in Pakistan and abroad. Regardless of their differences, Bhutto and Musharraf concluded this power-sharing agreement, not based on any party political agreement but on the basis that Washington and London urgently needed Islamabad to continue the fight against the Taliban.

Musharraf's government had been in power since his coup in October 1999 against the elected government of Nawaz Sharif, but had failed to resolve the country's longstanding problems of misgovernance, instead banking on the same politicians whom he had earlier debunked as corrupt and inept. His support for the Western invasion of Afghanistan, the rounding up of dissidents, activists, and militants, followed by the military operations in the border regions, had not only escalated suicide bombings in urban centers in Pakistan, but had also weakened his own political stature.

By sacking Pakistan's chief justice on 9 March 2007, then imposing a State of Emergency on 3 November 2007 in order to prolong his own controversial and weakened tenure, Musharraf had become a liability. In desperation, he sought the political backing of Benazir Bhutto, who had grown tired of living in exile in Dubai and London. However, Bhutto's tragic death so soon after her return threw a spanner in the works for many, including Musharraf, who had earlier allowed the Americans to undertake air and ground operations against militants inside Pakistan's tribal territories. As a result of the snap elections held in February 2008, Zardari emerged as the foremost powerbroker in the complex politics of the country.[1]

Zardari tried to forge a larger political consensus across the country, mindful of pressure from Washington and other countries for Musharraf's policies on the Pushtun border regions to be continued and the need for a return to stability and normality. He even invited Afghan President Hamid Karzai to join him at his inaugural press conference on 20 September 2008 in Islamabad. A few hours later a group of pro-Taliban militants blew up the Marriott Hotel using a truck loaded with high-velocity explosives.[2] It was a bleak message from the militants to the new government. Soon there were more blasts targeting Peshawar, Swat, and Wah and even the tribal agencies of Waziristan, Bajaur, Khyber, and Orakzai, causing serious alarm for the Pakistani government.

These violent outbreaks raised grave concerns about the competence of the country's administrative machinery. With domestic security already so volatile, the US ground and aerial offensives on Pakistani territory grew in frequency, with an impatient and desperate Bush administration intent on mounting more decisive operations before completing its unpopular tenure.[3] Pakistanis in general and Pushtuns in particular watched this callous violence with horror as US and Pakistani troops pursued a hammer-and-anvil strategy in the tribal belt, causing numerous deaths and dislocating hundreds of thousands of people from their native villages and settlements. *Pushtunwali*, the Pushtun code of honor and revenge, was joined by strong anti-Western rancor, fanning the flames of the militant movement. Chaos and disorder on both sides of the Afghanistan–Pakistan border only helped the Taliban regroup and replenish their recruits from inside Afghanistan, where Western military campaigns since October 2001 had failed to eliminate them. The Kabul regime, mired in corruption and ineptitude, had been unable to introduce reforms, and its dependence on warlords, ethnic firebrands, and drug barons, alongside an army of expatriates and expensive consultants, substantially helped the opposition forces.

By the time Barack Hussein Obama was sworn in as the 44th president of the United States on 20 January 2009, Afghanistan was far from peaceful, leaving many observers and participants of the conflict in despair. In his inaugural speech President Obama specifically mentioned both Afghanistan and Pakistan, promising a new series of policies prioritizing diplomacy and dialogue over military action. He appointed Richard Holbrooke as his special envoy to the region, raising hopes of a breakthrough in the region's politics.[4] However, despite some guarded hope for the new US administration,[5] Pakistanis were dismayed when two US drones targeted houses in North and South Waziristan and five US missiles killed 22 people on the ground three days into the new presidency.[6] The next day, a similar US aerial attack on Laghman province in Afghanistan killed 15 people. These incidents combined to highlight the fact that Washington, far from prioritizing political channels as promised, had continued to place its faith in firepower.

Shock and widespread public anger emerged across southwestern Asia, with protests from Zardari and Karzai, yet US Vice President Joe Biden strongly defended the increased military operations as well as warning his fellow citizens of more casualties to come in Afghanistan.[7] These drone attacks along both sides of the border continued even as Karzai and Zardari visited Washington in May 2009 to confer with the new US administration.

The main reason for appointing Richard Holbrooke as regional envoy was to deal with the wider political problems permeating the whole region—Afghanistan, Pakistan, and India—and to bring about tangible peace among these uneasy neighbors.[8] His appointment highlighted the fact that a concrete Indo–Pakistani agreement on Kashmir could help secure peace and security in the entire region, yet under pressure from Delhi, India was immediately excluded from Holbrooke's remit. Not only had India lobbied against the internationalization of the age-old dispute, it had equally refused to be equated with Pakistan, thus causing the first

U-turn of the Obama administration. The drone attacks, paired with India's exemption from Holbrooke's remit, further underlined Pakistan's apprehensions about the unevenness of US policies toward South Asia.[9] While British Foreign Secretary David Miliband, much to the consternation of his Indian hosts in Mumbai, urged a resolution of the Kashmir dispute in order to neutralize extremists, the new US administration appeared reluctant to see the dispute as a major flashpoint for regional instability.[10]

Regional observers, including military strategists, had been pushing for new policy options in Afghanistan rather than continuing to rely on aerial bombardment, which only served to popularize the Taliban. Brigadier Mark Carleton-Smith, commanding British troops in Helmand province in Afghanistan, had earlier voiced a pragmatic view of the situation: "We need to lower our expectations. We're not going to win this war; it's about reducing it to a manageable level of insurgency that's not a strategic threat and can be managed by the Afghan army."[11]

Through much of his tenure, Afghan President Hamid Karzai was confined to his palace, while his colleagues behaved in such a way that they were accused of collaborating with their enemies, money laundering, and drug trafficking. The Kabul regime was viewed as "the most corrupt, most venal" of its type by the British Conservative MP David Davis on his return from a fact-finding visit to Afghanistan in October 2008.[12] Even President Karzai's supporters within the Western media were now skeptical of the deteriorating situation and feared a bleak future for the country amidst corruption, graft, inefficiency, and rising violence.[13]

The serious economic crisis that had begun in the US before spreading around the globe, paired with the stalemate situation in West Asia, had already dampened enthusiasm in the West for waging wars against Islamists. Many Pakistanis feared that in desperation the Bush administration had callously turned its firepower on Pakistan, and that Western powers along with India were accomplices in destabilizing their nuclear Muslim state. Each fatal drone-led missile attack pushed more Pushtuns and their supporters toward the Taliban, neutralizing any sympathy that Islamabad might have gained after each Taliban/al-Qaeda-inflicted atrocity. Pakistan found itself between the proverbial rock and a hard place. Like Cambodia in the 1970s, Pakistan, bordering a weak and unstable Afghanistan, had itself become the casualty of vengeful and unpopular Western interventionism.[14] This clash of "fundamentalisms" had begun to bleed Pakistan, unleashing numerous mutinies in its Pushtun regions, and now a civilian elite was pushing the country toward a grave situation.[15] In October 2008, 63 million Pakistanis signed the largest petition in human history, entitled *"Yeh Hum Naheen"* (This is Not Us), condemning the violence while demanding substantial changes in official policy.[16]

During 2009–10, Pakistan was faced with the most serious challenge to its existence, with the country's economy and security undermined by apprehensions about the dissolution of this nuclear state.[17] For the most part, Pakistanis were aghast at the rapidity of the whirlwind that was engulfing their nation—a nation otherwise endowed with strong-willed and immensely patriotic people, and with bountiful natural resources. Pakistan's security had also been undermined by the terrorist attacks in Mumbai on 26 November 2008, which caused the deaths of over 170 people, with Indian leaders and the media blaming Pakistan-based militant groups for this atrocity. In addition to causing acute human misery and the attendant economic losses, the emerging peace process between the two countries came to a standstill, with New Delhi pressuring Pakistan to hand over leading Muslim firebrands for masterminding the Mumbai attacks. Not only did the events rekindle old tensions between the neighbors, they also exposed the fragile nature of the peace process that civic groups and governments on both sides had pursued since 2002.

With continued American drone attacks on the already restive border zone of FATA, and now India demanding its pound of flesh, Pakistan found itself in a state of double jeopardy. Faced with India's pressure, Pakistan's leadership tried to assuage public anger, while the public itself sought a more autonomous and confident policy, ironically restoring the army as the "real guardian of national security."[18] It appeared that, in their vehement dislike of New Delhi following decades of human rights violations in Kashmir and the 2002 massacre of 2,000 Muslims in Gujarat, militant groups had taken it upon themselves to damage India as well as bringing the two nuclear states to the brink of war.

Throughout 2009, spawned by increasing encroachments by the TTP in Swat and FATA, Pakistani public opinion backed its armed forces' military operations to restore order across the battered nation. Negotiations by the ANP regime with Swat's radicals led by Maulana Sufi Muhammad and his son-in-law Fazlullah had failed, and instead a parallel coercive authority established its own writ by demolishing schools and eliminating any critical voices. Militants from all over the country and across the borders began to filter into Swat and Malakand, and suicide bombings multiplied. The Swat operation began in April 2009 and resulted in the displacement of more than two million people from their homes; laudably, the government was able to provide them with shelter and food, and most returned to their homes following the ousting of the

Taliban from the scenic valleys and surrounding districts.

The armed forces also embarked on a three-pronged operation in South Waziristan—by now the headquarters of Pakistani and al-Qaeda militants intent upon destabilizing the country in order to defeat a demoralized West. The drone attacks claimed many lives, including those of some known militants—on 3 August 2009 Baitullah Mehsud, the titular leader of the TTP, was killed in such an aerial attack. His successor Hakimullah Mehsud intensified the suicide attacks across urban centers in addition to spawning a new phase in anti-Shia militancy. Finally, on 17 October 2009 Pakistani troops began their putsch into Waziristan and gradually began to capture villages and outposts earlier controlled by militants. However, these operations in South Waziristan and Swat resulted in an escalation in bomb blasts and suicide attacks across the country, making the autumn of 2009 an unusually bloody time in southwest Asia.[19] Concurrently, it proved a most violent phase for the NATO troops, with the Afghani Taliban inflicting casualties on Western troops. Hamid Karzai's election for a second term in August 2009 has been highly controversial, with proven cases of corruption and vote rigging. Led by an inept leadership and bedeviled by corruption and endemic violence, Afghanistan did not seem any closer to peace and stability, nor did Washington and its Western allies appear to have agreed upon any alternative policy options to steer the world out of this nine-year-long conflict.

The global war on terror and Pakistan's role

But how had Pakistan arrived at this precarious place? Some of the answers lie with the previous generation of leaders, one of whom held dictatorial sway over Pakistan for almost a decade. We return once again to the legacy of General Pervez Musharraf. Like his military predecessors, the general remained unwilling to accept that his 1999 military coup and its successive policies had exacerbated his country's problems of governance and security.

Musharraf's preeminence was largely the result of global events following 9/11, including Western security imperatives across the Muslim world, which found in him a dependable ally. That fateful night in late September 2001 General Musharraf was awoken by a call from the US Secretary of State Colin Powell offering him a stark choice between Washington and the Taliban, alongside other demands that were to underpin America's dangerous and multi-pronged war on terror. The stern message had already been conveyed by US Deputy Secretary of State Richard Armitage to General Mahmud Ahmad, Pakistan's director of

Inter-Services Intelligence (ISI), who happened to be visiting the US during 9/11. Musharraf recorded Washington's dire threats in his own memoirs: "Armitage added to what Colin Powell had said to me and told the Director General—not only that we had to decide whether we were with America or with the terrorists, but that if we chose the terrorists, then we should be prepared to be bombed back to the Stone Age. This was a shockingly barefaced threat, but it was obvious that the United States had decided to hit back, and hit back hard."[20] The United States had suffered a devastating blow and now sought deadly revenge against Afghanistan, a country already devastated by the Soviet invasion and subsequent Afghan infighting.[21]

For Musharraf, these US threats were something of a godsend. Following his dismissal of Nawaz Sharif's elected government in October 1999, the Pakistani army chief had become a pariah, ostracized by all Western countries, but now the Bush administration was offering him much-needed legitimacy as well as an opportunity to assume a front-line role in the emerging global war on terror. Musharraf was certainly not the first general in Pakistani history to dismiss a sitting government; moreover, his coup had not only been validated by an obliging Supreme Court, that same court had also ironically allowed him to amend the country's constitution as and when he chose.[22] In July 2000, through a Provisional Constitutional Order (PCO), Musharraf asked all senior judges to swear an oath of loyalty to him. Many obliged and stayed on, whereas any dissenters were promptly retired. Musharraf was to attempt to repeat the same exercise eight years later through another PCO, but that time it would not be smooth sailing.

Pakistan's political culture, marooned by incessant military inter-ventionism and incompetent politicians, certainly posed no formidable challenge to Musharraf during his early presidential phase, but his global isolation continued to haunt him. The events of 9/11 signaled an end to Musharraf's global marginalization; he had discovered powerful and well-equipped friends in the North Atlantic regions and had no qualms about following along so that he could revel in his own newfound status as a global statesman. Meanwhile Pakistan's ongoing problems of govern-ance seemed to be nobody's concern.[23]

Several long years later the country's chronic problems of governance and uneven economic development remained as entrenched as they had been when the general took over with promises of transparency and honesty. Suicide bombings had never been commonplace in Pakistan, even during the stormy days of the Afghan Jihad in the 1980s. Beginning in January 2007, however, and continuing to this day, Pakistan has not stopped bleeding: the death toll rises daily. The problems of poverty and sectarianism remain as acute as ever, and in Balochistan, Swat, Kohat, Bajaur, Kurram, Orakzai, and Waziristan, Pakistanis are suffering unnecessary bloodshed that could have been avoided through proper political and economic measures, and by isolating the militants from the mainstream civilian population.

Musharraf undone The closing weeks of 2007 had seen the unfolding of several significant developments, including preparations for the presidential election and the return of Benazir Bhutto and Mian Nawaz Sharif, former prime ministers who had both been in exile. In the meantime, Musharraf got himself reelected through the emasculated assemblies, and his imposition of Emergency rule on 3 November 2007 targeted the vocal senior judiciary and an increasingly critical media—a desperate act aimed at fortifying his faltering position and manipulating his own reelection. Since dismissing the chief justice on 9 March 2007, the general-president had faced persistent but mostly peaceful protests from groups of lawyers, students, journalists, laborers, women's organizations, and human rights activists. His dramatic and disputatious acts only added to his and Pakistan's woes.

Pakistanis, by and large, felt gravely disappointed in Musharraf when he took the presidential oath for another five-year term, administered by his own hand-picked chief justice on 29 November 2007. Musharraf always held the concurrent offices of president and chief of the army staff. The civic protest movement began in earnest in March 2007, starkly exposing the serious systemic contradictions that led to an increasingly isolated Musharraf taking extreme measures merely to shore up his own position. With the dissolution of the country's largest cabinet, headed by the expatriate banker Shaukat Aziz, Musharraf hoped for a hung parliament in the forthcoming elections of 2008. Instead, the Pakistani electorate gave a defiant verdict on 18 February by electing mainstream political parties including the Pakistan People's Party (PPP), and by rejecting the pro-Musharraf elements. However, concerned Pakistanis and foreign analysts feared that the ongoing crisis would be aggravated by the army's interventionism and Musharraf's own stubbornness propped up by support from Washington and London.

By the summer of 2008, between the PPP's election victory and the start of the new presidential term, Musharraf might have assumed a low-key profile, spending his time playing golf and attending private parties. But his country was now being viewed as a "dysfunctional" state by the civil and military officials in Washington; the entire Frontier was astir with volatile armed defiance led by the Pakistani Taliban, and Hamid Karzai's regime in Kabul continued its undiminished criticism of Islamabad amidst a rising tide of insurgency and bomb blasts in Kabul and eastern Afghanistan.[24]

Zardari's victory at the polls Following the assassination of Benazir Bhutto her party garnered a major electoral victory with her widower Asif Ali Zardari as its new leader. The political set-up in the country was led by Prime Minister Syed Yousaf Raza Gilani, PPP vice chairman from Multan. Suffering from inexperience and caught between a controversial yet stubborn President Musharraf and powerful party chairman Zardari, Gilani was embarrassingly aware of his own limitations. Tensions with the coalition partners over the reinstatement of deposed judges, concerns about Musharraf's accountability, plus the specter of vast swathes of the NWFP falling before menacing Talibanization needed patience, courage, sagacity, and, most of all, astute policies. Amid apprehension and high expectation, Pakistanis and the outside world were willing to allow Gilani time to find his own way to escort Pakistan out of its domestic and regional quagmire. Pakistani parliamentarians voted for Zardari to succeed Musharraf as president and, despite doubts about Zardari's integrity, a wider sympathy factor neutralized opposition to the new head of the state.

Past coups, past disasters

How had Musharraf won and lost the preeminent position he held in government and how did this fit into the narrative that is Pakistani politics since Partition? Pervez Musharraf's military coup of 12 October 1999 against Nawaz Sharif's government fitted in with the country's cyclic pattern of bad governance in which brief weak democratic interludes have been bracketed by longer spells of military rule.

In the early 1950s, the army began to assume a central governmental role in partnership with the civil bureaucracy, and in the process political forces grew weaker. Problems with India and closer ties with the US during the Cold War further entrenched the military establishment until it blatantly overthrew the civilian authority in October 1958.[25] General Ayub Khan, a self-styled field marshal, was determined to modernize the traditional society by ridding it of allegedly corrupt and indolent politicians.[26] Despite the semblance of some controlled elections, the economic stratification and political suffocation eventually led to agitation in the streets in both regions of the country. Eventually the general-president lost his nerve and was replaced by his army chief, Yahya Khan. Like his predecessor, General Yahya Khan began to cobble together a pliant political defense for his own survival that was challenged by the Awami League (AL), the majority party led by Sheikh Mujibur Rahman in East Pakistan. The generals dithered about transferring powers to the Awami League's elected deputies in 1971, leading to a repressive military operation in East Pakistan against fellow Pakistanis. This turned into a civil war, resulting in the Indian invasion of Pakistan's eastern region in 1971. This third Indo–Pakistani war resulted in an independent Bangladesh, as well as dishing out a humiliating defeat to Pakistan's armed forces, mostly due to the bad planning of its commanders.[27]

The scheming generals were spared by Zulfikar Ali Bhutto, the PPP leader of the remaining region of Pakistan, who dedicated more funds to the disillusioned military establishment as well as initiating Pakistan's nuclear program. Bhutto was eventually overthrown in 1977 by those very generals who, led by Zia-ul-Haq, executed Bhutto and imposed a selective form of Islamization on the country. The generals not only ruled the country through repressive martial law, they also imposed an exclusive ideology in which women, minorities, and democratic forces suffered under partisan laws, often justified in the name of Sharia law.

The Iranian Revolution of February 1979, followed by the Soviet invasion of Afghanistan, turned Pakistan into a front-line state for the West and its allies, giving Zia's regime a new lease on life and a sense of legitimacy. Zia's death in a mysterious air crash in 1988 allowed a modicum of democracy to return to the country, but a weakened political culture further fragmented by bickering between Benazir Bhutto and Nawaz Sharif could not deter General Pervez Musharraf from imposing his authority eleven years later in October 1999.[28]

Pakistan's own security with regard to India was massively costly in resources, and made the entire political culture, economic planning, and foreign policy formulation and implementation dependent on the army's support. Explanations of why the army has such an interventionist, dominant role have varied from viewing it as a state within a state, to having the role of a deliverer. Critics consider the Pakistani army to be a liability, whereas its supporters consider it to be the only institution that has escaped "the systemic chaos" allegedly let loose by the Pakistan People's Party (PPP) and the Pakistan Muslim League (PML) regimes during their decade-long, often factionalist civilian rule of the 1990s. However, non-polemical observers consider that the military lacks a clear perspective on its extra-professional role due to the absence of serious reviews and reforms of its role. Just such reforms were proposed by the Hamoodur Rahman Commission Report, headed by the chief justice after the separation of Pakistan in 1971, but this review has never been implemented.

Musharraf's coup and Sharif's downfall

General Musharraf's coup in 1999 against Nawaz Sharif's second administration had become rather less contentious after Sharif's agreement to leave the country for Saudi Arabia. During Sharif's trial on allegations of attempting to kill Musharraf by refusing to allow his plane to land, Sharif's Pakistan Muslim League (PML-N) held sporadic rallies to obtain his release. Despite the party's protestations, the Supreme Court not only rejected Sharif's plea of innocence, but found him guilty of hijacking and conspiracy to murder.

Curiously, while still in power Sharif had given Pervez Musharraf a two-year extension as chief of army staff, but Sharif got cold feet and attempted to dismiss Musharraf while he was returning from Sri Lanka in October 1999. As in the past, the corps commanders stood by their chief and arrested Sharif instead, imposing military rule without actually classifying it as martial law. Sharif's about-turn was largely temperamental and based on bad advice from some of his cabinet colleagues, who had somehow convinced Sharif of his own invincibility.

Sharif's exile to Saudi Arabia with his family members in December 2000 not only weakened his following within the PML-N, it also strengthened Musharraf's own position, although the judiciary had demanded the restoration of electoral politics by late 2002. In addition, senior judges had allowed Musharraf to amend the constitution unilaterally, a dire development that was to lead to a serious constitutional crisis years later. Several of Sharif's incarcerated colleagues had offered apologies and one by one they were all released. However, the military regime could not hammer out a similar deal with Benazir Bhutto (twice prime minister in the 1990s before opting for exile), especially following the April 2000 court verdict that found her guilty of corruption. Pakistan's third major political party, operating as a key power broker and closely tied to Musharraf, is the Muhajir/Muttahida Qaumi Movement (MQM), whose firebrand leader Altaf Hussain has lived in exile in London since 1992.

The absence of Bhutto, Sharif, and Hussain from the country amid an organized official campaign of depoliticization and cooption of splinter elements from the PPP and the PML-N initially helped Musharraf's regime. While democratic forces clamored for the restoration of unfettered politics and viewed the coup and subsequent cobbling together of a subdued political facade as a usurpation of power by ambitious military elements, many members from the two main parties, along with the MQM and several fence-sitting independent politicians, bided their time.

Using accountability as a pretext, the military regime mounted a selective campaign against the politicians who had ignored their earlier blandishments. The regime attempted to win support for Musharraf by applying coercion and directing temptation at dissenting politicians. However, despite media reports of corruption and inefficiency in the defense establishment, the regime and its National Accountability Bureau (NAB) only arrested politicians who were, in most cases, eventually let off if they agreed to support Musharraf.

However, by late 2001 the drive for accountability had petered out when the military regime started to look to its own long-term survival. It was clear that Musharraf was there to stay and was ready to make compromises with "like-minded" political elements. Some smaller ethnonational parties such as the Awami National Party (ANP) of Abdul Wali Khan, now headed by his son Asfandyar Wali Khan, felt that the military regime could still be nudged toward full democracy. By denouncing the Taliban in neighboring Afghanistan, they not only demonstrated the growing gap between the religious extremists and the moderates, but also a major shift in their former policy of Pushtun political identity. The ANP's former colleagues in the two factions of Jamiat-i-Ulama-i-Islam (JUI), largely confined to the Pushtun areas of the NWFP and Balochistan, were eager to reassert their ideological fraternity with the Taliban, but Fazlur Rahman, despite being ethnically Pushtun, felt uneasy with the Taliban's extremism. Such divisions served Musharraf's military regime well, as it could isolate the few pro-Taliban splinter groups from mainstream Pushtun society, which was not that enamored with Taliban-style anti-urban extremism. In retrospect, the current situation with a re-energized Taliban could have been averted had more judicious policies been in place at that time.

By the middle of 2001, it had become apparent that Musharraf was engineering a set-up, combining the legacies of his two military predecessors from the 1960s and 1980s, namely Ayub Khan and Zia-ul-Haq. He held local elections and promised decentralization, as well as reserving one-third of the seats in the National and Provincial Assemblies for women—although he stopped short of an immediate end to separate electorates for minorities in which non-Muslims had reserved seats for which only non-Muslims could vote. The Muhajir/Muttahida Qaumi Movement (MQM) stayed away from local polls in Karachi, but several other parties under different guises allowed their followers to contest polls for local councils. Headed by a general, an agency called the National Reconstruction Bureau (NRB) that promised grassroots empowerment had worked out the plan. Many critics felt that in bypassing national and provincial politics, the regime was simply interested in entrenching localism. Some observers felt that since Musharraf had no political constituency as such, he might use these councilors and the elected heads of district councils—called *Nazims*—as an electoral college. However, when this new system of local bodies was finally introduced on 14 August 2001, confusion prevailed regarding the separation of powers between the local bureaucracy and these elected councilors. In addition, some economists worried that this duplication of a rather ambiguous administrative setup would be very costly.

It is interesting to note that Musharraf, unlike Ayub Khan, did not bank on these councilors to get himself elevated to the presidency in 2001; instead he simply eased out President Rafiq Tarrar and took his place just before he undertook a visit to India in late July 2001. However like Zia-ul-Haq, in April 2002 Musharraf pursued a referendum to seek the highest office in the country; though the turnout was dismally low, a submissive bureaucracy delivered the desired result. While Musharraf had already seized the presidency, it was important to give the appearance of legitimacy and this referendum served as a useful legal ploy. Within Pakistan, there was little outcry as the largely disaffected nation could see history repeating itself for the umpteenth time.

Musharraf now held all the highest and the most powerful offices in the country, with no possible role for either Sharif or Bhutto. Musharraf's critics did not represent any major political opposition, nor did the criticism from Qazi Hussain Ahmed of the Jamaat-i-Islami (JI) register any response. The military, the most powerful organ of the state, had simply reasserted itself, irrespective of the fact that Pakistani civic groups and some Western voices reiterated their demand for the restoration of democracy. Musharraf knew his corps commanders were behind him and the judiciary had already given him extraordinary power to change the constitution to fit his own desires. The few dissenting judges had been eased out, while those remaining had sworn to stay loyal to the general by accepting his PCO. Meanwhile ordinary Pakistanis worried about their day-to-day existence.

In his much-awaited speech on Pakistan's Independence Day, he took credit for establishing democracy at the grassroots and reiterated his commitment to hold elections for the National and Provincial Assemblies in October 2002.[29]

Three-in-one leader After getting himself elected president through the dubious referendum, Musharraf—by now the head of state, the Army Chief, *and* the prime minister all in one—proceeded to hold "sanitized" elections, in which intelligence agencies and the police delivered the results of Musharraf's choice. Here, mainstream political parties such as the PML-N and the PPP expectedly received the official wrath, while Islamist and ethnic organizations such as the Muhajir/Muttahida Qaumi Movement (MQM) along with an army of loyalists, were allowed to dominate the assemblies. As Musharraf had fixed the elections, the uneven playing-field was of his own devising. Religio-political parties espousing a purist form of Islamic order such as Jamiat-i-Ulama-i-Islam (JUI) and Jamaat-i-Islami (JI) were the main beneficiaries in the elections due to an increased accent on Political Islam in the Muslim world amidst a formidable wave of anti-Americanism. In Pakistan, these groups were more acceptable to Musharraf, as he feared mainstream political parties and through the presence of religio-political elements in the assemblies, he could also flag his own indispensability to his Western friends as "the last bastion against an encroaching extremism."

These religio-political parties structured themselves into the Combined Action Forum (Muttahida Majlis-i-Ammal, or MMA) and, despite forming provincial governments in Balochistan and the North West Frontier Province (NWFP), they remained suspicious of Musharraf as did many supporters and beneficiaries of this tailored political system. However, their own interests and expediency kept them together until 2007, when serious cracks within the MMA began to emerge, especially because of the anti-Musharraf campaign led by the civil society.

Other than the landowning elite and the MMA coopted by Musharraf's sleuths, another major ally for Pervez Musharraf and his handpicked Prime Minister Shaukat Aziz, was the Muhajir/Muttahida Qaumi Movement (MQM), the Karachi-based ethnic party of Urdu speakers who often vacillated between bullet and ballot to keep Pakistan's largest city under its unchallenged control. Its leader Altaf Hussain, though settled in London, controlled Karachi according to his whims as well as to suit Musharraf's personal prerogatives. Using the politics of coercion and violence, Hussain relished pressurizing power brokers in both Islamabad and Sindh.[30]

The serious political and constitutional imbalances within the country's body politic persisted, owing in large part to the enduring tradition of military dominance. This allowed Musharraf's apologists, especially the splinter groups from the PML and the PPP, to cobble together an interest-based alliance known as the Pakistan Muslim League (Quaid-i-Azam Group, or PML-Q).

The PML-Q was, in fact, delivered through an official initiative on 20 April 2002 to provide support and second-tier defense to Pervez Musharraf. Very few analysts were ever taken in by the premise that it was only the military that could contain the mullah—a dictum his spokespeople used too often to curry favor for the General, who with each passing day found his position even more untenable. On the contrary, most Pakistani observers believed that democracy would only ever flourish in the country if the army retreated to its barracks and surrendered its predominant role in the country's political, economic, and foreign affairs. To these groups, only the ballot and civil society could deter an encroaching Talibanization and rising violence. According to this growing consensus, it was understood that the longer military power dominated the country, the more serious its problems of governance and nationhood would become. Moreover, the army's own professionalism was seen as being seriously eroded by the politicization of its generals who zealously maintained their untouchability over every other institution and section of Pakistan.[31]

Chasms across the borders

Kabul's routine criticism of Musharraf, as well as critical statements from Washington and London for not doing enough to eliminate support for the Taliban, were exacerbated by his own domestic vulnerabilities. He was made even more defenseless by his dependence on corrupt and inept supporters in the assemblies, as well as by genuine concerns about his legitimacy given the serious anomaly of serving as army chief and president concurrently. It had been true that Musharraf was safe as long as the corps commanders remained loyal to him with all their benefits guaranteed. His position was made more secure by the fact that his North Atlantic backers needed him to rein in the tribal Pushtuns—a premise Musharraf used to his own advantage. By undertaking an undefined military operation in Waziristan in 2006, Musharraf was seen as having been weakened even by some of his former liberal supporters. However, for Washington and London he was valiantly roadblocking a feared Taliban uprising in nuclearized Pakistan, and for that it was worth overlooking his serious democratic deficits.

The West's prioritization of security over democracy worked in Musharraf's favor, but this was at the expense of the country's long-term prerogatives. After more than 2,000 Pakistani soldiers were killed fighting fellow Pakistanis between 2005 and 2007 and the near-loss of control over the tribal regions, ordinary Pakistanis were not pleased when the resulting suicide bombings began to happen more frequently.

In the same vein, Hamid Karzai's own fragile situation, including his continued inaction and scores of Pushtun deaths hastily identified as Taliban insurgents, had created a serious moral and political dilemma for the Afghan leader. Instead of addressing his own unquestioned dependence on the US-led Coalition and NATO, Karzai fired off periodic verbal missiles at Musharraf. The Afghan scapegoating of Pakistan for Kabul's own problems as well as the unrelenting Western criticism of Musharraf for not doing enough, only aggravated Pakistani cynicism and anger. To many of his domestic critics, it was obvious that Musharraf was becoming a liability to the US. Another body of opinion posited that by putting pressure on Musharraf for more military operations against tribal Pushtuns, his Western allies actually wanted to squeeze more blood out of Pakistan; however, the West believed that the Pushtuns were providing succor to the Taliban and al-Qaeda stragglers.[32] By default, this multi-directional pressure and unrelenting criticism not only emboldened Musharraf's opponents, it also appeared to be taking its toll on Musharraf himself during 2007, evidenced by his short fuse with Pakistani journalists at the time.

The nuclear question

Long before 9/11 and the destabilization of southwestern Asia, Pakistan's nuclear program had been viewed with intense skepticism and distrust by the West. The security threat posed by a nuclear India has never been far from official Pakistani concern and this threat has only multiplied with the loss of East Pakistan with New Delhi's full involvement. Pakistan's ruling elite—often dominated by military forces—decided to seek "an ultimate" deterrent at a time when nuclear proliferation had become a global preoccupation.

Throughout the 1970s, Pakistan's effort to gain nuclear knowledge, equipment for enrichment, and eventually, nuclear arms happened under the watchful eyes of an increasingly hostile Washington. Pakistan's re-alliance with the US after the Soviet invasion of Afghanistan meant that official Western watchdogs politely looked the other way although the CIA continued to gather evidence on suspicious movements of men and materials. Among the reportage on Pakistan's nuclear bomb tested in May 1998, some journalists focused on the activities of Pakistani nuclear physicist Abdul Qadeer Khan and his alleged sharing of nuclear know-how with North Korea, Iran, and Libya. Both India and Pakistan pursued nuclear arms programs in the 1970s, yet one wonders why commentators have been so single-mindedly obsessed with Pakistan.

By 2007, frequent leaked reports about the possibility of Pakistani nuclear assets falling into the hands of extremists and ominous predictions about Pakistan becoming a failed state not only caused despair among Pakistanis, it also put Musharraf's policies under the spotlight. Owing to its travails in the Middle East, it was evident that Washington had already backtracked on its worthy espousal of democratization in the Muslim world, and instead found it expedient to bank on dictators. Moreover, the Bush administration had allowed serious contradictions in its policy on nuclear proliferation in South Asia by offering several reactors to India. Once again, Pakistanis felt very strongly that their country had been singled out for discriminatory treatment. In Pakistan, Musharraf and his associates were being held responsible by the people for the nation's predicament. Given the country's problematic relationships with India, Afghanistan, and Iran, Pakistan's geopolitical isolation had provided a stark reminder to its concerned citizens that the country urgently needed to resolve the domestic political malaise, as well as to rethink its foreign policy within a new security framework.

Indo–Pakistani relations and the problem of Kashmir

Musharraf's attempts to build friendlier relations with India also seemed to have come to a dead end despite his major concessions on Kashmir. Of course there were pro-war hawks on both sides thwarting every effort for regional peace, but for a time Musharraf and the former Indian Prime Minister A. B. Vajpayee received plaudits for breaking the deadlock between the two countries. However, in 2002, following a terrorist attack on the Indian parliament, they had taken the nuclearized subcontinent to a proverbial eyeball-to-eyeball situation. India and Pakistan held two extreme positions on the Indo–Pakistan quagmire at that time— Pakistan's insistence on Kashmir as the defining issue of Indo–Pakistan relations contrasted with India's dithering and unhelpful focus on semantics. There was no tangible progress on contentious issues and no agreement on the freer movement of people and goods across the borders. In spite of this, a precarious peace prevailed between the two neighbors for a time; India had shown commendable restraint by not immediately accusing Pakistan of numerous violent past events, but the bomb blasts in Mumbai and Varanasi in November 2008 were used by Delhi's hawkish elements to reiterate their hatred of Pakistan. This incriminatory pattern became more obvious following the bomb blasts and shootings in Mumbai in the final days of November 2008, which led to over 170 deaths and hundreds of casualties.[33] The Mumbai attacks exposed the immensely weak nature of the Indo–Pakistani relationship, and it appeared that the underlying mistrust and the unresolved issues of Kashmir and water rights would block any substantial normalization.

While dissuading both Delhi and Islamabad from intensifying their mutual recriminations in early 2009, British Foreign Secretary David Miliband advised a "resolution of the dispute over Kashmir [which] would help deny extremists in the regions one of their main calls to arms, and allow Pakistani authorities to focus more effectively on tackling the threat on their western borders."[34]

The endgame?

Musharraf's presumed indispensability and his role as trustworthy bulwark against Islamists worked in his favor as it sidelined Pakistan's democratic and civil imperatives. This remained the case until the pinnacle of his career in 2006 when he published *In the Line of Fire*. His extended visits to the US and the UK were soon followed by a reckless move on 9 March 2007 to dismiss the country's chief justice. Brimming with resentment over one more serious betrayal, Pakistan's civil society rose to defend Justice Iftikhar Muhammad Chaudhry. The restoration of Chaudhry and other empowering verdicts by a reawakened Supreme Court on 20 July 2007 only enraged Musharraf. Described by the *New York Times* as "a shameful win," Musharraf's reelection on 6 October 2007 by the few hundred remaining members of the National and Provincial Assemblies (in the closing days of their tenure) further agitated a civil society that had already evolved a consensus on constitutional government and an independent judiciary.

Demands for unfettered democracy and an end to the involvement of the generals became the cornerstone of a national movement, which was spearheaded by thousands of lawyers, journalists, and human rights activists. Mismanagement and the army's contested dominance amid a rising tide of anti-Americanism in the Pushtun belt led to a deteriorating situation in the tribal regions and Swat. The escalating tensions in these already volatile areas required fresh ideas and well-planned policies. Once again, the impetuous and insecure Musharraf turned to coercive measures. His secret parleys with Benazir Bhutto in 2007, largely directed by Washington and London, appeared to work only in the interests of the four main parties involved, lacking any serious consideration about the cost to Pakistani civil society and democratic norms.

At this juncture, the Supreme Court again came under moral and professional pressure to disallow the extraconstitutional practice of gerrymandering or altering constitutional boundaries to favor a particular party. The senior judges heard well-argued petitions against Musharraf's control of the highest offices of the country—otherwise disallowed by the Constitution—along with his blanket pardon to all those who had amassed fortunes from the national exchequer and whose support Musharraf now needed to shore up his weak position. He preempted the Supreme Court in his usual rash manner and on 3 November 2007 imposed martial law on the country, terming it Emergency rule, which harshly singled out judges, lawyers, human rights activists, and journalists. In addition, Musharraf once again dismissed the chief justice and several other senior judges.

Deaf to the countrywide demand for his removal so that democracy, the primacy of law, and an independent judiciary could be restored, Musharraf hung on by the skin of his teeth. The same country that he had promised to rescue from a feared meltdown eight years earlier he was now describing as a failing state. For an honorable leader, this would have been reason enough to resign, but for a man prone to rash decisions and an unrealistic belief in his own survival, the writing on the wall remained blurred. The burning issues of Musharraf's own survival and the army's dominance were unraveling the resolution of the dangerous crises facing the country. The nation required his unmaking in order to be remade itself, and the civil society was ready to turn that corner, with or without him.

Vast territories in the NWFP had fallen under the ever-increasing authority of Taliban-style extremists who doled out harsher forms of tribal justice while frequent bomb blasts in the cities targeted vital defense and police establishments. The message these actions signaled was clear. Firstly, Pervez Musharraf was already an immensely unpopular ruler, and like the proverbial sinking ship, was beyond salvage. In an opinion poll conducted by the International Republican Institute in Pakistan in late 2007 only 15 percent of those polled had supported Musharraf, while two-thirds demanded his resignation as the solution to the violence gripping the country.[35] In another poll conducted by the BBC's Urdu Service in January 2008, the majority of Pakistanis viewed Musharraf as a liability and harbored doubts about the legality of his reelection. To more than two-thirds of those polled, his departure from the political scene would pave the way to a peaceful future ahead.[36]

The second message was that the country was crucially bound up in the sinister fallout from the stalled bloody war on terror in Afghanistan, though the actual security threat permeated from within its own tottering body politic. A sense of resignation prevailed among Pakistanis as they suffered perhaps the most serious crisis of their short history as a sovereign nation. The absence of a mechanism for the peaceful transfer of power had never been more apparent, and thus the replacement of Pervez Musharraf by General Ashfaq Parvez Kayani as army chief was received with new hope and apprehension. Against the backdrop of this wider dismay, Pakistanis went to the polls on 18 February 2008 and overwhelmingly voted for the Pakistan People's Party (PPP), the Pakistan Muslim League (PML-N), and the Awami National Party (ANP), all of which had been stifled during Musharraf's regime.

Amid the resulting euphoria, a unanimous parliamentary vote installed Syed Yousaf Raza Gilani (PPP) as prime minister, and committed itself to restoring parliamentary sovereignty, judicial independence, and constitutionalism, which further energized the fractured national morale. Political parties and the civil society displayed a strong consensus on resolving the economic crises along with prioritizing dialogue in addressing the various conflicts. Several months after the formation of the PPP-led coalition, and with growing unrest across the Frontier region, Washington, London, and the new army chief began to distance themselves from Musharraf. Shortly afterwards, following assurances from the new government about his future safety, Musharraf resigned in August 2008.

Benazir Bhutto's murder, the February elections, and Musharraf's resignation culminated in Asif Ali Zardari's ascendance as the most powerful person in Pakistan's uneven political system. Amidst raised expectations for new policies on security, the economy, and politics, Zardari appeared out of touch with the political realities of his society. He seemed unwilling to return those constitutional powers amassed by Musharraf through radical constitutional amendments back to parliament. Zardari also reneged on his promises to Sharif and others to restore the deposed Chief Justice and other senior judges. He also did not undertake any steps towards resolving the difficulties between Sharif and the governor of Punjab Salman Taseer, a Musharraf protégé now supported by Zardari. Zardari's political honeymoon headed towards turbulent times due to his strained relations with the lawyers, civil society, and the Sharif brothers. Musharraf, on the other hand, has settled in London, while his legacy continues to prolong Pakistan's agony and the country remains far away from its cherished ideal of good governance.

DICTATORS AND DYNASTIES

THE DRAMA THAT IS Pakistan's labyrinth in political history has been peopled with a cast of personalities who have, in their own ways, shown great loyalty to their country. But like tragic heroes, they have all failed to fulfill the promises they made.

For some of the post-independence generation of politicians—the likes of Benazir Bhutto, Nawaz Sharif, Altaf Hussain, and to a lesser extent, Imran Khan—their redemption may be possible to discern in their personal life stories featuring death and exile, but for Musharraf it has been a different journey with an uncertain outcome. Personality, family, resources, networks, and even the Western context have all been crucial in each of these cases. It is useful to examine the personalities and use their biographies and ideas within their own cultural and class structures to help us better understand the continued hold that dynastic- and personality-based politics still exercise within Pakistan.

Pervez Musharraf came from the urban, professional middle class, and his early days in power promised the very principles indicative of his background—a fresh start and "enlightened moderation." However, after eight years of sitting at the apex of an outdated and contentious system, Musharraf proved to be no different from his predecessors; surrounded by sycophants and unnerved by criticism, he became increasingly detached and resentful of civic criticism. He could have used these civic groups as a source of strength, but a mix of insecurity, unrealistic ambition, and misguided self-belief hastened his downfall.

On the other side of the fence, Benazir Bhutto always took pride in her education at Harvard and Oxford, but like her Oxford-educated father Zulfikar Ali Bhutto, she surrounded herself with a small coterie of hangers-on and often made decisions on her own rather than by committee. Even her will, briefly displayed by her widower Asif Ali Zardari after her funeral on 28 December 2007, nominated Zardari and their adolescent son Bilawal to take over the leadership of her party, the Pakistan People's Party (PPP). In her Urdu speeches, she often used the plural pronoun "we" for herself and took pride in being the daughter of one of the biggest landlords in Sindh. Like Musharraf, she was unwilling to listen to critical views, and ruling Pakistan and its masses through increasingly dangerous times seemed not only her passion but also her obsession. Sadly, it was also her downfall and death.

Mian Nawaz Sharif has an urban, industrial background and, like the Bhuttos, his politics have been pursued as a family affair reflecting dynastic ambitions. Sharif's dependence on his late father and brother for vital decisions, as well as his eagerness to amass power amidst great insecurity, propelled him towards confrontational politics.

Altaf Hussain, the leader of the Muhajir/Muttahida Qaumi Party (MQM), has been based in London since 1992. Coming from a poor background, he spoke of defeudalizing the country; however, Hussain not only collaborated with feudal lords and generals, he also assumed an almost spiritual status—he is called *Altaf Bhai* (brother) by followers in London and Karachi, and is often addressed as *Pir Sahib* (saint). Hussain combines the mafioso-style politicking of a venomous tribal chieftain with that of a ruthless feudal lord, and relishes subjecting people in Karachi to his endless speeches. He has never been known for magnanimity toward his critics. In the full knowledge of British and Pakistani security agencies, Hussain controls the city of Karachi like a Mafia godfather figure.

Imran Khan may be a heartthrob for millions of young Pakistanis, but his popularity has never translated itself fully into votes. Projects, such as the Shaukat Khanum Cancer Hospital in Lahore, his cricketing career, his stance on corruption, and his vocal criticism of Altaf Hussain and the MQM have endeared Khan to many. Despite his charisma, however, his Justice Party remains weak while the indomitable Khan has ended up as a coalition partner to a variety of political forces. Despite periodic planted news stories about his involvement in scandals and romantic escapades, Khan is a hero for ordinary, educated Pakistanis; like them, he is faced with the formidable barrier of ethnic, religious, and feudal leaders who have sleek party machines and local loyalties to oil their ambitions. Pakistan is a fertile land for all types of leadership, though one needs influence, resources, charisma, and some sort of support base. In addition to money, ethnic and local loyalties come in handy, though there have been times when citizens have supported parties with programs focusing on their basic issues.

In the pre-1947 era, Muhammad Ali Jinnah was a unique case—his integrity and the power of his message reached emerging middle-class Indian Muslims, who then took it to the masses. His liberal lifestyle and absence of religiosity were not issues for these segments of the population, who eventually became the foot soldiers for an emerging Pakistan. In the same vein, Benazir's father Zulfikar Ali Bhutto was also known for his liberal lifestyle, but succeeded in reaching the hearts and minds of millions who felt that he really communicated with them on their terms. People waited for hours to listen to his emotional speeches, which were always an amusing mix of raw Urdu and colloquial Sindhi; it was his ability to communicate directly with the masses and focus on their predicament that turned his Pakistan People's Party (PPP) into a grassroots organization. After his tragic hanging by General Zia-ul-Haq on 4 April 1979, Bhutto took on the aura of a Sufi saint and a folk hero. His tomb, built by his daughter in their native village of Garhi Khuda Bakhsh, has become a Sufi shrine, and with the graves of his two sons and Benazir Bhutto situated next to him, the dynastic and mystic traditions have reached the level of Greek tragedy. Rather like the Kennedys in the United States and the Nehrus in India, the Bhuttos are as strong in death as they were in life, and this powerful element of tragedy within the family has given it an aura of immortality.

Pervez Musharraf, the indulgent commando

Pervez Musharraf was born on 11 August 1943 in his paternal family home in Old Delhi and traced his Syed ancestors, who had migrated to India from Arabia several centuries ago, from the Prophet. His father, a graduate of Aligarh Muslim University, was an accountant in the foreign office of the new Pakistan government, while his mother, after obtaining a master's degree from Delhi University, had become a schoolteacher. Like millions of other Muslim refugees at the onset of Partition, the family undertook a perilous journey from volatile Delhi to Karachi. On their way lay a riotous Punjab, where Sikhs, Hindus, and Muslims engaged in killing sprees amidst a complete breakdown in law and order.[1] The British had refused to impose martial law and the civil authorities had either been withdrawn or, in many cases, were partisan and often participated in the ongoing communal violence.

A hot dusty journey on 14 August 1947 brought the Musharraf family to Pakistan's new capital, having witnessed massacres and arson on the way to their new home. Throughout the journey Musharraf's father held on to an important box that concealed 70,000 rupees meant for the newly formed Pakistani Ministry of Foreign Affairs, vital funds needed by the new government since India was refusing to share its assets with its new neighbor.[2]

When his father was posted to the Pakistani embassy in Ankara, the family moved to Turkey where the young Pervez learned Turkish and grew up admiring Mustafa Kemal, the founder of modern Turkey. The Musharraf family returned to Karachi in 1956 where Pervez attended a Catholic school and flew kites in his spare time in the tough neighborhood of Nazimabad. The exposure to a more cross-cultural, rather liberal lifestyle in Ankara while growing up in a professional family allowed Pervez to mix his studies with an extroverted social life.

From Lahore, where he attended Forman Christian College, his education took him to the Pakistan Military Academy in Kakul in 1961, which proved to be a voyage of self-discovery. Not only did his military training match his temperament, Musharraf's profession was also the best for him in terms of security and prestige. In September 1965 Musharraf saw military action near Kasur and, feeling "very proud," walked on the captured Indian territory of Khem Karan.[3] In 1966 he was selected for the Special Services Group, his top choice and Pakistan's elite commando regiment, and he was then sent to Cherat. Over these trying but exciting years Musharraf gained self-confidence as well as an ingrained belief "in leading from the front by setting a personal example." He could not go to East Pakistan in 1971, and blamed the separation of Pakistan on the "wily" Zulfikar Ali Bhutto, although he found General Niazi's surrender "the saddest episode in Pakistan's history."[4]

After his tenure in Balochistan in the late 1970s, Musharraf spent time administering General Zia-ul-Haq's martial law in the Punjab. During this time, Musharraf claimed to have witnessed lashings being meted out to ordinary Pakistanis in his zone and credits himself with stopping them. The fact remains that these repressive activities occurred in the glare of officially sanctioned cameras, as the military authorities wanted to create fear among ordinary people.

Following General Zia-ul-Haq's death in August 1988, Pakistan slowly moved back towards quasi-democracy, alternating between the prime ministerships of Benazir Bhutto and Nawaz Sharif. Musharraf's autobiography blames Pakistani politicians for running "the dreadful decade" of the 1990s, as he observes: "Never in the history of Pakistan had we seen such a combination of the worst kind of governance—or rather, a nearly total lack of governance—along with corruption and the plunder of national wealth." In October 1998 Musharraf was summoned to Islamabad after receiving a call from Prime Minister Nawaz Sharif. Uncertain as to the nature of the call and given his low opinion of the "errant" prime minister, Musharraf was surprised to hear that he had just been appointed army chief.[5]

Musharraf does not comment on the attitudes of the three military chiefs regarding the visit of Indian Prime Minister A. B. Vajpayee to

Lahore in January 1999 when the two national leaders signed the Lahore Declaration, committing themselves to peace and cooperation in all areas, including the thorny issue of Kashmir. This accord did not go down well with senior military commanders, and the conflict over Kargil a few months later further increased suspicions between Nawaz Sharif and army chief Musharraf. Musharraf remained critical of Sharif's role in the Kargil conflict, since the latter sought President Clinton's help in stopping hostilities from further escalation. While Musharraf felt upbeat about the military aspects of the conflict, Sharif feared its ramifications since India threatened to widen the conflict by employing its air force. Certainly, for many Pakistanis, the Kargil campaign was a "debacle," although in Musharraf's view it was cause for celebration. According to him, 600 Indian troops were killed and more than 1,500 had been wounded in these skirmishes, but despite his claim of few Pakistani casualties, he has shied away from giving any figures.[6] Needless to say, Sharif challenged Musharraf's triumphalism by highlighting the lack of preparation and coordination during the skirmish. According to Sharif, Musharraf soon realized the delicacy of the situation and pleaded for a political solution, prompting Sharif to undertake his hastily organized trip to Washington on 4 July 1999. According to Musharraf, it was actually international pressure that "demoralized" Sharif into his Washington trip, offering a "sudden capitulation" to President Clinton, despite Pakistan allegedly having captured 500 sq miles (1,300 sq km) of Indian territory. President Clinton accommodated an anxious Sharif and found a way out of the volatile situation.[7]

Musharraf offers interesting details on developments leading up to his coup, and is unforgiving toward Sharif who was influenced by his overpowering father Abaji; the family schemed to replace General Musharraf with somebody more pliant: "He was trying to consolidate his power, but he failed to understand that he was actually about to lose power. This happens to people who don't understand the dynamics of power or its extent and limit." In light of Musharraf's controversial decisions of 2007, followed by the massive national ballot rejecting his polices in February 2008, one wonders if Musharraf ever took on board his own dictum. Instead, he persisted with his own bid for political survival, while the nation strove toward a new beginning by rejecting him completely.[8]

Later chapters in Musharraf's autobiography are devoted to his personal contributions to economic recovery and political reform that began with his own referendum on 30 April 2002. This was followed by "cobbling together and launching" the Pakistan Muslim League (PML-Q) on 20 August 2002 that included his own supporters and dissenters from the Pakistan People's Party (PPP) and the Pakistan Muslim League (PML-N). Musharraf glorifies himself for spearheading these constitutional and political developments, in which the PML-Q, the Muhajir/Muttahida Qaumi Party (MQM) and other religio-political parties turned out to be the main beneficiaries.[9] These groups reciprocated by indemnifying all his actions through the umbrella Seventeenth Amendment to the constitution, which took away powers from parliament and the prime minister in order to strengthen Musharraf's presidency.

By this time, a confident Musharraf found himself the beneficiary of the new US–NATO security imperatives in South Asia as a result of 9/11. Despite some muffled international criticism, Musharraf continued to hold the two most powerful offices of president and chief of army staff, while the post-9/11 war on terror bestowed upon him much-longed-for international status. At the same time, it secured his position through a tier of loyalists both from within the assemblies and the army.

Within *In the Line of Fire* Musharraf records his dealings with the Taliban, his allowing of facilities to the US, the rounding up of high-profile suspects and militants, and the circumstances surrounding the mysterious disappearance and murder of American *Wall Street Journal* reporter Daniel Pearl. Musharraf goes to great lengths in recording Pakistan's heroics during the arrest of known al-Qaeda sympathizers and activists by becoming "the one country in the world that has done the maximum in the fight against terrorism."

In the area of religion, Musharraf certainly believes in a progressive form of Islam, yet he shied away from commenting on the political practice of Kemalism, which espoused the importance of a modern, democratic, and secular nation, ideas he admired from his early days in Turkey. But his argument that Pakistan is a largely feudal society with a high illiterate population inherently unable to practice unfettered democracy is not a persuasive one, especially when one sees it working next door in India. His views are similar to those of Ayub Khan and smack of the stereotypical military opinion of politicians.

Musharraf's self-righteous refusal to negotiate with Benazir Bhutto and Nawaz Sharif dissolved the moment he needed to build constitutional and political safeguards for his own diminishing political situation. A list of his bad judgements easily deflates Musharraf's claims about his political legitimacy: his initial military coup, the Provisional Constitutional Order, conviction and exile of the Sharif family, his dubious referendum and acquisition of the presidency by easing out the incumbent, the creation of a supportive and subservient political dispensation, the disappearance of many Pakistanis, ill-planned military operations, the mishandling of clerics in the Red Mosque in Islamabad in July 2007,[10] and the abrasive treatment of the judiciary, constitution, and the media—this list is by no means exhaustive.

In spite of the fact that the interface between the state and society had deteriorated to a state of dysfunction,[11] Musharraf felt that his military status and his political and strategic importance to America in light of the post-9/11 situation would protect him. But cracks were beginning to show. Financial scandals involving the Karachi Steel Mills and the Stock Exchange during 2005–6, were deeply resented in the country until the Supreme Court took the authorities to task. In addition to rebuking the government on its hasty privatization of national assets, the Supreme Court began questioning intelligence agencies about the hundreds of "missing Pakistanis," whose relatives had been campaigning since late 2001. The Supreme Court issued notices to the police and intelligence authorities to provide information on these individuals. This only multiplied official unease.[12]

Musharraf, unused to criticism and judicial rebuke, unceremoniously dismissed Chief Justice Iftikhar Muhammad Chaudhry on 9 March 2007, a few days after a long letter of accusation concerning Musharraf's regime had circulated on the Internet.[13] The chief justice's dismissal gave rise to the "Lawyers' Movement," which advocated his reinstatement, and he was restored to office by the Supreme Court on 20 July 2007 among great jubilation.[14] On 6 October 2007 Musharraf was contentiously elected to another presidential term through the lame-duck Assemblies; on 3 November 2007 he proclaimed Emergency rule and issued the second Provisional Constitutional Order (PCO) of his tenure, once again dismissing Chief Justice Chaudhry along with 60 of the justice's senior colleagues. Once again the Supreme Court experienced a major reshuffle—any judge reluctant to take an oath of loyalty to Musharraf was promptly retired, while others, including Chief Justice Chaudhry, were put under detention.

Faced with domestic and international criticism over these extreme measures, Musharraf attempted to soften public resentment by quitting the more powerful of his two offices, that of army chief, on 28 November 2007, allowing General Ashfaq Parvez Kayani to succeed him. The next day his newly appointed Chief Justice Abdul Hameed Dogar administered the oath for his new term as President. By now, Musharraf had become extremely unpopular, with two-thirds of Pakistanis demanding his resignation. His repressive measures only reinvigorated the campaign led by civil society and politicians for his removal.[15]

Buckling under domestic and foreign pressure, Musharraf finally lifted Emergency rule on 16 December 2007, but only after ensuring the detention of several senior judges including the house arrest of Chief Justice Chaudhry, and, more significantly, shifting the concentration of crucial powers to the office of the president.[16] Musharraf tried to defend himself through his envoys abroad, as well as by writing letters to various international organizations before embarking on a European tour in 2008. In spite of this, he failed to change negative world opinion.[17]

Beginning of the end By February 2008, Pakistan was back to square one. Musharraf, whose almost decade-long tenure had been spent repudiating Sharif and Bhutto for operating a "sham democracy" now found himself having to confront public defiance in the form of an electoral verdict favoring these two leaders.

After the new Provisional Constitutional Order (PCO) of 2007, Musharraf had expected his allies to gain majority seats; instead his favored branch of the Pakistan Muslim League, the PML-Q, had been tarnished in public perceptions, while the general's constitutional tamperings followed by the imposition of Emergency rule had turned him into a pariah.

In spite of Musharraf's mistrust of Benazir Bhutto, the two found themselves in the midst of power-sharing discussions under Anglo-American persuasion. These would have allowed Musharraf another presidential term, even if it meant that he would have had to share it with his enemy, but Bhutto's assassination, on 27 December 2007 put an end to the negotiations.

By the time the election was held on 18 February 2008, the rise in suicide bombings, the public disgust over the breakdown of law and order, Bhutto's assassination, and severe public disenchantment with US-led policies in the region translated into an overwhelming anti-Musharraf vote.

Increasingly, he confined himself to his Rawalpindi Camp Office, busying himself with prolonged drinking sessions in the company of a few old friends. The strong man who believed himself at the top of his power suddenly found himself no longer able to ignore the reality on the ground—the Pakistani public had spoken. Musharraf resigned on television, then left the country in late 2008 and bought a residence in London while simultaneously conducting a series of lecture tours throughout the West.

Benazir Bhutto: redemption for the Daughter of the East?

Tragically assassinated during a bomb blast at a political rally in Rawalpindi on 27 December 2007, Benazir Bhutto had attracted millions of supporters during her second homecoming to Pakistan. She was murdered while aspiring to the prime ministership for the third time, after negotiating a mutually beneficial power-sharing deal with General Musharraf; fate, however, had something else in store for both.

The first-ever Muslim woman to head a modern government in 1988, Bhutto was one of the most charismatic political leaders of her time due to her attractive personality, good education and, of course, her dauntless courage. It was this courage that led her to refuse to back down or cancel mass rallies, even after hundreds of deaths in Karachi on 18 October 2007, and her own close brush with death that day. Glorified to mythic proportions as one of the Bhuttos, a prominent landowning dynastic family from rural Sindh, Benazir Bhutto was known as "BB" among her friends and "Pinkie" to her immediate family. She is buried next to her famous father, Zulfikar Ali Bhutto, and close to the graves of her brothers, Shah Nawaz who died mysteriously in Cannes, France, in 1985, and Mir Murtaza who was killed outside his home in Karachi in 1996, during his sister's second tenure as prime minister.

Zulfikar Ali Bhutto (ZAB) was the son of Sir Shah Nawaz Bhutto, a Sindhi feudal landlord and former prime minister of the princely state of Junagarh. Shah Nawaz initiated the family's political ambitions and sent ZAB to the University of California, and then on to the University of Oxford. In contrast to his father's privileged background, Zulfikar Bhutto's mother came from a humble Hindu family, and it is no surprise that ZAB's temperament vacillated between extreme arrogance toward his colleagues and friends and great compassion for the ordinary masses.

As the eldest of the four Bhutto children, Benazir Bhutto spent time with her flamboyant father as he delivered passionate speeches, first at the UN during the 1971 war with India, then at Simla in 1972, where negotiations between her father and Indira Gandhi were finally concluded in a treaty. BB was not only groomed for politics by her father, her own education at Harvard and then at Oxford—and especially her active role as the President of the Oxford Union Society—honed her political and analytical instincts, though at the time she was aspiring to a position in Pakistan's foreign service.[18] Sadly, her time at Oxford coincided with the overthrow of her father, his incarceration, and the disputatious trial leading to the death penalty from a divided Supreme Court. Benazir's own political memoirs offer a firsthand account of these crucial developments and her central role in steering the Pakistan People's Party (PPP) through the long, trying tenure of Zia's eleven-year regime, which attempted to crush the morale and ranks of her party. Zia and his administration tried to maneuver the political and physical ruin of both the Bhuttos and their party.

Bhutto's book, *Daughter of the East*, became a bestseller as it ended triumphantly with the closing phase of Zia's regime. Based on her own notes, family history and the resistance against the longest military regime in Pakistan by the PPP, the book is a penetrating account combining tragedy, heroism, defiance, courage, persistence, and retribution. While Musharraf's autobiography is based on his interviews and notes, which helped ghost writer Humayun Gauhar[19] reconstruct the narrative, Bhutto's book, despite being the story of the Bhuttos, comes across as reportage accurately recording the activities of various sections of Pakistani society in their resistance to Zia's military dictatorship. In Musharraf's account, the Pakistani people either do not exist or only merit perfunctory references. The general finds his people largely illiterate, poor, and vulnerable to the machinations of self-serving politicians, while BB's Pakistanis are valiant, warm, and resolute while standing for justice. Her Pakistanis are willing to sacrifice their today for a better tomorrow. Despite the denigration of the Bhuttos by Zia, Musharraf, and a host of intelligence agencies, the resurgence of people power as espoused by the Bhuttos and as seen in the rallies of 2007–8 and the crucial 2008 election ballot is certainly not a minor achievement.

Benazir Bhutto was a Westernized woman owing to her upbringing and Western education, but like her father she was mindful of her traditional background. Like her father, her childhood had been insulated from the harsh realities of Pakistani life and even her knowledge of the Sindhi and Urdu languages remained scanty until she made subsequent efforts towards fluency.

BB's memoirs begin with the grievous account of her father's hanging in a dank Rawalpindi cell in the early hours of 4 April 1979. Nusrat and BB remained incarcerated a few miles away in Sihala Jail, hoping that some last-minute pressure might dissuade Zia from carrying out ZAB's execution. The previous day, mother and daughter had been brought to his cell to see him for the last time, but they were not allowed to participate in his funeral in Garhi Khuda Bakhsh, their native hamlet outside Larkana. After his hanging, ZAB's body was quickly flown to Sindh, where a helicopter took it to the ancestral village for a hurried funeral. Eventually, the military regime allowed them to visit his grave, as she remembered: "Mummy and I sat at the foot of the grave. I couldn't believe my father was under it. I dropped down and kissed the part of the mud where I imagined his feet to be."[20] Her autobiography covers the life and traumatic end of her father, and her own struggle against a tyrannical military regime intent on disabling her party and eradicating the possibility of any other Bhutto taking on ZAB's mantle.

Earlier she had lived a carefree life in Massachusetts away from the dreary existence of a Pakistan that had already succumbed to General Yahya Khan's martial law. The general's personal and professional weaknesses converged with the rising tide of Bangladeshi nationalism in East Pakistan, while Indira Gandhi's India waited in the wings to claim its pound of flesh from its neighbor. Islamabad fought an unpopular war and ZAB's speech, followed by a dramatic walkout from the UN in December 1971, did not halt the loss of the country's eastern wing. BB, herself used to debating international issues with Professor Walzer and other Harvard professors, sat behind her father in the UN chambers and heard his impassioned plea for an international effort to block the partitioning of Pakistan.

The years of solitary confinement and house arrest in Sihala, Lahore, Karachi, and Larkana had been unnerving—her mother developed lung cancer and her brothers left their studies and moved to Kabul to dislodge the military regime through the militant organization al-Zulfikar. BB's efforts now concentrated on keeping the PPP together, as well as resisting Zia's attempts to weaken the party. She was an active member of the Movement for the Restoration of Democracy (MRD), which was formed with several opposition parties in 1981, although the PPP became the main recipient of official wrath. In 1983, the MRD assumed a more vocal stance and in retaliation the martial law authorities focused on rural Sindh, which was already simmering with resentment. The disappearance of thousands of Sindhis as well as the growing unrest in Karachi among Urdu speakers intensified the seething ethnic conflict, further weakening the federation of Pakistan.

In London, Benazir spent the next two years organizing expatriate Pakistani support against martial law, undertaking visits across the UK as well as lobbying in Europe and the United States. Her brothers Murtaza and Shah Nawaz had also moved to Europe with their Afghan wives, where the latter was found dead in mysterious circumstances. Despite pleas from her mother and her brother Murtaza, Benazir Bhutto decided to bury her younger brother at Garhi Khuda Bakhsh near her father's grave. Ignoring restrictions imposed by martial law, Pakistanis demonstrated their loyalty and affection for the tragic Bhuttos and as a consequence Benazir soon faced fresh detention, followed by another spell in London.[21]

In the meantime, Zia-ul-Haq held a farcical referendum in December 1984 to claim the presidency of his country while also continuing as chief of army staff. Nationwide elections followed in February 1985, but the major parties were barred from participating unless the candidates claimed to be independent or joined Zia's favorite Pakistan Muslim League. The new assemblies were not permitted to function until they had indemnified all his martial law regulations and other ordinances, including those that largely disempowered women and minorities. Many of ZAB's former colleagues in the PPP were either forming their own parties or simply joining the Zia–Junejo duopoly. However, ordinary Pakistanis, PPP exiles, and Benazir's former classmates such as Peter Galbraith, stood by her.[22] With a political arrangement now in place under Muhammad Khan Junejo, some of Benazir's colleagues felt that she should return to Pakistan to lead the disgruntled masses against the general. Accompanied by an international press corps and advised by the American public relations consultant Mark Siegel, Bhutto landed at Lahore Airport in April 1986, where a million people gathered to welcome her. Her rallies and a surge in the party's ranks unnerved the Zia regime, whom she blamed for masterminding the wild shootings at her subsequent processions.

Marriage and power On 29 July 1987, Bhutto married fellow Sindhi landlord Asif Ali Zardari; her marital arrangements were facilitated by her aunts and the "prompting of my family."[23] Younger than her by two years and not renowned for his academic or political pursuits, Zardari was a polo player with a modest landholding who managed to impress Benazir with his persistent interest in her.

While the Bhutto family and their party appeared to be gaining in popularity and strength, Zia was running out of options after dissolving Junejo's government and the assemblies on 29 May 1988, blaming them for corruption and the slow pace of Islamization. Within three months, Zia had died in an air crash along with many of the senior army command and the US Ambassador Arnold Raphel, allowing Pakistan a rare chance to pursue party-based democratization. Bhutto's party won a majority of seats in the elections of October 1988, making her the first female prime minister of a Muslim nation a mere few weeks after the birth of her son Bilawal. Amidst euphoria and hesitation on the part of Acting President Ghulam Ishaq Khan and the generals, Bhutto began her tenure on 2 December 1988 and faced immediate challenges including a restive Karachi, defiance in Indian-controlled Kashmir, and a civil war in Afghanistan. Bhutto's government was dismissed by Khan 18 months later on 6 August 1990—only four days after Saddam Hussein's invasion of Kuwait—as the world's attention was diverted to events in the Gulf. She was removed from office and the assemblies were dissolved in spite of the fact that technically they should have been allowed to complete their five-year term. New elections were held under the auspices of an interim government, giving Nawaz Sharif a slight majority. Sharif began his tenure as prime minister on 6 November 1990, but despite support from civil and military groups who had been beneficiaries of the Zia regime, Sharif's government met the same fate. Sharif was dismissed by Khan in April 1993, yet his administration and the dissolved Assemblies were restored through a judicial verdict in the same month. The next spate of elections took place some months later under another interim government headed by international banker Moeen Qureshi, and on 19 October 1993, Bhutto was brought back as prime minister for a second time. Despite a parliamentary majority, it would not be smooth sailing for Bhutto and Pakistan soon fell back into confrontational politics. Differences with President Farooq Leghari, a former PPP stalwart, led to Bhutto's second dismissal on 5 November 1996 allowing Sharif another term. His government soon lodged cases of corruption against Bhutto and her husband.

Bhutto was already in self-imposed exile when Musharraf's coup occurred on 12 October 1999, but contrary to her expectations, the general decided to keep both former prime ministers away from the country until they were able to maneuver their return toward the end of 2007.[24] While working on her second book, she wrote a new preface and an additional chapter for her first book, *Daughter of the East*, which detailed her political life including her two administrations and exile. While dedicating this volume to her three children and to the children of Pakistan, Bhutto observed: "I didn't choose this life; it chose me." Crucial developments after 9/11 had put Pakistan under the international spotlight and Bhutto felt that her country needed her more than ever: "Pakistan is no ordinary country. And mine has been no ordinary life"; her destiny was intertwined with that of her nation.[25] In her new chapter, Bhutto commented on the twin threats of dictatorship and extremism, as the former gave rise to the latter: "In my view, it is the Zias and Musharrafs of this world who have fuelled the xenophobia and sense of victimisation of Pakistanis and Pakistani émigrés in the West…Extremism has been nurtured, empowered and exploited by military rulers for generations."[26]

Within a few weeks of her return to Pakistan, Benazir Bhutto was killed in Rawalpindi—one more Bhutto entombed in Garhi Khuda Bakhsh amidst national mourning. Her second book, *Reconciliation: Islam, Democracy and the West*, was published soon after her murder and focused on the reconstruction of a culture of democracy in Pakistan, while commenting on national and global affairs in her capacity as an astute analyst. In addition to her sadness over the violence and political drift within her country, she was deeply aggrieved about the difficult relationship between Muslims and the West, especially after 9/11, recommending that significant reconciliation on all sides was necessary. She condemned violence in the name of Islam and abhored al-Qaeda and the Taliban. She was also uncomfortable with Western inconsistencies and interventionism in Muslim regions, especially over the uneven policies in West Asia, including the invasions of Afghanistan and Iraq. However, she was sensitive to Islamophobia as a sad and regular feature within some segments of the Western media.

It appears that she was working on the manuscript right up to the time of her death and had not had time to revise the manuscript. The book was published posthumously with an explanatory note by her PR consultant Mark Siegel, who had also helped with the research. To Siegel, "Benazir Bhutto was the bravest person I have ever known and a dear, irreplaceable friend," who had worried about the misinterpretation and misuse of her religion by some extreme elements.[27]

Her sudden and dramatic death underscored Bhutto's courage, winning her second book plaudits as it offers a balanced commentary on contemporary intra-Muslim relationships and the difficulties between Western regimes and Muslim communities. The book is reflective in its analysis and shines a searchlight on three interrelated areas. Firstly, it is a resumé of Bhutto's own political career, especially her two terms as prime minister. Secondly, it reviews the imbalances within the Pakistani political structure that allowed the army and intelligence agencies to dominate over democratic forces. Thirdly, the book reminds the West of its responsibilities within the context of contradictory polices toward the Muslim world, as well as being a reminder to the latter to seek out a tolerant, progressive, and democratic discourse away from intra-Muslim schism and negativity towards the West.

The narrative begins with her emotional return to Pakistan on 18 October 2007, reminding the reader of her similar journey from London to Lahore on 10 April 1987. Holding the *Quran*, she stepped from the aircraft and felt deeply moved by her homecoming: "But as my foot touched the ground of my beloved Pakistan for the first time after eight lonely and difficult years of exile, I could not stop the tears from pouring from my eyes and I lifted my hands in reverence, in thanks, and in prayer. I stood on the soil of Pakistan in awe." Dangerously, her army-controlled country had become "the epicentre of an international terrorist movement" urgently in need of a democratic retrieval.[28] Bhutto's first encounter with this mass violence was during a rally in Karachi hours after her return, when two blasts went off near her bulletproof van, killing 179 of her supporters and grievously injuring 500 more.

According to Bhutto, Pakistan was once again seething under "military dictatorship," and on 3 November 2007, by imposing draconian restrictions, Musharraf had "removed all pretense of transition to democracy by yet another extraconstitutional coup d'etat."[29] With hindsight, Bhutto was right in claiming that elements within the Musharraf administration, especially the security agencies, were traditionally hostile towards democratic forces in general and the Bhuttos in particular. Before returning to Karachi, Bhutto had alerted Musharraf's government and the global media to possible threats on her life and had even named certain officials who she suspected of plotting against her.

Subsequently, she is critical of inconsistent Western policies toward the Muslim world over the past two centuries, yet stops short of zeroing in on Western military interventions amidst an unrelenting war on terror, which she feels crucially triggered this latent phase of violence. Even at the height of the Soviet intervention in Afghanistan and the displacement of millions of Afghans, suicide bombings, and intra-Muslim violence had remained absent. This makes it clear that the current violence is the result of several intertwined factors and is certainly not due to any inherent Muslim penchant for bloodshed.

While dealing with the Islam–West relationship, Bhutto underlines the unanimous Muslim world view and outrage over the invasion of Iraq in 2003 and the lack of any UN sanction. She also believes it is crucial for Muslims to show their resentment more vocally over the rising tide of sectarianism. Citing Quranic and Prophetic traditions, she is worried about the misappropriation of jihad for violent ends, though she has no qualms that jihad would stipulate a defensive resistance against an external aggressor. Focusing on Islam's inherent respect for Christianity, Judaism, and other religions, she abhors violence against civic populations and is equally critical of the restrictions on women by some Islamists. She is emphatically supportive of many Muslim modernists and not at all enamored with purist-revivalists such as Syed Mawdudi and Syed Qutb.[30]

Bhutto finds no inherent conflict between Islam and democracy, but is critical of Washington's readiness to work with dictators while simultaneously lecturing the world on democracy. While she acknowledges the ideological fault line within the Muslim world between dictatorship and empowerment, she is equally alert to colonial legacies and the ongoing unequal relationships that powerful nations have established to suit their own prerogatives. Within *Reconciliation*, Bhutto covers a brief political analysis of several countries where efforts to establish representative and transparent systems have often faced a range of challenges. According to Bhutto, Turkey, Indonesia, Mali, and Senegal are the only Muslim countries where democracy, despite serious structural problems, has stayed ascendant, while scores of other countries present a "mixed record of starts and stops, of progress and regression, of missed opportunities and roads not taken."[31] However, she does not merely blame the West for roadblocking democratization and economic development, but also allocates responsibility for the political malaise to the Muslim ruling elite.

The fifth chapter of her book is perhaps the most persuasive and articulate, with its awareness of the historical and contemporary nature of the debate on the clash of civilizations and her own views. "Preventing a clash of civilizations, at least in terms of the Islamic world, requires that we put our trust in the power of trade, exchange, technology, education and democratic values to accelerate the process by which Islamic societies can build bonds and trust with Western societies." She suggests:

> The West must be ready to acknowledge the residual damage of colonialism and support for dictatorships during the Cold War. The West, and especially the United States of America, must be ready to revisit the rippling impact of the so-called global war on terror, which is perceived by perhaps hundreds of millions of Muslims as a "global war on Islam." Many Muslims fear that the Islamic faith is under attack and Muslims are under siege.

Benazir Bhutto was killed while the manuscript was in its final stages; however, the brief afterword by her widower and three children reiterates their determination to carry on what Bhutto believed in, as they observed: "Time, justice and the forces of history are on our side."[32]

Other players on the Pakistani political stage

Pakistan's struggle to establish good governance through constitutional means, delivered by parliamentary sovereignty, and safeguarded through an independent judiciary and a vocal civil society, remains an heroic fight against the odds. Questions about the competence, motives, and class dimensions of its leaders abound. The population of Pakistan is complex and pluralistic, and it can be difficult to separate out the power bases from the various sections of civil society. Pakistan's middle classes come from salaried sections of its population, and some businesses cluster where army and bureaucracy emerge as two powerful echelons, while politicians predominantly hail from landowning families whose politics are usually interlocked with the former through a complex pattern of dependency. The urban-based ethnic and business leadership also vacillates between opposing feudal and reformist groups, although the civil society run by lawyers, journalists, and other activists has been attempting to push them toward holistic democratization for the benefit of the nation.

Nawaz Sharif Mian Nawaz Sharif emerged as the head of a middle-class political dynasty largely due to General Zia-ul-Haq's patronage. He became chief minister of Punjab province under Zia and was twice prime minister (1990–3 and 1996–9). He lost his position as a consequence of a coup in October 1999 led by General Musharraf and spent a number of years in exile in Saudi Arabia. Sharif led the Muslim League (N) and was blocked from participating in elections on 18 February 2008, but his party won the second-largest number of seats in the National Assembly and in Punjab. After Benazir Bhutto's murder, he emerged as the most popular leader in the country. The Supreme Court controversially disqualified him from holding any public office on 25 February 2009 during Asif Ali Zardari's reign but a subsequent appeal overturned that decision, and other similar cases against him dating from the Musharraf era were thrown out by the court. He was a vocal supporter of the lawyers' campaign to reinstate Justice Chaudhry and other senior judges, and remains one of the most powerful and influential leaders in the country.

Imran Khan He established his own independent credentials as a popular cricketer before becoming politically active in order to highlight corruption as a major national issue. Khan's tirades against politicians, generals, and ethnic militants, and demands for an independent foreign policy made him one of the most popular and dependable politicians in the country. But the absence of a nationwide party machine and the fact that most grassroots people of influence opt for the main parties has meant that Khan has been unable to translate his ideas into an electoral force.[33] He took a visible stance against Musharraf's policies in FATA, which he believed were proving counterproductive and increasing alienation amongst the Pushtun population. In an interview, Khan observed: "This is a civil war in the making. One million refugees have been created. Innocent people are being killed; children left without arms and legs. All under the magic mantra of fighting Islamic extremism. If people understood what is really happening, they would not countenance it. It is time to change tactics on the so-called war on terror. There is hope in President-elect Obama."[34]

Altaf Hussain On the other end of the political spectrum from Imran Khan is Muhajir/Muttahida Qaumi Party (MQM) leader Altaf Hussain.

Hussain controls Karachi through a very alert party apparatus, despite the fact that the party grew out of a movement espousing ethnic separatism and has been involved in several alleged cases of violence. From his safe-house in London, Hussain has been able to direct his party as well as block any challenge to his authority both in Karachi and in the UK. For non-Urdu-speaking Pakistanis, Hussain is a complex, enigmatic, violent, and aggressive leader, though in Karachi it is only in private that one comes across any criticism of this ethnic rhetorician.

Other leaders Pakistan's other middle-class leaders include Asfandyar Wali Khan—the son of Abdul Wali Khan and the grandson of the legendary Abdul Ghaffar Khan, both of whom were known for their steadfast views and for which they were often victimized by colonial and national regimes. The Khans ran their party, the Awami National Party (ANP), against numerous obstacles and despite a visible emphasis on Pushtun identity, they have advocated reformist politics. The elections held in February 2008 led to an ANP victory in the NWFP, trouncing the pro-Musharraf elements as well as weakening the religio-political groups. In the end, all of these groups agreed to form a coalition government. The new chief minister of the NWFP is Amir Haider Khan, a young Pushtun nationalist who began his tenure with cross-party support and the determination to defeat terror and violence through negotiations and dialogue. Other significant middle-class leaders include Rasul Paleejo, Asghar Khan, Aitzaz Ahsan, and certainly the leaders of religio-political parties such as the Jamaat-i-Islami and Jamiat-i-Ulama-i-Islam, which have often preferred the ballot over violent means. Expatriates such as Tariq Ali, Ziauddin Sardar, and activists Mahmud Achakzai, Afrasiyab Khattak, Nafeesa Shah, and retired judges, advocates, poets, artists, human rights activists, NGOs, and talk-show hosts offer Pakistan a wide array of talented individuals who continue to challenge the system in the face of unending challenges.

GEOPOLITICAL ISSUES

LYING AT THE HEART OF THE INDUS VALLEY, Pakistan sits within what were the borderlands of the British colonial subcontinent before independence, and since 1947 has played a high-profile geopolitical role in the region. Pakistan has deep roots in the Indo–Islamic tradition and its cultural affinities with its eastern neighbors go beyond a shared ancient past; South Asia has the largest Muslim population in the world. A predominantly Muslim state itself, Pakistan has had volatile relations with India but the relationship cannot be viewed simply as a conflict between secular and religious states. This has been especially true since the ascendance in the 1990s of the communalist parties in India and the 2002 massacre of Muslims in Gujarat.

Currently, both India and Pakistan are showing a bias towards their dominant religions, often at the expense of minority religions, sects and ethnic communities within their borders. This pressure springs from a wide variety of religious, historical, demographic, economic, political and demagogic sources, fueled by the media and the pulpit. In both countries, the civil societies are striving to safeguard their diversity and the equal rights of their citizens, but despite positive steps towards regional co-operation, interstate conflicts have often undermined any significant progress. This chapter suggests that a political dispensation for Pakistan need not include Islam as the only systemic ideology. Pakistan's significant position within the subcontinent, as well as its current geopolitical role mean that a functional ideology must seek to incorporate domestic and international pursuits, including its relationships with the Taliban, India, and the US.

Cultural divide or communal schisms

Adherents of Huntington's *Clash of Civilizations* theory concerning religious and cultural identity as the source of conflict might well see South Asia as being dangerously poised over a civilizational fault line. The events leading to Partition in 1947 as well as the troubles since could easily be interpreted as evidence of an unbridgeable chasm between Hinduism and Islam. In the same vein, viewing Pakistan as a front-line state challenging Western-led modernity by training and sending out violent militants would be equally mistaken. Like other young nation-states, Pakistan is situated in a challenging region, away from the settled and buffered regions of mainland South Asia. Its location means that not only is it at the forefront of India's defense against threats from the northwest, but it is also a melting pot of diverse ethnicities and cultures. Its economic and political travails have often converged with its politicized ethnic tensions, further accentuating the rifts between its rural, urban, and tribal groups; global and regional geopolitics have been no less crucial in exacerbating these dissensions.

The new state of Pakistan promised to coexist with pluralistic ethno-regional identities within a fair and just society, however, living up to this ideal as envisioned by the nation's founders Muhammad Ali Jinnah and Muhammad Iqbal has been a Herculean challenge. But this predominantly Muslim country with its large population of non-Muslim Pakistanis has neither witnessed a brutal separation from its Indian past nor has it imposed an Islamic theocratic purism. The nation's forefathers were middle-class and predominantly modernist reformers who came from a wide variety of ethnic backgrounds. To these men, the notion of "Muslimness" provided the means to bind together disparate ethnicities in order to prevent the Balkanization of the Indus and Gangetic regions.

The nature of the post-1947 Indo–Pakistani relationship, their communal volatility and the dominance of the elites in both countries have shaped perceptions of Partition in a way that has not helped either country over the last six decades. A mutual interdependence anchored on a more positive understanding of Partition as a "rearrangement" rather than as a "separation" could have saved South Asia from much conflict, war, and depletion of good will and precious resources.

The Kashmir dispute

From the outset, a positive relationship between the two newly created nations was not likely. The thorny issues of the transfer of assets and equipment, demarcation of boundaries, communal killings and kidnap of women, and contentious disputes over the princely states of Kashmir, Hyderabad, and Junagarh further exacerbated an already tense situation. The latter two states were promptly annexed by India, leaving Kashmir divided between the two new neighbors.

On the eve of British withdrawal from the subcontinent, Kashmir's population was predominantly Muslim ruled by Hindu dynast Maharaja Gulab Singh. His dithering over the political future of Kashmir resulted in internal revolts and external interference by Pakistani tribals. The rebels expelled the Maharaja's forces in October 1947 from the western regions of Kashmir, leading to the formation of Azad (Free) Jammu and Kashmir, a largely Pakistani-administered region seeking union with Indian-controlled Kashmir. That region had come under India's control when Delhi flew in troops to save Srinagar from Kashmiri activists and their Pakistani Pushtun tribal allies.[1] Subsequent wars and skirmishes over the Kargil Heights added to the growing conflict. A Muslim–Kashmiri insurgency erupted in 1989 and has continued ever since despite a severe crackdown by Indian troops. This military intervention has resulted in serious human rights violations, further aggravating the distrust between Islamabad and Delhi.[2]

For some observers, the fracas over Kashmir, frequent Hindu–Muslim riots in India, and the wars between these two neighbors are symbolic of irreconcilable Hindu–Muslim differences that preceded Partition. Hindu–Muslim relations have too frequently been characterized as being pulled by diametrically opposed forces of separatism versus syncretism. In other words, attempts to reconcile the two religions within one nation have struggled against the efforts of those who have sought to engineer continued division and conflict. It is tempting to lay the blame for communal conflict on the British Raj for not ensuring public safety and peaceful mobility during Partition. Whether an intentional ploy or not, this only widened the growing gulf between Hindus and Muslims.[3] However, this does not explain the religious- and caste-based divisions already in existence, which have aggrieved even the most tolerant rulers as far back as the great Mughal Emperor Akbar (1542–1605).

While redefining Indian and Pakistani/Muslim nationalist aspirations, the emerging nations used Partition as a tool for political expediency. On the Indian side, the government and nationalist historians blamed the British Raj and Jinnah for butchering an ingrained Indian unity. According to this belief, Pakistan was not just a newly carved state emerging from the debris of a dying colony, it was also a grim reminder of India's terrible division. The accession of Kashmir, as well as the growing unrest in other princely states against the backdrop of the world's largest and tragically mismanaged migration made such a discordant view of Pakistan and Partition appear expedient. This antagonism was not merely confined to the denizens of the new Indian state and the proponents of *Hindu rashtra*;[4] it was also fully subscribed to by Indian nationalist Muslims and secularist writers. These arguments have yet to evolve into a more all-encompassing explanation of Partition, away from the current need to find convenient heroes and villains.[5] Despite Jinnah's exhortations for peace with Delhi, Indo–Pakistan politics was destined to become a tale of two hostile nationalist discourses. Pakistan was put forward as a culturally ordained nation that had always existed without any clear-cut sovereign demarcation. Emphasizing cultural distinction, religion, language, history, cuisine, and other identifications naturally became the mainstay of this separatism, which was promptly transcribed as Muslim nationalism.[6]

Pakistan undoubtedly has its own problems of governance, but this does not mean that the country does not have genuine grievances with its bigger neighbor to the east. Even after several dramatic retreats on Kashmir and reconciliatory measures under Pervez Musharraf since 2002, India has refused to undertake any substantive concessions on the issues of Kashmir and water resources. Not only has India continued to chip away at Pakistani territory, as in the case of the Siachin Glacier, it has never shown any commitment to resolving the most serious dispute between the two nations. Instead, the normalization process begun in 2002 is seen within India as Pakistan's withdrawal from its stance on Kashmir. After the Mumbai attacks of November 2008, India threatened Islamabad with severe consequences and by 2009 the entire process of normalization had ground to a halt once again as the old issues and suspicions were revived.

The terrorist attacks in Mumbai on 26 November 2008, causing 177 deaths at luxury hotels, railway stations, and an Israeli center, had been perpetrated by ten Pakistanis who had apparently been trained by jihadi elements in Azad Kashmir. The negative effect of the attacks on Indo–Pakistani relations continued even after a year, while Muslims on both sides of the border felt immense shock at this bloody act. The Indian police arrested only one terrorist—Mohammad Ajmal Kasab—as the rest had been killed in shoot-outs or simply committed suicide to avoid arrest. Kasab provided valuable information on the recruitment, training, and execution of this attack while India and Pakistan continued to exchange dossiers with details on the perpetrators and their group affiliations. Such was the horror provoked by the bloodshed, that Indian Muslims, even a year after the event, refused permission to bury the embalmed bodies of the nine assailants.[7] While on his first visit to Washington during the Obama presidency, India's Prime Minister Manmohan Singh accused Pakistan of harboring terrorists in order to pursue a war through proxy on his country.

Previous attacks have also been attributed to Pakistani groups, though one cannot dismiss the possibility of homegrown violence, given the thousands of deaths and rapes in the Kashmir Valley over the two decades and the massacres of more than 2,000 Muslims in Gujarat in 2002. It is equally important to note that in February 2007, a Lahore-bound Samjhota train was ambushed in the Indian Punjab where terrorists unleashed violence against its mainly Pakistani passengers. It was reported that diehard Hindu groups had masterminded the operation, locking the carriages from the outside and killing 67 passengers by torching the train. Pakistanis were shocked and upset, yet Islamabad refused to put pressure on Delhi, despite media reports of Indian involvement in volatile events in Balochistan following the opening of several Indian consulates in Afghanistan.[8]

The escalating pressure from India was strongly resented by Pakistanis who felt that the Indian authorities were scapegoating Pakistan in order to hide their own inefficiency; Indian authorities, on the other hand, were angered over the haste with which counter-accusations were made. On 28 November 2008, a mysterious phone call, presumably from India's Ministry of External Affairs, had threatened President Asif Ali Zardari with dire Indian retaliation. This threat alarmed Pakistan's civil and military leadership amidst reports that New Delhi was planning violent strikes against Pakistan.[9] This heightened tension, further hyped by the media on both sides, resulted in a visit by then-US Secretary of State Condoleezza Rice, followed by a visit from her UK counterpart David Miliband in January 2009. Rice tried to calm the situation amidst reports that in response to the Indian threat, Pakistan was planning to move 100,000 troops from the tribal areas to its eastern borders. Naturally, this unnerved the West, given that such a move could have allowed the Taliban and other anti-Western groups some respite, as well as pushing South Asia closer to the precipice of a potential nuclear war.

External pressure from India and elsewhere was perceived within Pakistan as an affront, denigrating its state as the epicenter of global terror. It was shocking but not wholly unexpected that this pressure resulted in a concerted Pushtun assault on the NATO refueling and storage facility outside Peshawar on 7 December 2008, torching more than 140 vehicles loaded with equipment meant for NATO troops in Afghanistan. The precarious nature of these routes and the consequences of military supplies being waylaid by Pushtun activists compelled NATO to seek longer routes from Central Asia into northern Afghanistan.[10]

Political Islam, the Taliban, and the West
From a post-9/11 perspective, it is tempting to simplify Muslim politics into a dichotomy of fundamentalists and moderates in the same way that it is convenient to identify Political Islam as Islamofascism or sheer

terrorism.[11] More accurately, it is the selective use of Islam for segregational and restrictive purposes that has opened up several battlegrounds across Pakistan with disastrous results. It is interesting to note that Pakistan's tribal regions and Balochistan remained peaceful throughout the 1980s in spite of the fact that these areas were inundated with millions of Afghan refugees as well as serving as a conduit for armed support to the Mujahideen.

The post-9/11 militarization of these regions and the transformation of Pakistan's borderlands into "badlands" is the result of complex geo-political factors including the US–Muslim relationship featuring invasions as well as Islamabad's continued disenfranchisement of the Federally Administered Tribal Areas (FATA). In 1893, while demarcating borders between India and Afghanistan, the British Raj divided the tribes into several semi-autonomous agencies to be run through political agents. This greatly disenfranchised vast majorities of people and consolidated land-based parochialism and intra-tribal rivalries. The tribes fought over land while their leaders vied for official power facilitated through political agents, whose job it was to maintain peace across the passes so that the "Great Game" (the struggle between Britain and Russia for domination over the region) could continue and the rest of the "settled districts" remained unaffected.

The imperial system came down hard on traditional communities since their way of life was often diametrically opposed to contemporary Western notions of ownership and community. Imperial dictates were put in place, wresting property ownership from the collective tribe and putting it into the hands of individuals. This resulted in the confinement of the tribal Pushtuns within their own areas, creating islands of suffocated populations denied the modern civic facilities accessible to their counterparts in towns and settled areas across the administrative divide. Under this system of control many roads, railway tracks, listening posts, and cantonments were protected by locally recruited militia, or *khasadars,* who were to remain loyal to the tribal hierarchy as well as to their paymasters, the political agents of the colonial government.[12] The tribal *maliks* were allowed to carry guns, which absolved British officials of the responsibility for law and order. This system has often been romanticized through imagery of a brave but "violent" and "untrust-worthy Pathan" alongside the tough colonial officials hardened on the Frontier,[13] turning the NWFP into one of the most attractive subjects for travelers, anthropologists, and journalists.[14]

With its focus on containment and its inherently divisive nature, the control mechanism eventually began to crumble due to the emergence of clerical groups. Inspired by resistance dating back to the stormy events of the 1857 Rebellion as well as the Anglo-Afghan Wars and other conflicts,[15] these reenergized clerics triggered the downfall of control. This is where the terms "mad mullah and Wahabbis," or purist Islamist were first used to caricature these defiant elements whose presumed bloodthirst was out of sync with contemporary sensibilities. They were portrayed as barbarians intent on destroying the "settled" regions of India with the emotional battle cry of jihad. No wonder more than 100 years later that a similar characterization has reappeared while describing the turbulence in FATA and the adjoining regions of Afghanistan.

The post-First World War Khilafat Movement in India aimed to defend a weakened Ottoman Caliphate while also trying to break the political agent–khan duopoly over the stalemated tribal societies. Many in the Muslim world viewed the Ottoman Caliphate as the last remaining symbol of their political and cultural past. The caliphate was responsible for overseeing the holy sites of Makkah and Medina, and during the First World War it took on huge significance for educated Muslims everywhere, as it appeared that the Allies were intent upon its destruction. As such, the stability of this institution became a major concern of the movement. An offshoot of the Khilafat Movement, the Red Shirts Movement was led by Abdul Ghaffar Khan, whose austere but dynamic politics based on self-reliance, liberation, and social service tried to forge unity between the tribal and settled Pushtuns.[16] Even as late as the 1930s, the Royal Air Force (RAF) mounted bombing sorties over the tribal belt, and following the Second World War, a major section of the British Indian Army remained concentrated in these areas.

Jinnah befriended the tribes and withdrew troops from their forward positions back to their specific cantonments. This policy of non-interference within the tribal regions was pursued by successive Pakistani regimes until Musharraf initiated his military operations in 2005. Pakistani militia and troops made pincer movements from the eastern reaches of the Durand Line while American and Afghan troops pressed on from the other side. In 2007 Predator drone attacks opened up a new phase in trans-border interventionism, and continue to claim the lives of militants and civilians alike on this side of the Durand Line.

Afghanistan, the Soviet invasion, and Talibanization
Originally part of the Mughal empire, Afghanistan became an independent country in 1747. During the 19th and early 20th centuries, that region was the focus of conflicting British and Russian interests, with

Britain fighting three wars against the Afghans between 1839 and 1919. In 1930, the country became a constitutional monarchy, although this classification failed to draw a line under the tensions in the area. Afghanistan was at a crossroads of external conflicts soon after the Second World War, with global powers competing to gain the upper hand in this landlocked country. The Soviets eventually mounted an invasion in 1979 to protect a fledgling leftist regime.

Afghanistan's position as an active theater of war shaped contemporary Pakistan into a front-line state with anti-Soviet states coalescing to arm and support the Afghans against the Russians. True to their liberationist history and rooted in Political Islam, the Afghan people fought and incurred immense losses, yet prided themselves in ultimate victory. The forces of nationhood and Islam, derided during the colonial era, now became celebrated among academics and policy planners, especially in the North Atlantic regions.[17]

The Soviet withdrawal, in 1989, unleashed chaos and intra-Afghan violence. Afghan Pushtuns attempted to turn over a new leaf in their history, and a major shift in the power structure saw these Pushtun elements being led by clerics whose credibility had increased by spear-heading a successful armed resistance movement against the Soviets. As in neighboring Iran, a religio-political force emerged amidst the lawlessness, promising peace, justice, and order. Given their background in the seminaries on the Pakistani side of the border, they came to be known as "Taliban," or students. Their controversial form of Political Islam emphasized a penal code and summary judgments. The Taliban's pivotal role in allowing Osama bin Laden to remain in Afghanistan soon brought the group under the global spotlight. In addition, their mistreatment of women and minorities also began to weigh heavily against them in the world media.

Links between the Taliban and Pakistani groups such as the Lashkar-i-Jhangvi (LJ), Lashkar-i-Tayyaba (LT), and others continued after 9/11 due to the porous nature of the Pakistani–Afghan borders and as a consequence of increased sympathy for anti-American resistance. With pressure building inside Afghanistan, the Pakistani tribal areas of Waziristan and Bajaur became the next abode for such elements due to the terrain, proximity to Afghan Pushtun regions, and a wider sympathy for Taliban fighting elements in Afghanistan. The punitive campaigns by the US and its allies largely focusing on Pushtuns on both sides of the border created a greater sense of solidarity against the West and Islamabad. In the Pushtun tradition of *Pushtunwali,* or tribal revenge, an overspill took the form of intermittent suicide bombings, which soon engulfed Pakistan. This became even more pronounced after 2005 when

Pakistani troops began to mount punitive campaigns in the tribal belt against suspected al-Qaeda elements and their local sympathizers.

Pressure came from Washington, London, and Brussels to carry out more surgical campaigns in tribal regions, while American drone attacks killing "militants" became a routine policy that claimed hundreds of civilian lives. Such civilian deaths were often rudely brushed aside as collateral damage, and casualty figures on both sides of the Durand Line were never made public.[18] While many Pakistanis were aggrieved over the escalating bomb blasts, suicide bombings, and school closures in Swat and FATA by militants calling themselves Pakistani Taliban, the same people felt cynical about Pakistani involvement in a war that was seen as a global crusade against Muslims. India's accusations following the Mumbai bomb attacks, American pressure and increased Predator attacks only served to exacerbate anti-American sentiment and increase the sense of grief and helplessness across the country.

The relationship between Pakistan and the US dates from the early Cold War period when both countries had their own domestic and international reasons for joining alliances such as the Central Treaty Organization (CENTO) and South East Asia Treaty Organization (SEATO). Pakistanis often felt sidelined whenever they required more sensitivity from America in their travails with India.[19] On issues of Kashmir and nuclear proliferation, Washington was either lukewarm or vocally critical of Pakistan, though the increased security imperatives following the 1979 Soviet invasion of Afghanistan brought the strained allies together. Washington, Islamabad, and their respective intelligence organizations collaborated in arming the Mujahideen and their supporters such as Osama bin Laden. Following the Soviet withdrawal of 1989, the US soon lost interest in Pakistan and Afghanistan. Instead, Pakistan was confronted with economic and security sanctions from Washington over its nuclear program, while India received preferential treatment from the Clinton administration. Throughout the 1990s, Pakistan's "Islamic bomb" made headlines in the Western press, with "leaks" provided by intelligence agencies.

While most concerned Pakistanis did not support the attacks of 9/11, they could sense the forthcoming American fury and Western resolve to pursue Muslim activists and militants, and feared an eventual blowback for their own country. The October 2001 invasion of Afghanistan by the US and its allies and Musharraf's hasty Washington alliance quickly brought Pakistan into the whirlwind of political turmoil. For vast sections of Pakistani society, this action affirmed the idea that the war on terror was, in fact, directed against Muslims generally and Pakistan in particular.

Pakistanis feared that the invasion of Afghanistan, amidst frequent reports of trans-border Pushtun solidarity, was a pretext to erode Pakistani sovereignty. The US ground offensives and scores of missiles targeting Pakistani hamlets were viewed as the logical next step in a well-orchestrated policy to cripple a nuclear-armed Pakistan. To these Pakistanis, their country was becoming the true casualty of a venomous and multidimensional campaign rooted in Islamophobia.

South Asia or Central Asia: where does Pakistan belong?

In 1947, several departing British officials and some critics within the Indian National Congress expressed the opinion that Pakistani statehood was nothing more than a fiction. Its anomalies would soon weaken it, and the smaller country with disparate constituent units and deficit economies would not be able to afford the huge cost of national defense. India's size, its consolidated land mass and functioning bureaucracy were viewed as its assets; Pakistan's western borderlands were to weigh it down heavily—the unsettled tribal situation and Kabul's claims on Pakistani Pushtun regions further solidified the Afghan belief that this territory could be acquired somehow.

Pakistan's vociferous critics felt that by opting for Muslim nationhood, the Indus regions had sought an unpardonable separation from a larger unified South Asia. In the same vein, East Pakistan, despite its pronounced cultural homogeneity, was a flood-prone peninsula comprising the border regions of Bengal and Assam, which might find it difficult to remain self-sufficient since Calcutta and the upper Gangetic regions had gone to an unfriendly India. Pakistan's two separated regions certainly posed serious challenges to nation-building, however, for various external powers, the inherent problems of such a configuration represented an opportunity to pursue their own geostrategic interests.

Significantly, the desire to gain Kashmir from India, in addition to ensuring security against a perceived Indian threat, pushed Pakistani civil and military planners towards alliances with SEATO and CENTO. The concurrent perceptions of Pakistan as an Islamic community and Islam as a non-Indian/West Asian religion by several non-Muslim nations not only compelled Pakistan to seek common ground with the Muslim world to the west, but also coincided, rather dangerously, with the Hinduization and Hindiization of India.

The perception of Islam as an external force had its roots in the Hindu revivalist movements of the 19th century, such as the Arya Samaj, which underpinned a strong desire to convert poorer Muslims in eastern Punjab and Alwar.[20] The Hindu evangelical movements of Shuddhi and

Sangathan pursued these campaigns in the early 20th century. In addition to intensifying communalism, they strengthened Muslim revivalist movements such as the Tabligh.[21]

Efforts to strengthen Hinduism coincided with several reformist and cultural initiatives among Muslims, including the formation of dozens of *anjumans* (cultural bodies) and *tanzims* (associations), the establishment of schools and colleges as well as many political parties. It was in Punjab and in areas around Delhi that these Muslim organizations undertook to represent the interests of the community, which, in most cases, depended on the common language Urdu as the shared denominator of north Indian Islam. In Bengal, the economic concerns of the landless peasantry—an historical grievance spawning earlier movements such as the Faraidhi during the 19th century—soon converged with the demands for a sovereign Muslim state. Of particular interest to this group were the promises of cultural and economic well-being as well as political empowerment.[22]

Thus Pakistan came to be seen as a meeting ground for various cultural, economic, regional, and political aspirations, which might provide an escape from the feared majority rule in some Muslim sections. The two border regions in South Asia comprising the Indus Valley and Eastern Bengal concurrently underwent parallel processes of separation (from India) while ascribing to a trans-regional "Muslimness." At the same time, the rising tide of belief in India as a separate Hindu state, or *Hindutva*, continued to view this separation as a major betrayal of an historic and trans-regional India. Within this belief system, India's own Muslims were viewed as "outsiders" whose hearts and souls belonged to Pakistan and not to Hindustan. Realistically, Pakistan could not provide for *all* Muslims in South Asia, yet its appropriation of Islam amidst a growing de-emphasis of its own Indianness added fuel to the venom emanating from anti-Muslim groups. Bereft of hundreds of millions of Muslims, India's refurbished Hindu majority should have had no reason to be apprehensive of their fellow Muslim citizens. Their presence had served a useful purpose in keeping the communalist agenda alive at a time when Indian Muslims were seen merely as a vote bank for secularists/ nationalists.[23]

This discretionary viewing of Islam and Pakistan followed by the 1971 independence of Bangladesh with India's active intervention only pushed the Indus Valley nation into seeking greater commonality with West Asia and other Muslim states. Zulfikar Ali Bhutto's holding of the summit of Muslim countries in Lahore in 1974 stemmed from this perspective and oriented Pakistan more towards the Muslim world, whereas South Asia came to be seen only as negative baggage that could drag down an already weakened country.

Islam as Arab imperialism? The recent perception of Islam as Arab imperialism, with its continued yet exacting foreignness outside the Arab regions has been proposed by several authors including the Nobel Laureate V.S. Naipaul. Born in Trinidad of Indian origin, Naipaul is a strong supporter of *Hindutva*. Since his early travels through Iran, Pakistan, Indonesia, and Malaysia, Naipaul has found the Islamic creed of non-Arabs problematic.[24] He is even more critical of Iranians, Pakistanis, and other Asian Muslims, who, in their commitment to "Arabism" have denied their historic roots as Persians, Indians, and so on. According to Naipaul, the demands of this Arabian cultural imperialism are both unending and debilitating, but that does not seem to have stopped millions from pursuing this collective self-denial.[25]

Like Islam, Judaism and Christianity are Middle Eastern Abrahamic religions by origin, yet the latter two are followed by millions of non-Middle Easterners, including Europeans, Asians, Australasians, Africans, and Americans. Comparing the widespread global uptake of all of these religions, one wonders whether Naipaul's dictum of Islam being culturally imperialized holds any parallel truth in these religions. Naipaul's enthusiastic support for organizations spearheading a totalitarian agenda in India further compromised his criticism. While the Nobel Laureate's well-articulated argument shows flaws when held up to the light, it would be wrong to see him as an exceptional case.[26] Naipaul's work represents a body of literature imbued with such Arab-specific views of Islam as to deny its historical, cultural, and trans-regional diversity. However, it would be a travesty to deny such open tendencies for Arabization as held by some non-Arab Muslims. Such recourse is certainly evident in those religio-political groups who have been inspired by Salafi and Wahabbi precedents and may include some sections of Muslims in the diaspora.[27]

In a society like Pakistan's there are pulls toward a more scripturalist and exclusive form of Islam among some groups holding revivalist inclinations, yet by and large they do not propagate any rejection of democracy or human rights. In most cases, the traditional seminaries have never encouraged militant programs and it is only recently that some have begun incubating Political Islam, which found an outlet in Afghanistan following the foreign invasions. Additionally, these institutions feature many technical and professional deficiencies that also beset public sector education.[28] The exploitation of Islam for nation-building purposes is not unique to mainstream and religio-political parties; nonrepresentative rulers, including Musharraf and others across the Muslim world, have equally used Islam as a tool for legitimacy.[29]

Islam was not the cause of Pakistan's failure in national integration, nor does it prevent Muslims from reinterpreting it to work alongside democracy, gender empowerment, and other basic human rights. In reality, it is only the selective use of this faith that has led to the growing critique of its narrow remit. The idea of Pakistani nationhood was couched in constitutional politics, economic welfare, and equal citizenship. This form of nationhood was intended to allow the emergence of Muslim/Islamic democracy that could harbor a much-needed interface between tradition and modernity. In their adulation for modernization, Pakistan's founders were neither rejecting Islam nor were they apologists for some theocratic state. They felt that sovereign Muslim state(s) would eventually lead to "spiritual democracy" in the larger interests of a stratified and violence-prone world.[30]

Throughout Pakistan's history, the positing of Islam as inherently anti-democratic and anti-modern has only caused unnecessary problems within this otherwise workable interface. In fact, as seen by many modernist intellectuals, Islam has often displayed its own processes and attributes of reinterpreting texts and Prophetic examples to suit new challenges throughout its history.[31] The Muslim empires and kingdoms of the past avoided the universal evangelization of non-Muslims, pursued politics more in tune with mundane realities, and promoted arts, literature, and diverse cultures. The tolerant manifestations of Islam allowed open space in which civil society could flourish, and thus neither Islam nor the Muslim ruling dynasties turned into annihilating forces.[32] Positing Islam merely as a violent ideology, defining jihad as free-for-all violence, and finding every Pakistani madrassa operating as a jihadist factory may be rooted in an all-too-familiar premise of a prevailing clash of cultures, yet this does not explain a visible Muslim consensus on universal empower-ment and economic welfare.[33]

PARTITION AND PUNJAB

THE LONGSTANDING CONFLICT between India and Pakistan, stretching as it does from the time of Partition, has prevented the politics of good neighborliness. The respective views of Pakistan and India's own past is based on the need to only see each other's "otherness," where histories, landscapes, faiths, languages, political systems, and geopolitics have all fed into this polarity.

The grand narratives on both sides of the border continue to get in the way of any resolution and the expropriation of the past by both nations makes otherwise consensual terms such as "independence" or "Partition" suddenly contentious. Whereas many Pakistanis view 1947 as the beginning of independence for a pluralistic subcontinent, their Indian counterparts see the same event as a vivisection of what was a singular Indian entity. Such overarching views permeate official debates and academic texts and are forced on the public imagination by an obliging but powerful media. These versions of the region's history, as well as the attitudes and policies based upon them, filter down to the local and even to the individual level, where they are internalized readily as the *only* truths. It is little wonder then, that for ordinary Pakistanis, India seems full of scheming Hindus with nothing more to do than hatch policies intent on eliminating Muslims from South Asia. In the same way, for many Indians, Pakistan is a land full of uncouth and untrustworthy warriors who will not miss an opportunity to humiliate India.

Interaction between the two has also reflected these prejudices. Considering the humanitarian tragedies created in the wake of the 1947 Partition, as well as Punjab's recurring position as the battleground for Indo–Pakistani Wars, these attitudes of mistrust are understandable. Ironically, one-to-one relationships between individual Indians and Pakistanis within the region are astounding to observe, owing to both curiosity and a shared guilt over the ongoing hostility on both sides.

Thus, the predominantly Sikh visitors from India to Lahore and the Indian Sikh pilgrims visiting shrines in Nankana Sahib and Punja Sahib all exude a sense of belonging that can only be found in people who have come home after a long absence. A similar impression is often given by

Pakistani Punjabis visiting Amritsar, Jullundhar, Ludhiana, and Chandigarh, or while traveling through cities such as Delhi and Ajmer.[1] Some people see in this growing warmth the easing of the painful memories of 1947, and this is especially true among the younger generation on both sides of the border, a fact that is often overlooked amidst the prevailing distrust.[2] The evolution of a middle-class, mobile, and largely conservative diaspora has helped Punjabis on both sides of the border to realign their positive cross-border connections—a luxury not available to their counterparts elsewhere in the Indus Valley.

Other than economic constraints, mobility across the Indo–Pakistani borders in this region is strictly controlled by the respective states. Both regimes either deter their citizens from undertaking interstate visits by implementing difficult visa barriers, or set in place unnecessary bureaucratic hurdles allowing only a handful people to travel across the borders.[3] Kashmiris on both sides of the Indo–Pakistan border remain the most disadvantaged group among these interstate travelers.

It is interesting to note that the Sindh province of Pakistan has not attempted the same engagement across the borders as has occurred in Punjab. Despite a shared linguistic and historical heritage, Sindhis do not pursue the same cross-border connections even though Partition caused less violence on both sides of the border and migrations were comparatively peaceful. In Sindh, Partition appears tangibly real although a few urban Sindhis on both sides have tried to retain some limited contact. Thus, the Sindhi identity was more fractured along class and communal lines as a result of Partition than that in the Punjab, where fissures were strictly faith-based among all four communities—Muslim, Hindu, Sikh, and Christian.

Despite these distinctions of faith among Punjabi people before 1947, communities could still mount common alliances as was seen among the Punjab National Unionist Party and the Ghadrites,[4] a movement started in the early 1900s by Sikh and Hindu Punjabis living in Canada to eject the British from India. One may be wary of the rural parochialism of the pre-1947 Unionists, yet their successful efforts to keep together the three main communities for a sustained period was no mean feat. For this, credit is due to leaders such as Fazl-i-Husain, Sikandar Hayat, and Chhotu Ram who succeeded in anchoring the cross-communal politics during the inter-war years, resisting internal as well as external challenges. Founded in 1923, the Unionist Party upheld the territorial, cultural, and political vision of a united Punjab at a time when bickering had already succeeded in transforming it from its early composite cultural identity to more assertive political creeds with strong communalist undertones.[5]

The evolution of a modern Pakistan

The major transformation that occurred among these South Asian societies during the final years of the Raj is certainly linked to the evolution of Pakistan, both as a product of Partition and as a culmination point for divergent forces in India. Pakistan was the handiwork of reformers who were themselves products of modernity. These reformist forefathers projected Pakistan, in the 1940s at least, as a cultural utopia where Muslim political and economic interests would be safeguarded. Their form of Muslim nationalism was akin to the German folk spirit of *volksgeist* rather than a nostalgia for lost Muslim glory.

These reformists were enthusiastically challenged by Islamists including Jamiat-i-Ulama-i-Hind (JUH), Majlis-i-Ahrar-i-Islam (MAI), and several other such doctrinal groups. The Islamist nationalists did not share common ground with the All-India Muslim League (AIML), and wanted to see a rehabilitation of Islamic life within a united, independent India. Thus, Pakistan (a new independent Islamic nation) and Hindustan (a united and independent India) were two ideological trajectories contested by both the culturalist-modernists and the Islamist-nationalists, and pre-1947 Punjab was the battleground for this intra-Muslim dissention. Rejecting both the modernists and the Islamists, another group within the contemporary Muslim elite sought regional solutions to the Indian quagmire and defined themselves simply as Punjabis, Bengalis, Pushtuns, Sindhis, and so on. To this group, India was an entire continent, and the provincial territory-based demarcations guaranteed by independence could allow a peaceful transfer of power without assuming any frightening sectarian transformations.

The three major opinion groups among Muslims had been formed in the wake of the Raj in India, specifically after the provincialization of Indian politics in 1919. These groups remained the main players in Muslim India for the next three decades until the 1947 Partition. In that year, both the regionalists and nationalists lost out to the culturalists, who had been successful in mobilizing a significant Muslim majority behind their notion of Muslim nationalism in the form of a separate nation. Pakistan represented a territorial arrangement, where faith, culture, and economy were combined to create a position that was larger than that of the regionalists, yet smaller than that of the Islamist-nationalists. Many regionalists had also joined the movement for Pakistan, leaving their former parties such as the Unionists and the Red Shirts in a quandary. In the same vein, many Islamists deserted the JUH, MAI, and others by shifting their support to the Muslim League's demand for Pakistan.

Consequently, between 1946 and 1947, newer, powerful, and more diverse political alliances emerged within India. As a result of the cross-party changes to get behind the idea of an independent Pakistan, the Muslim League had become a stronger, more pluralistic organization, and was able to confront the Raj, the Indian National Congress, the regionalists, and Muslim nationalists with confidence. To be fair, the modernists, nationalists, and regionalists never spoke of breaking down their mutual relationship, and perhaps this is part of the reason why no serious debate ever took place on the specifics of Partition, the religious and communal tensions, and the possibility of population transfers.

Mass migration in the wake of Partition By the time the processes for Partition were underway, communalism and migrations had become a *fait accompli*, the same sad sight that was seen in Palestine, Ireland, Cyprus, the Balkans, Rwanda, and post-2003 Iraq. The architects of modern South Asia, responsible for the dissolution of the Raj by replacing it with a modern territorial state system, were humanists and had never imagined that the relationships among the postcolonial states would be based on hatred and violence. Mohandas Gandhi's last fast, for example, was undertaken in order to help protect Muslims in India from Hindu and Sikh aggression, and to put pressure on the Nehru government to release funds and assets due to Pakistan.

Like the subcontinent itself during the summer of 1947, Punjab was engulfed in the simmering cauldron of communal violence—a bitter reality that continues to reverberate to this day. Despite all the pious statements about peace, a painful polarity persists, whether considering Indo–Pakistani warfare, the strict interstate visa regimes, or the bizarre daily flag-hoisting ceremonies on both sides of the border, farcically cheered by their respective supporters.

In the early decades after Partition in both India and Pakistan, national integration was the official priority and all kinds of tools were applied to de-emphasize regional and local agendas. In Pakistan, in particular, the country's evolution was explained with reference to the top leadership of the Muslim League working within the context of a binding Islamic ethos. Due to the nature of the Pakistani state's bifurcation along the east and west of the subcontinent as well as the plurality within West Pakistan, any discussion of regional dynamics or prerogatives was considered subversive to the country as a whole.

In many cases, Pakistan's ruling classes assumed increased roles, ignoring the fact that in order for their national project to succeed the country needed equal recognition and participation from all segments of society. Such an impatience with the nation's inherent ethno-regional diversity soon turned into a complex of fear, resulting in a greater centralization of government through administrative measures such as the One-Unit scheme of 1955.[6] Under this scheme, all existing provinces within West Pakistan were integrated into one single unit, which fostered considerable resentment against the ruling elite, who predominantly came from Punjab. This fear was also expressed against intermittent military takeovers and the oversimplification of the official language, brushing aside or trivializing the pluralism of its people.

Early historical narratives either attributed the formation of Pakistan to a presumed unified Islamic ethos or simplistically attributed it to the needs of the Urdu-speaking elite from Muslim minority provinces such as the United Provinces (UP—the former British India province that united Agra and Oudh). Consequently, the constituent regions of Pakistan were either denied a significant role in the process of decolonization or were derisively viewed as apolitical monoliths. This depoliticization of the Pakistani regions including Punjab led to vast sections of the country being left out of events as momentous as the dissolution of the Raj. Most of these regions' indigenous intellectuals and activists understandably had serious misgivings about their lack of input into the unfolding events and felt it unlikely that they would carry any more weight in helping to forge the new nation of Pakistan.[7]

One Punjab or several?

Within the context of the history of Punjab, there are three main areas of debate, however, there are no clear cut answers and these debates continue as intellectual challenges.

Firstly, beginning with the expression of parallel or even competitive identities since the Rebellion of 1857, why has the Punjabi consciousness branched into separate politicized and communalized strands of Hindu, Muslim, and Sikh groupings rather than building up a single, unified platform? Secondly, why did Punjab suffer the most during Partition; was the violence that occurred here unique to or inherent in this region only? Thirdly, unlike its Indian counterpart, why did Pakistani Punjab assume a larger-than-life role within the new state, a position that has earned negative criticism and few plaudits?

The Punjabi ethos was based on a rural population with total dependence on agriculture and some involvement in soldiery, controlled through local intermediaries. Towns and cities existed but did not operate as battlegrounds between competing interests. The rulers—the Mughals and the Sikhs—usually kept a confederal arrangement without drastically interfering with the local mores and practices.

The advent of the British Raj unleashed significant economic, political, and administrative changes that transformed both rural and urban societies within the Punjab. The canalization and settlement of new colonies coincided with the introduction of modern communications networks along with an educational system that transformed the sociopolitical patterns of the province within a generation. The Indus Valley's geological and ecological systems, as well as its location as a bridgehead across the regions of Hindustan, Persia, Afghanistan, and Turkistan, afforded the area a degree of self-sufficiency. Within a generation, modernization transformed the sociopolitical patterns of the province. Major projects harnessed the Indus water systems for irrigation, however, these reduced the importance of the Indus River as the main artery of communication in favor of railways connecting Punjab with Karachi and the Middle East.

The introduction of English, Western education, printing presses, canals, a complex revenue and taxation system, the reorganization of private property, the arrival of Christian missionaries, as well as the focus on Punjabis as a martial race certainly offered new opportunities to the people, but also increased mutual competition. Mobility through education, jobs in the armed forces or commerce, and population transfers within the newer colonies soon resulted in new cultural configurations. As a result, language and religion became the prime bedrocks of community identity at a time when Punjabis were on their way towards a transformation on a scale never encountered before in their previous history.

The displacement of Persian by English as the language of governance, as well as the change to printing books, newspapers, and pamphlets in English, Urdu, Hindi, and Punjabi, brought in trans-regional linguistic competitors Urdu and Hindi, which would soon merge with Islam and Hinduism respectively. Like the United Provinces (UP) of the 1860s, Urdu–Hindi competition in Punjab became a symbolic Muslim–Hindu tussle, while the Punjabi language was allowed to languish in the backwaters. Colonial textbooks portrayed India as a land of multiple, segmentary, and primitive identities with a religion-based, chaotic view of traditional Indian societies.[8] The codification of identities, based on religion, caste, and even class, was used in the census reports and district gazetteers, further solidifying this redefinition of collective identities where Hindu, Muslim, European/Christian, and Sikh emerged as completely separate categories. This is not to suggest that this entire process was harmful, yet the speed and scale of reclassification underlying these transformations were unprecedented.

Religion as a cultural marker Within urban Punjab, the Muslims, Hindus, and Sikhs began to organize revivalist and modernist/reformist efforts in order to preserve their own cultural identities. The groups at the forefront of these efforts were the Arya Samajis (a Hindu reform movement), the Probhandak committees (which managed Sikh shrines and holy places), and the Muslim anjumans (clubs and associations). Within these efforts, simple identity markers such as being Punjabi or coming from a particular caste- or kinship-based affinity were not sufficient. In their place, religious identity markers—Muslim, Hindu, and Sikh—began to subsume these smaller categorizations. Emanating from the larger cities of Lahore, Amritsar, and Gujranwala, the sense of competition among religious groups began to grow until it assumed political dimensions; the march from cultural redefinition to political nationalism happened within one generation.[9] This is not to suggest that the three major religious communities had unified and consensual political programs in place, as they simultaneously debated and argued among themselves.

Almost all those involved in such movements were literate or educated professionals who interacted with the state in their own ways, related to other communities, read and debated press reports and shared links with wider Indian communities. In the case of Muslims, they were a class unto themselves and quite distinct from their urban poor or rural landed elite counterparts across the province. They had more in common with their counterparts from the United Provinces, Bengal, and Bombay by virtue of their shared views on Islam, colonial administration, Muslim history, Indian past, the Urdu language, and the importance of education.

These groups divided loosely along revivalist/traditionalist and reformer/modernist lines, but they all agreed on the urgent need for change. The traditionalists might have idealized returning to their roots, yet they used modernity for their own ideological interests. Modernists such as Sir Mohammad Shafi and Nawab Muhammad Hayat Khan had no hesitation in supporting the colonial regime as well as reformers such as Sir Syed Ahmed Khan. The city of Lahore, in particular, became the forerunner of literary, educational, and intellectual pursuits, spearheaded by bodies such as the Anjuman-i-Islamia and Anjuman-i-Himayat-i-Islam, which accounted for the renaissance in Urdu literature.[10]

From this base it was a short jump for these movements to politics, with the All-India Muslim League, Punjab Nationalist Unionist Party, Khaksar Tehrik (a Muslim revivalist and social movement aimed at releasing India from foreign rule), and Ahrars (a Muslim separatist movement) earnestly following one another to spearhead their own political programs, until eventually the Muslim League surpassed all other regionalist rivals.

Another possible explanation for the parallel expressions of Muslim, Hindu, and Sikh identities in place of a single, loosely defined Punjabiat can be found in the regionalization of these groups. For instance, Muslims were concentrated in the western regions while Hindus and Sikhs lived mainly in eastern regions. Also Muslims and Sikhs were predominantly rural while Hindus tended to be mostly urban dwellers or engaged in non-agricultural professions. The rural nature of Punjab's economy further augmented by political-economic engineering during canal construction, created several new and transient communities that failed to develop relations across traditional boundaries. A number of Sikh and Muslim families from the eastern districts who had settled in the new canal colonies were still developing their roots when the events of 1947 overtook their third generation and set them on the move once again.

Communal violence: the Punjabi experience

The most persuasive explanation for the violent breakdown of pluralism in Punjab can be attributed to the dissolution of the colonial administration. Partition was originally planned for 1948 but was then brought forward a year; as a result troops were not yet installed in the border areas and subsequently these deteriorated into a free-for-all during the huge migration. Responsibility should also be laid at the doorstep of British and Indian leaders for their inability to forge common strategies for the likely transfer of populations, whether voluntary or enforced. The absence of any discussion concerning the actual practicalities of independence was not only an abysmal failure on the part of the colonial administration, it was equally apparent in the carelessness demonstrated by South Asian leaders.

The demands for Partition were not new in Punjab. Otherwise responsible Hindu leaders such as Lala Lajpat Rai and Har Dayal had supported the community-based division of the province back in the 1920s. Muslim and Sikh leaders also spoke of utopias based on separatism, which, in these cases meant joining up with their counterparts elsewhere to form larger units. Sikhs wanted a separate state in which to safeguard their own interests, as they saw themselves caught between the two larger communities of Muslims and Hindus. As such, the Punjabi elite within all three religious groups of the 1940s only focused on their own paths without building bridges across the fault lines of their respective religions.

An additional factor behind this malaise was the breakdown of local networks, which meant there were no mechanisms in place for protecting the impending refugee caravans. Within their specific localities, displaced people had some sense of protection among their familiar neighbors and friends, yet once out in the open and away from their native regions, they simply became the "other." The breakdown of a common political ethos against the backdrop of a failing state hastened the processes of ethnic cleansing and revenge in South Asia. In this respect, 1947 Punjab is not unique within the history of modern decolonization, in which the processes of partition and the accompanying reality of population transfers have occurred in several locations around the globe.[11]

It remains possible to argue that Punjab is an extreme example of such communal violence, certainly when placed alongside its Sindhi and Bengali counterparts. The experiences of these two regions make for an illuminating comparison. Despite their locations on opposite corners of the subcontinent, pre-1947 Bengal and Sindh were more similar to each other than they were to Punjab, which actually shared a border with Sindh and would be expected to share more similarities. The provinces of Bengal and Sindh were divided between Hindu and Muslim sections, yet they shared common languages and culture and even, in spite of their religious- and class-based differences, a sort of consensual identity (Muslim Sindhis with Muslim Bengalis and Hindu Sindhis with Hindu Bengalis). Both had wealthy Hindu classes that often lived in urban districts, while their Muslim counterparts lived in rural areas. However, these regions' experience of Partition was less volatile than that of Punjab. But as soon as class and creed took over as the most decisive identity markers in these provinces, one could detect a propensity towards a rift, with a separation between Sindhi's Muslims and Hindus and Bengal's Muslims and Hindus.

For a long time, Sindhis had resented being seen as an extension of a larger Bombay presidency and sought their own separation through the demand for a Sindhi province. The urban and rural elite—both Hindu and Muslim—converged over this matter, seeking a common political goal. As Karachi's importance grew following the construction of the railway lines and large-scale barrages on the Indus, the influx of rural Punjabis into Sindh was widely resented. Both the urban Bombayites and the rural Punjabis were seen as common foes to the Sindhis. As a result, the rural Muslim landholding elite almost forgot their distrust of the Hindu *amils* (low-ranking bureaucrats) and *baniyas* (moneylenders) who ran businesses, credit, and other services based on their higher levels of education, mobility, and resourcefulness.[12] Both the *amils* and the *baniyas* belonged to the Lohana caste—similar to the Hindu business castes of *khatris* in Pothowari Punjab and *sethis* in Peshawar—who were also involved in extra-regional commercial enterprises.[13]

Following Sindh's separation from Bombay in 1936, this former consensus broke down, giving way to new configurations in which an emerging Muslim bourgeoisie built up alliances with the *pirs* (spiritual mentors and saints) and *waderas* (feudal landlords),[14] while the Hindu wealthy classes sought out extra-regional alliances. Given its earlier secession, it is not surprising that Sindh was the first province to support the demand for a separate Pakistan. It did so through its provincial assembly in 1943 where feudal and urban nationalists passed a resolution in favor of a separate Muslim state.

Despite the cultural and linguistic unity of Bengal, economic tensions began gathering momentum between the castes of the *bhadralok* and *ashraaf*, as they sought economic, political, and administrative influence for their respective communities. While the Bengal renaissance of the nineteenth century had reenergized the Hindu elite, contemporary aristocratic and rural Muslim elements tried to invigorate a unified Bengali Muslim identity.[15] This movement shared similarities with the Lahore Urdu renaissance, which reinvigorated the Muslims of Punjab. Unlike Punjab however, Muslims in Bengal were predominantly concentrated in eastern regions. Similar to the situation in Sindh, the 1905 Partition of Bengal had occurred at a time when a strong Muslim cultural identity had already become vocal at the grassroots.[16] The administrative arrangement made by George Curzon (Viceroy of India 1899–1905), though annulled six years later, had opened up significant prospects for Bengali Muslims while curtailing the power enjoyed by the upper classes. Bengali partition was annulled in 1911 following an intense Self-sufficiency Movement to remove British control. This outcome certainly made Indian political groups aware of the efficacy of modern acts of rebellion such as boycotts, as well as the possible success of peaceful yet persistent civil disobedience. On the flipside, the partition annulment was a damper for Bengali Muslims. It was not surprising that amidst the economic disenchantment further exacerbated by the uncertainties of annulment, both the Indian National Congress and the Communist Party of India failed to gain a foothold among the Bengali Muslim peasantry and bourgeoisie. When the All-India Muslim League, led by Abul Hashim and Huseyn Shaheed Suhrawardy began addressing the economic disparities faced by Bengali Muslims, an independent Pakistan appeared as "a peasant utopia," promising a cultural assertion.[17]

Within Punjab, the Muslim, Hindu, and Sikh communities were scattered all over the province, whereas in the Sindh and Bengal, Hindus lived in urban areas while Muslims were found predominantly in rural regions. Due to its location and size, during Partition, Punjab became the crossroads for mass migrations as refugees made their way from NWFP to India. Similarly, most refugees heading for Pakistan—Punjabi Muslims and millions of others from all across India—had to traverse expanses of eastern Punjab where communal violence had already intensified, with the exception of Faridkot.[18] Sindh also received and sent out millions of refugees during those turbulant months, however, not many refugees came from Balochistan on their way to India as better air and sea links allowed some refugees safer passage across the southern Indus Valley.[19] Population transfers between Indian and Pakistani Punjab were all land-based and refugees moved away from the populous areas where acts of collective violence were causing greater havoc.

While Sindh's boundary was, to a great extent, demarcated during its 1936 secession and Bengal had already experienced the division of 1905, Punjab's boundary line remained unclear and highly contentious until long after the Radcliffe Line, the official border between Pakistan and India, was decided by the Border Commission and awarded on 17 August 1947. In particular, the unknown future of certain subdivisions within the Ferozepur and Gurdaspur districts was unnerving for their inhabitants and equally controversial from the Pakistani viewpoint especially with the growing Indo–Pakistani tension over the fate of Jammu and Kashmir.[20] Gurdaspur's location was quite precarious as, according to Pakistani accounts, it allowed India a land bridge into the princely state as well as causing the outflow of the Ahmadi population from Qadian into Pakistani Punjab.

The "Punjabization" of Pakistan

Now we come to our third major area of study—the degree to which Punjabis came to dominate the formation and government of the new state of Pakistan and the degree to which this was achieved at the expense of the the nation's other provinces. Soon after Pakistani independence, the finger of blame began to point toward Punjabis for their perceived monopolization of the national resources and administrative offices, either on their own or in collaboration with the Urdu-speaking Muslim migrants or Muhajireen from India. It is certainly true that the majority of Pakistanis lived in the Punjab region, and many important national institutions were concentrated there, including the defense establishment and the new national capital. But it is also true that the existing unchallenged system of a Punjab-centered and often undemocratic polity justifies some criticism, although a few Punjabi intellectuals may call it "Punjabi bashing."

There are some Punjabis, however, who believe that by assuming the role of the country's flagship, Punjab has sacrificed its own linguistic and cultural distinctness. To this group, Punjabis appear to have been negligent in maintaining their own language and culture and have opted for trans-regional preferences, including Urdu. To such critics, even considering the Punjabi language as a medium of instruction or the recognition of Punjabi identity at a collective level could be viewed as anti-Pakistani. Critics also feel that Punjabis have too often inflicted self-immolation, and by divesting themselves of Punjabiat, have distanced themselves from Pakistan and one another. During the tensions between the central government in Islamabad and the provincial administration in Lahore—both cities in Punjab—such Punjabi grudges may secretly or indirectly receive official encouragement so as to embarrass the national leadership.[21]

The preeminence enjoyed by Punjabis in the country's internal and external policies and institutions continues to be problematic, given the federal and plural nature of Pakistan. In addition, the region's self-assumed de facto role is astounding when one looks at the parallel divisions and marginalization of its counterpart in India. Unlike the painful march toward a Punjabi-speaking autonomous state, and the creation of the separate states of Haryana in 1966 and Himachal in 1971, Punjab in Pakistan has enjoyed a larger-than-life role within the structure of the country. This state of affairs is due to pre-1947 politics when Punjabi Muslims opted for extra-regional alliances of a cultural and political variety. Despite its partition between India and Pakistan, Pakistani Punjab found itself endowed with significant human and institutional resources, allowing it to take center-stage in the new state.

This positive outcome enjoyed by Punjab is in contrast to the experience of other provinces after Partition. The division of Bengal had given rise to East Pakistan in 1947. In addition to the disadvantage of their physical distance from West Pakistan, Bengalis/East Pakistanis lacked the unique institutional and strategic wherewithal that allowed Punjabi bureaucrats, commanders, and entrepreneurs a pivotal national role. After the 1971 creation of Bangladesh, Punjab's dominance has become even more significant and disputatious, which often causes Sindh and Balo-chistan to react strongly.

Interestingly, a new axis of power was established in the 1980s, allowing Pushtuns from settled districts to join Punjabis as partners in governing the country. Given the closer Pushtun–Punjabi alliance as well as the Pushtun expansion as an economic reality across the country, the turbulence in neighboring Afghanistan during the 1979–89 Soviet occupation did not cause any concerns about secession in the NWFP or

Balochistan. However, the anomalous situation of FATA Pushtuns finally gave way to an implosive militancy, which in 2005 had evolved out of post-9/11 geopolitics.

At another level, Urdu speakers have felt a greater sense of marginalization after Bengalis/East Pakistanis, and the Muhajir/Muttahida Qaumi Movement (MQM) ensured that its street politics were directed against Islamabad and other ethnic groups in Karachi. The MQM plays an important role for many Urdu speakers as it claims to be the mouthpiece of the Indian-born Muhajireen who speak Urdu as their mother tongue. In the 1980s and 1990s the controversial leader of the MQM, Altaf Hussain, led an urban backlash against Karachi's other ethnic communities in response to what was considered the ethnic and cultural marginalization of his community of Pakistani-born Muhajireen.

Punjab today

Following the civil society movement of 2007–8 advocating a return to democratic government and the primacy of the judiciary, major changes took place across the country, including Benazir Bhutto's assassination, Musharraf's eclipse in the elections of 2008, and the ascendance of Bhutto's widower Zardari, now head of the PPP. The MQM joined forces with the PPP-led centrist regime and the provincial government of Sindh. President Zardari's reticence on substantive issues including the full restoration of deposed judges and the removal of the controversial Seventeenth Amendment, which allowed too much power to reside in the presidential office, created a gulf between the PPP government in Islamabad and the Pakistani Muslim League (PML-N), led by the Sharif brothers in Punjab. The League had done well out of recent changes and following a spectacular victory in the 2008 elections, it formed a provincial administration in Punjab. However, it was not smooth sailing and the party faced stiff resistance from Governor Salman Taseer. Nawaz Sharif had worked with Zardari in removing Musharraf from power, yet he withdrew from the coalition over Zardari's procrastination on constitutional and judicial reforms as well as Zardari's close ties to Taseer.

By early 2009, the political leadership in Islamabad and Lahore appeared to be heading toward a new confrontation. Mired in controversy over their ties with Musharraf, the judges of Pakistan's highest court deliberated over the cases filed against the Sharif brothers, challenging their eligibility to hold any public office.[22] Finally, on 25 February 2009 the Supreme Court, headed by Justice Dogar, disqualified the Sharif brothers from holding any public office, thus pushing Pakistan into a new phase of political instability. Even before the judicial verdict was made public, Governor Taseer, on

Zardari's advice, imposed governor's rule by dismissing Shahbaz Sharif's provincial government and replacing it with senior bureaucrats from Islamabad.

This latest phase in the crisis of governance not only highlighted Musharraf's continuing legacy under Zardari, it demonstrated that the country remained a long way from achieving its desired political consensus.[23] A defiant Punjab and an Islamabad tied to the status quo while aiming to defend its own dominance certainly did not bode well for a post-Musharraf political setup. The disqualification of the Sharif brothers not only pushed the country back into a familiar polarity, it showed that Zardari was intent on consolidating his hold on power to the extent of antagonizing his former allies. The situation did not bode well for his own PPP, already weakened by Zardari's procrastinations on judicial and constitutional reforms. Pakistan was once again in the throes of political drift and schisms with Punjab becoming a battleground when Zardari assumed presidency as an increasingly unpopular successor to Musharraf. Parallel to that, following a majority vote in the elections, PML–N emerged as a ruling party in the province.

Things were to change again in the summer of 2009. The increasing Taliban-led insurgency in Swat and the Supreme Court's reversal of the verdict of the Sharif brothers' eligibility restored a semblance of a working relationship between Zardari and Sharif. The Sharif brothers had helped to restore the senior judges, yet stopped short of adding to Zardari's problems. But turbulent geopolitics in the NWFP and its fallout for the rest of the country, demanded a greater overhaul of the system. Even though a year had passed since Musharraf's exit, the country was still waiting for solutions to its enduring problem of misgovernance and domestic and international challenges to its stability. While the political culture remained weak, the army was able to resume its pivotal role within the state structure.

THE MIDDLE CLASSES

MOST BOOKS ABOUT PAKISTAN have examined the evolution of the country as a predominantly Muslim state in terms of its viability, problems of nationhood, and governance as well as addressing issues of ideology, ethnicity, pressure groups, and geopolitics. While one does not want to underestimate these factors, sometimes the complex interplay between state and society and the intricate issues of class formation and gender politics are overlooked. Due to the rather state-centric nature of much academic study, the entire society appears frozen in a time warp, with the country stuck in a predictable cycle of repetitive history.

Since 9/11, the issues of security and Political Islam have monopolized the entire discourse on the region, either completely ignoring society itself or seeing it as a brittle monolith of anti-Western clusters hastening the state's demise. The limited focus on jihadis and their invincibility, or on the army's indispensability as the last defense before the bestiality of Islamic fundamentalism, has allowed Pakistan to be portrayed as a failing state in which society itself has no role. The assertions of the warlords in FATA and Swat are not representative of the society at large. At the other end of the spectrum, middle-class Pakistanis seek peace, progress, universal education, and political and economic empowerment, and view militancy in the name of Islam as inept at best.

Several recent books have offered similar generalizations about Islam and Pakistani Muslim society, laced with the threat of nuclear bombs, imbued with anti-Americanism, and set on a course of self-immolation.[1] Pakistan has been presented as an exceptional case, a Muslim country untimely ripped into existence by Partition and on a permanent life-support machine provided by "Allah, America, and Army." These views, purported by some journalists, academics and even the country's own leaders and pressure groups, betray Jinnah's dream of a civic, tolerant, and progressive nationhood.[2] These negative attitudes are not unique to Pakistan, as similar attitudes pervade other Muslim countries.[3] Despite concerns about misgovernance and disturbing fundamentalist forces, these simplistic views routinely describe madrassas as jihadi training camps where hatred and militancy are intermeshed with an archaic, discretionary, and sexist curriculum.[4] In the same vein, such books may also posit Pakistan as a country permanently in turmoil, which, despite having a population of 175 million people, is still lacking in nationhood.[5]

There is no disputing the fact that Pakistan has been confronted by acute domestic and regional challenges, and that a system incorporating capable leadership, a sound judiciary, and an equitable economy backed by an all-encompassing foreign policy is long overdue. Crucially, one must locate the existence of positive forces, such as the emerging middle class to provide the glue between Pakistan's diverse groups and create a stable and even system.

However, there are several basic questions that must be addressed in order to pursue this thesis, and chief among them is: does Pakistan have a middle class? Can Islam, the army, modernity, the West, and ethnicity all provide helping hands in solidifying this middle class or will they simply cause even more fractures? Is it the economy or politics that determines the mental horizons of the middle class? And is there any guarantee that by assuming a mature, trans-regional, national character, this middle class will move toward modernist/secularist politics and an overhaul of the country's infrastructure on education, gender, and pluralism? Before delving into these questions, we shall explore the ways in which Pakistan and its people have been viewed. Finally, we will look at the factors that spawn as well as shape Pakistani middle-class opinions and stances on a variety of issues.

Western opinions, multiple views

An American specialist on the Middle East visiting Pakistan in March 2007 viewed Pakistan as perched on a precarious balance. Mark A. LeVine began his story with a rather dramatic narrative of the Frontier as he crossed the Indus near Attock. Unaware of the region's subtleties and its society, he found Peshawar symbolic of all of Pakistan, "filled with contradictions" as "each meter of Peshawar brings new contradictions." It was not just Peshawar, but almost every other city, including Islamabad, Quetta, Lahore, and Karachi, where "violence permeates the society" and wherein "hotels and airports are bombed with increasing frequency."[6] He also noticed, however, that students and teachers raised tricky issues, even at conservative institutions such as the International Islamic University in Islamabad, where instead of embracing Talibanization, he discovered students learning Hebrew and teachers eager to offer "secular courses." He was mindful of the fact that the media enjoyed more freedom in Pakistan than in Jordan and Egypt. His worries about

Pakistan's future contrasted with his impressions of an emerging and assertive middle class, as he noted: "An IT-driven middle class is emerging that is drawing into Pakistan the kind of tech services and call-center jobs that have helped drive economic growth in India." But he remained apprehensive about the country's vulnerable and precarious situation, domestically and internationally. He warned: "The disastrous repercussions of a disintegrating Pakistan are almost too frightening to contemplate. Iraq pales in comparison. Yet the policies of Bush, Blair and their European allies are pushing the country towards precisely such an outcome. Someone had better sound the alarm before it's too late."[7]

While a few Pakistanis might have welcomed the military coup of October 1999, most critics felt that the answer to the country's survival and progress lay in democracy and tolerant nation-building. Stephen Cohen, a longtime observer of the Pakistani military, had advised Washington to re-engage itself "with Pakistan's most powerful organization, the military." In a pre-9/11 article, Cohen wrote that it was the country's civil society that remained the most important asset for its stability. Cohen's mixed views about Pakistan's viability became clearer in his next book where his main hope rested with the middle class in the belief that they could direct the country towards better alternatives.[8]

Several Western analysts found the army to be at the root of Pakistan's problems of misgovernance, increased fundamentalism, and other socio-economic distortions. According to Frederic Grare, the generals embodied discretionary and centralized preferences at the expense of Pakistani universal rights, spawning problems in Balochistan and the NWFP. He believed that the Pakistani establishment was using jihadi elements to further geopolitical interests in Kashmir and Afghanistan and was oblivious to the domestic and regional fallout of such reckless tactics. Musharraf and the army presented themselves as the last bastions of liberalism before the looming threats of disintegration and volatility, while in reality they should have been viewed as the main culprits. Grare felt that the army created the specter of jihadism and was now exploiting it to squeeze additional benefits from the West.[9]

Vali Reza Nasr concurred with Grare's views, stating that in Pakistan's democratic deficit a major entry point for destructive forces could be found. To Nasr, "Pakistan [under Musharraf] is more in danger of an Islamist takeover than it was under democracy, because Pakistan had far stronger political parties, which is a rare thing in the Muslim world." He urged the restoration of democracy: "Right now the main obstacle to democracy in Pakistan is the military, not the Islamists. After the military takeover, it essentially set about destroying civilian parties and civilian institutions, and even made a pact with Islamists in order to do so."[10]

Compared with its misgovernance by the military and by elected politicians, the country's economic situation before 2007 often received plaudits from the West, though most happened after 2002. Largely, this was due to the West's need to cozy up to Musharraf in order to push its new geopolitical imperatives. Prior to that date, Pakistan's economy had been faltering due to stagnation, low foreign exchange reserves, corruption, global sanctions, massive tax evasions, and loan defaulting. The injection of $10 billion of US aid over the next six years (most of which was filtered into an unaudited defense sector), remittances by expatriates and partial restructuring of national debt all helped to encourage the emergence of a prosperous but equally consumerist middle class. Real estate, private education, and automobiles, in addition to a growing service sector, underwrote this prosperity amidst the growing poverty of its population.

In several speeches made during their visits abroad, Pervez Musharraf and Shaukat Aziz asserted the positive news about Pakistan's economic growth as a major achievement.[11] A report by the Associated Press of Pakistan (APP) opined that "the middle class is growing and a widely spread out, organized banking system offers a basis for sustained and fast-paced growth."[12] According to prominant *Dawn* journalist M. Ziauddin, the benefits were failing to reach the country's poor citizens who accounted for one-third of the population: "The rich have become very rich since 9/11, and the middle class is better off, but not the mass of Pakistanis."[13]

The gradual rebuilding of relations between the UK and Pakistan spawned visible commercial interest in Pakistan. British investments and aid allocations increased and British companies such as BP began to show interest in the country's energy sector. In spite of this outside interest, Islamabad itself did not undertake any projects to enhance its energy output. This failure would soon become a major strike against the Musharraf–Aziz regime. But as Pakistanis grew increasingly weary of longer power cuts, the situation reached a crisis point toward the end of 2007, when this power shortage converged with exorbitant oil prices and dwindling supplies of food and flour. The miracle of Pakistan's economy was shown to be deeply flawed and the middle class turned against the General's government. Musharraf could offer no tangible solution to Pakistan's economic and political woes at a time when life for his people was so insecure and daily bomb blasts began to take a horrific toll among the urban population.

Pakistani expatriates, driven by fear of Islamophobia following the erosion of civil liberties and a full-blown media assault on Muslims in the

West, invested their money in Pakistan, on real estate and sectors of the service economy. While this may have helped to expand Pakistan's middle class, it may also have exacerbated preexisting class-based stratification. The convergence between military-sponsored defence housing projects and expatriate Pakistanis caused a surge in property prices as well as the evolution of "gated communities," putting more strain on the lower strata of the middle class.

Hope as well as despair Visiting Pakistan soon after Benazir Bhutto's assassination in December 2007, William Dalrymple witnessed the national election campaign at close quarters. In the Sindhi heartland of Khairpur where feudal leaders had controlled local politics, electoral challenges from middle-class professionals heralded a welcome change. An activist against honor killings, Nafeesa Shah is the daughter of a lawyer-politician, and a post-graduate student at Oxford who stood against the well-entrenched feudal leader Sadruddin. Shah had previously served as the district *nazim* and now, supported by students, lawyers, journalists, and human rights activists, this Pakistan People's Party candidate defeated her rival. Dalrymple noticed similar trends in central Punjab and the NWFP, where sons and daughters of professionals were taking on and defeating powerful dynasts: "What happened in Khairpur was a small revolution—a middle-class victory over the forces of reactionary feudal landlordism. More astonishingly, it was a revolution that was reproduced across the country."[14]

Pakistan now has an expanding middle class challenging feudal leaders, generals, and mullahs and, according to Dalrymple, concerns over a serious rise in targeted bomb blasts and gloomy predictions about Pakistan were overstated. Politicians, lawyers, journalists, activists, and critics were containing religious extremism and official highhandedness and proving the middle class had come of age.[15]

However, after playing such a significant role in the 2008 elections and expelling Musharraf, this middle class was shocked by the indolence of the Zardari–Gilani regime that appeared to be failing on domestic and foreign fronts. Faced with the growing specter of Talibanization across the NWFP, daily US Predator drone attacks in FATA, and an aggressive India exerting pressure on Pakistan's eastern borders, Pakistan's chattering classes were losing patience with Zardari and the PPP. The country's constitution remained in tatters, the senior judiciary remained suspended well into 2009, and the growing division between Punjab and Islamabad did not engender optimism among this group. Against the backdrop of a restive Afghanistan and now an unstable northwestern

Pakistan, Dalrymple's optimism also seemed to have evaporated, as he subsequently noted:

> The blowback from the Afghan conflict in Pakistan is more serious still. Asif Ali Zardari's new government has effectively lost control of much of the North-West Frontier Province (NWFP) to the Taliban's Pakistani counterparts, a loose confederation of nationalists, Islamists, and angry Pashtun tribesmen under the nominal command of Baitullah Mehsud. Few had very high expectations of Zardari, the notoriously corrupt playboy widower of Benazir Bhutto. Nevertheless, the speed of the collapse that has taken place under his watch has amazed almost all observers.[16]

Indian views of Pakistan

For the most part, Indian commentators have seen the Pakistani state as synonymous with the entire society, and the entire society with a simplistic, militarist version of Islam that reduces Pakistanis to either a hapless mass run by a capricious military and the mullahs, or mere collaborators in sinister plots. Islam, Pakistan, the army, the actions of the Inter-Services Intelligence, and ethnic volatility are juxtaposed to present a judgmental and erroneous view of Pakistan.

A rather more balanced Indian attitude would like to see the political and economic advancement of Pakistan so that regional cooperation could secure a new beginning for South Asia, as well as allowing more freedom for minorities on both sides. In addition, a careful segment within this opinion group views Pakistan as a dependable—if not totally maneuverable—buffer between West Asian Muslim lands and a predominantly Hindu India.[17] Some Indian scholars give credit to Pakistan and its predominant Islamic ethos, especially its syncretic traditions, though find the lack of democracy is hampering any serious debate on Muslim civil society. Yoginder Sikand, a respected scholar of Islam in South Asia who has undertaken fieldwork on both sides of the border, has been aware of a general disenchantment in Pakistan among both liberal and Islamist groups. However, he has found that:

> ...the average Pakistani Muslim certainly is not a bearded, Kalashnikov-wielding, vehemently anti-Hindu or anti-Indian monster...For the average Pakistani Muslim, Islam is an integral part of his or her cultural identity, but it is not something that dominates every act or thought. This perhaps explains why religious parties have consistently won relatively few seats in Pakistani elections, with the discourse instead dominated by economic, personal, caste, *biradari* (brotherhood) and regional issues. [18]

In addition to the usual hateful, Muslim-baiting rhetoric from ultra-right Hindu parties, many serious treatises also refuse to acknowledge the diverse and positive aspects of Pakistani public opinion.[19] This othering of Pakistan is certainly motivated by a need to build up democratic, exceptional, and more tangible credentials for India, which is easier when Pakistan is seen as different and inferior. For instance, while commenting on the concept of the middle class and a vibrant civil society, Subhash Kapila of the South Asia Analysis Group, observed:

> In India there does undoubtedly exist a sizeable "civil society," which is a product of its politically liberalized society, democratic institutions and a general level of religious tolerance in a traditionally historic multi-racial society. It also emerges from a well-educated middle class and an enlarging one fuelled by its high rate of economic growth. Credit also needs to be given in this regard to the growth of political liberal institutions established during British rule and further nurtured in the last 60 years of independent India.

According to Kapila, Pakistan is deficient in liberal political institutions and, over the last 60 years, has regressed from the institutional framework left by the British, turning it into an autocratic military plus mullah gridlock.[20] This view of Pakistan is encountered among some Delhi elite who, like their counterparts in Islamabad or even Dhaka, might hold extreme opinions. The Mumbai attacks of November 2008 undoubtedly dampened efforts for regional amity, as extremists on both sides of the border assumed center stage. The view of Pakistan as an intolerant society of bloodthirsty jihadists with official patronage returned full force and the international media, with some notable exceptions, once again reverted to longstanding stereotypes.

The evolution of a middle class in Pakistan

So far, we have explored some external views of Pakistan, in which its political and ideological divisions have been examined with reference to the fragility as well as strengths of a middle class operating as a harbinger of change, tolerance, and empowerment. While a traditional Marxist explanation would present the middle class not as a solution, but inherently a problem, the fact remains that modernism is a middle-class project and modern Western history is certainly a culmination of the successes, ambitions, and even failures of the middle classes.[21]

From time to time, analysts within the Pakistani media offer interesting debates on their nation's class structure. A pervasive view of Pakistani society portrays it as inherently feudal, where military, civil bureaucracy, and urban ethnic leaders all operate within a patriarchal model when dealing with a vast majority of the "underclass." One explanation put forth for such a two-tier society is that historical land-based traditions with a Muslim preference for land and agriculture were further solidified by the colonial setup aimed at creating a loyal class of intermediaries. Pakistan's senior bureaucrats followed in colonial footsteps by coopting the landed interests, who were subsequently joined by the military elite, thus perpetuating the colonial framework.

The Islamic socialism of Zulfikar Ali Bhutto remained ambiguous in its definition of Pakistani class formation, despite having promised empowerment to the working classes, peasants, and lower-income urban groups. Bhutto's own feudal lifestyle and authoritarian populism demonstrated his lack of real commitment to a systemic overhaul while deeply politicizing people across Pakistan. It was a muffled form of liberalism that could have matured into a more progressive outlook, but the vagaries of Bhutto's rule followed by the military coup of General Zia-ul-Haq in July 1977 halted these processes.

The consolidation of the military within Pakistan, including its unrestrained coalition with the religious elite, further cemented by the Afghan Jihad, made it difficult for civil society to assert itself. However, restrictive measures, especially those focusing on women and minorities, did manage to politicize wider sections of society. The lack of land reforms, which were declared un-Islamic by some religious sections during the 1970s, not only strengthened traditional pressure groups, but also turned religious elements into power brokers. The direct availability of funds to politicians through Ayub Khan's basic democratic system, Zulfikar Ali Bhutto's People's Works Program and the provision of development money during General Zia's reign, strengthened the traditional patron-client relationship of feudal society. These changes effectively halted the expansion of a vocal middle class.

The state's neglect over loans, vacillations over tax collection, and resistance to land reforms certainly helped society's elite but created serious disadvantages for everyone else. By the 1980s and 1990s, the state had become an arena in which to seek urban land plots, business permits, bank loans, and other perks and privileges, and was only open to a small coterie of landed elite, senior state officials, and the capitalist-industrial class.

With so many avenues of authority barred to them, the Pakistani middle class began to vacillate between religious/sectarian and provincial/ethnic identities. Even today, it is still not totally possible for the middle classes to construct a trans-communal national character. Contemporary sociological studies of Pakistani society acknowledge the existence of a middle class but usually view it as lacking nationwide, forward-looking, and entrepreneurial initiatives, and sociologist Sabiha Hafeez even called it "artificial":

> The artificial middle class is characterized by income levels comparable to those of the real or ideal middle class but without comparable changes in their educational attainments and the nature of occupation. In Pakistan, the magnitude of status-centric norms is higher than the rate and magnitude of legitimized occupational mobility, with the result that an instant or artificial middle class has emerged as a new social structure, perhaps larger in size than the ideal or real middle class. The enlarged social formation competes with the ideal middle class and poses a threat to its emergence and growth.[22]

During the 1990s, some sociologists and historians preferred to identify urban, professional, and economically secure groups of Pakistanis as an "intermediate class," stopping short of designating them a fully fledged middle class.[23] However, the evolution of a private economy, remittances from abroad, urbanization, and a shared desire to seek improved education for the next generation offered new prospects for this burgeoning middle class. In the early 21st century, the Pakistani middle class was mostly urban and it began to assert itself through education, the growing media, property development, family and professional networking, and religious conservatism. This class became more aware of its Muslim credentials but would refuse to accept a narrowly defined Islam seen as tribal and largely rural—a form that often threatened the urban privileges of this emerging middle class. Immensely patriotic and concerned with the vagaries of national politics, it sought reforms and eventually aligned itself with the lawyers' movement.

Pakistani academics remain divided over the composition, direction, and even the existence of a Pakistani middle class. One group is skeptical of the current portrayal of an emerging middle class, instead viewing it as a shrinking class within a society that has become even more polarized, with economic and ideological disparities further disempowering Pakistanis. On the other hand, optimists see more opportunities in recent years for a growing middle class due to increased mobility, universal education, industrialization, the Dubai factor (offering jobs to skilled and unskilled South Asians, thereby increasing the income of many families), and the Green Revolution, all allowing greater financial autonomy to several sections of society.[24]

The third, and more balanced, opinion places itself between these two extremes. Despite being sensitive to pervasive poverty in the nation, this view accepts the enlargement of the middle class based on more capital injections, entrepreneurial skills, and wider economic opportunities. In addition, a better standard of living, multiple options for quality education and healthcare, and prospects for establishing small businesses have all vitally enlarged the precarious middle class of the past. According to this view, privatization has been a double-edged sword for this socioeconomic group. For instance, in the area of education, privatization has led to an increase in the number of schools, professional institutions, and universities, yet the quality of education has not kept apace due to a lower threshold of accountability. However, some private institutions in Lahore and Karachi have built excellent facilities, although these may only be accessible to a privileged few.

Contrary to the view of Pakistan as a feudalist society, some analysts believe that feudal land is already being parcelled out among more heirs, while the middle class is still not strong enough to assume a decisive profile on democracy, gender equality, land reforms, and minority rights, requiring more time and resources to reach that stage. Abbas Rashid in the *Daily Times* wrote:

> It [the middle class] does not appear to invest sufficient energy and resources in the task of building up social capital so necessary to improving on, even sustaining, its achievement...the state must give high priority to education and rural reform. Both are critical for empowering the middle class to play its vital role.[25]

The middle class and civil society

While the middle class is inherently urban and professional, the wider civil society contains this grouping but may also include rural and tribal elements working toward social reform. Within a Muslim society, it is crucial to take into account traditional bastions of local civil society rather than simply banking on non-governmental organizations (NGOs) or select groups of urban reformers.[26]

To the analyst Akbar Zaidi most NGOs are former state functionaries working within official parameters, and as such, any dependency upon foreign assistance compromises their autonomy. General Musharraf's coup was praised by these "liberal" groups who, in the beginning, saw in him a "savior" to safeguard the country against economic drift, political mismanagement, and ethno-sectarian violence. In many cases, these Westernized elements volunteered to work with the General to the extent that they supported him in holding democracy in hiatus. On the other hand, opposition to the military government mainly came from religious groups. Previously these groups would have been defined as anti-liberal, but here they were advocating empowerment, usually the prerogative of liberal groups. "For civil society in Pakistan, whether of the Westernizing, modernizing kind, or of the more fundamentalist Islamic kind, the question has not been one of democracy versus non-democratic norms, but of liberalism against perceived and variously interpreted Islamic symbols and values."[27]

By 2007, these "modern" segments of civil society had formed a consensus on an independent judiciary, constitutional primacy, free media, and an unrestrained form of parliamentary democracy and began to view Musharraf as a liability. At the same time, religious groups were becoming critical of Musharraf's role in the war on terror, yet continued to govern two provinces of the NWFP and Balochistan until December 2007. Through the Seventeenth Amendment, these groups had previously helped Musharraf in his presidential election while he was simultaneously chief of army staff. This complex relationship proved even more interesting when Westernized NGOs avoided vocal criticism of the Anglo-American invasions of Afghanistan and Iraq, whereas religious groups fronted the main opposition without hiding their anti-Western sentiments. Certain echelons of Pakistani civil society might have been skeptical of the democracy experienced under Benazir Bhutto and Nawaz Sharif in the 1990s, and under Musharraf they may instead have prioritized liberalism over democracy. However, this cannot be seen as the universal view of the entire civil society.[28]

The analyst Zaidi had previously found Pakistani NGOs to be unsupportive of democracy and more focused on liberalism, even where it occurred under military autocracy—a view that agitated several other analysts. The analyst and economist S. M. Naseem took exception to Zaidi's observations; to Naseem, not all liberal professionals had joined Musharraf by washing their hands of a "messy democracy" and Pakistanis were certainly no different to other societies, since they did not view democracy as a social need. Naseem concurred with Zaidi that people were becoming more hedonistically self-interested due to their disillusionment with the pursuit of democracy, though not essentially with democracy itself. Nor did he feel that this reflected on their lack of any rational choice. Although Ayub Khan's regime has traditionally been associated with rapid industrial development, Naseem traced the consolidation of the army's supremacy and the secession of East Pakistan to those years and policies. In addition, the army's dominance, buoyed up by US support, has become stronger over the decades.

According to Naseem, the absence of land reforms and the army's unchallenged control over budgetary allocations and all other processes resulted in a civil society that remained weak and "less argumentative" than its Indian counterpart. Zulfikar Ali Bhutto had attempted to contain the army's control by the introduction of a nuclear program, but then a military coup sealed the fate of such efforts once and for all. General Zia-ul-Haq and his military successors ensured that no civilian authority could be assertive enough to challenge the army's systemic primacy and that is where so many political regimes have been routinely dismissed. Against all odds, Pakistani civil society continues to speak out and Naseem suggests, might even seek credit for certain achievements:

> Today the argumentative Pakistani has a lowly existence in the columns of Pakistani newspapers, but he/she engages in a dialogue of the deaf, which does not translate into the formation of public opinion and, unlike India, has little impact on policy formulation, due to the low level of literacy and the minimal influence of public opinion on decision-making. However, the recent tactical retreat by the government in postponing the construction of Kalabagh dam is to some extent indicative of the fact that the rumors of the demise of the argumentative Pakistani may be rather exaggerated.[29]

Constituents and components of the middle class

The Muslim middle class of pre-colonialism included state functionaries, writers, merchants, clerics, and Sufis—the last two groups being largely dependent on land grants from Muslim rulers to shrines and seminaries.[30] Some Ulama and Sufis remained independent of state control and would often criticize the official policies of the sultan/caliph. Meanwhile, industrial and capitalist developments not only diversified professions, they intensified socioeconomic mobility, creating a modern class of entrepreneurs, intellectuals, academics, and artists in an increasingly urban milieu. As a consequence, the former kinship-based solidarity began to give way to professional and ideological congruities and individual choices gradually overtook collective preferences.

In Pakistan, the early traces of a middle class can be found among the smaller sections of society existing between the two extremes of rural landed gentry and landless peasantry. Small-time artisans suffered from limited economic means and social bias, so it was the state functionaries—both in the civil and military cadres—who assumed lower-middle class characteristics. Today, retired military officials, civil servants, urban industrial and business families, academics, physicians, writers, artists, lawyers, physicians, clerics, and journalists make up Pakistani middle class, which is itself crisscrossed by varying levels of economic prosperity and a multitude of ideological viewpoints. The major political parties and other regional and religious outfits have middle-class memberships that use modern media and urban rallies to further their causes. The most vocal groups among the professionals include lawyers, human rights activists, artists and poets, academics, transporters, hoteliers, employees of banks and foreign firms, and journalists.

Pakistani ethnic and religious organizations often display regional and denominational preferences resembling the power-based relationships of a small town, whereas professional networks are less simple and more effective in challenging the "received wisdom," thus remaining receptive to innovative ideas.[31] These professional associations—such as those of journalists, human rights activists, lawyers, political analysts, bankers, independent consultants, doctors, and even religio-ethnic movements— are the beneficiaries of information technology and use it with efficiency. Considering the clear contrasts within urban life—similar to rural divisions between rich and poor—some analysts see feudal patterns emerging among urban communities. To such observers, real urban dwelling is beyond the reach of ordinary people, and despite a growing consumerism, it is a small moneyed class who disallow the emergence of a steady and stable middle class. Discretionary policies and rules end up supporting incumbents already well ensconced in related businesses who try to squeeze out any newcomers. In other words, the rural-feudal politics of patronage—minus the dependence on land—is being replicated in cities, even where they are largely appropriated by defense personnel. Abdus Samad wrote:

> Our feudalism has, through its control of state power, expanded beyond the rural areas. In fact, our post-colonial policies have ensured that our cities are little more than villages. They contain countryside estates with the government in the middle. There is no urban density and no public spaces other than empty parks. Most of all our cities do not allow urban density in the heart of town.[32]

If we accept this view of urbanization as turning into small groups of "gated communities," then certainly the early-stage development of the middle class is being slowed. As a result, instead of increasing professional diversification, this group is more likely to become localist and conservative, especially when it comes to politics, gender equality, modernity, and relations with the West.

National poverty The concern over poverty within the country has been a significant issue among the chattering classes with professional backgrounds. In this regard, India and Pakistan are quite similar, as both countries have experienced vibrant economic growth alongside serious challenges creating a widening gulf between their citizens. Both Musharraf and Aziz claimed a sharp downward trend in national poverty, from 34 percent in 2000–1 to 23 percent in 2005. According to their critics, however, these statistics did not take into account the rising cost of living as well as a serious reduction in the numbers of middle-class citizens. Critics often mention the 40 million Pakistanis who remained "pauperized" in 2007 whereas in 1990, some 29 million people lived below the poverty line. These figures can be difficult to assess when one takes into account the steady rise in population—Pakistan's population has registered an additional three million people annually.

The millennium development targets call for a halving of poverty levels by 2015. This might be possible but for most critics such a reduction is unattainable without diminishing the acute disparity of income. The global economic recession as well as issues of national security will continue to impinge on any programs for improvement. Poverty is not only responsible for a loss of self-esteem among a vast section of society, it also adds strains to a precarious family structure that has historically served as a safety net. Zubeida Mustafa wrote:

> When the poor live alongside the rich—see the shanty towns that creep up to the boundary walls of the palaces of the rich in our cities—the psycho-social, economic and political repercussions of this phenomenon are devastating, more so when the rich are used to ostentatious living and flaunting their wealth.[33]

Such clear contrasts between the generations of young professionals portrayed in *Moth Smoke* (a novel by Mohsin Hamid set in the Lahore of 1998) and those of slum dwellers have certainly added fuel to militant forms of extremism.

With no democratic system allowing for participatory politics, Pakistani pluralism has occasionally become a source of conflict. In these cases, the traditional and parallel middle classes have used variables such as language, territory, and statistics to support the case for their own ethnic rights.[34] Bonds among the middle-class groupings over and above ethnic and sectarian ties have yet to emerge, though exceptions do exist and this model may change with increased social mobility and enhanced professionalization. Thus far, Pakistani class structure and citizenship remain ethnicized, especially outside Punjab. Given that the Punjab has a majority of the population and its existing dominance over government positions and the professions, the Punjab is not likely to activate itself on any ethnic basis, but may perhaps on religious grounds. Here, Islam and Pakistani nationalism become the two main driving forces while in Balochistan, Sindh, and the NWFP, ethnicity often operates as a more assertive medium for political will than religion.

The national education system with its emphasis on Urdu as the preferred language of instruction, standarized texts, and English curriculum, at least at private urban institutions, has certainly removed most of the "intensity" from former ethno-national movements seeking Pushtunistan, Sindhudesh, Greater Balochistan, and Jinnahistan. The late-1990s transformation of the MQM from an ethnic organization into *Muttahida* (united for all) was a major change that guaranteed peace in urban Sindh under Musharraf. A similar economic and professional integration of the urban NWFP into the mainstream Pakistani economy and state structures has also reduced ethnic separatism there. However, it has also escalated a tribal backlash against this imbalanced modernity.

It is still too soon to suggest that Pakistanis (and the middle class in particular) have become national in their ethos, beliefs, and political structure. Religion continues to be a major component of Pakistani middle-class consciousness, but sectarian identities (Sunni and Shia) and denominational divisions (Brelvi, Deobandi, Ahmadi, etc.) spawn religious divides that disrupt harmonious community relations. Irrespective of these varying interpretations of Islam, it holds true that these parties and groups draw sustenance from religion and may even espouse the case for an Islamic Republic—a concept perhaps situated between the existing models of Saudi Arabia and Iran. A smaller section of the Pakistani middle class, out of conviction and also disillusionment with extremist violence, remains secular and might even privately support a Kemalist solution on the Turkish model. Such views are found within several disparate sections of civil society and are under pressure from official authoritarianism as well as societal dissuasion. The Turkish model might be acceptable to a few opinion groups, but is generally seen as too far-fetched to hold much weight within Pakistan. The problems in Turkey include the prevalence of a hegemonic ideology and an ever-present threat from power-hungry generals, which may help to explain the diminishing support for such a movement in Pakistan.

The middle-class military Pakistan's defense forces are an interesting element of the country's middle class, as most serving and retired officials, as well as junior commissioned officers, have secure means and draw generous pensions upon retirement.[35] Excluding ordinary soldiers who are helped by pensions and better healthcare facilities, it is the privileged officers who easily qualify for middle-class status. The defense sector is not merely a huge fighting machine drawing a lion's share of the country's budget, it also accounts for the single most dominant political and cultural force within the state and society. The army has used Islamization as well as liberalization with incredible transformative results, but its role as the country's most influential and even "pampered" economic establishment is gradually provoking steady criticism. For instance, the Fauji Foundation and similar organizations aimed at the welfare of armed forces pensioners and their families, run scores of businesses, including banks, cereal factories, private schools, hospitals, housing societies, exclusive clubs, and industrial and commercial developments. Exempt from taxation, and like the defense budget itself, this "predatory capitalism" remains outside the range of national accountability. Even minor criticism of its role or extra-professional pursuits may cause a serious backlash.[36]

Emerging voices—middle-class women

Pakistani women, like the majority of their male counterparts, suffer from multiple disadvantages, especially if they are from tribal, rural, or inner-city areas and are also poor. For a long time a woman's role was limited to the home, and this only began to change after 1947 ushered in a process of transformation that was visible at many levels of society. Unlike the pre-1947 generation of upper-class women, such as those from the Mian family of Lahore, the Suhrawardies of Bengal, or the Hayats of Wah, most Muslim women in India had to content themselves with a basic, home-based education and a strict domestic role. Earlier nineteenth-century reformers such as Syed Ahmed Khan, Syed Ameer Ali, and Mumtaz Ali had advocated the case for women's education. Later, during the independence movement, women like Fatima Jinnah, Begum Jahan Ara Shahnawaz, and Begum Liaquat Ali Khan tried to politicize Muslim women from the emerging middle class. Following the formation of Pakistan, education, nursing, telecommunications companies, the service industries, and the financial sector all began to hire women, and organizations such as the All-Pakistan Women's Association (APWA), mostly run by upper-class women, campaigned for better socio-legal rights for women. This emerging group of middle-class women generally entered the aforementioned professions as well as branching out into law, medicine, media, and the arts while some went abroad to pursue higher education.

During the early days of Pakistani independence suffrage was limited, however, in 1956 women were given the vote on a massive scale. By the late 1960s, women were actively participating in politics, not merely as voters but also as elected councilors and ministers, despite institutional and patriarchal roadblocks. Unlike the Pakistan Muslim League (PML), Zulfikar Ali Bhutto's PPP reached out to these middle-class women through its advocacy of progressive and empowering reforms. At the same time, conservative parties such as Jamaat-i-Islami enlarged their female membership and an ideological rivalry soon emerged among these educated, urban, and self-confident women. The situation for women also changed in rural and tribal areas, but only to the extent that a woman's right to education and a vote were now accepted, but women's roles in these regions remained circumscribed. However, increased mobility within the country allowed many tribal Pushtun and Sindhi women more access to cities, especially Karachi, while migrations to Britain and the Gulf afforded better economic opportunities to women of Azad Kashmir and Pothowar.

The most serious threat to women's rights came in the wake of Islamization that occurred during General Zia-ul-Haq's rule (1977–88), when the limited gains made during the 1960s were overruled by a regime largely supported by extreme conservative elements. Female members of JI were able to find sympathetic ears under this regime, yet for their rival professional women such restrictions were not acceptable. In a spirit of "now or never" these middle-class women organized themselves into groups such as the Women Action Forum and the Aurat Foundation and began to play a pioneering role in civil society. Despite a serious setback for civil rights, the 1980s also turned out to be "the women's decade," in which activism against selective Islamist and militarist restrictions gave rise to human rights groups, rallies, watchdog groups, and domestic abuse shelters, and with issues further highlighted by magazines such as *Newsline*. The following decade was a rather sluggish era for women's empowerment, though the 1990s did herald a freer press, frequent elections, political debates, an IT revolution, and an increase in the numbers of women entering professions. Equally, cases of honor killings, dowry deaths, marriages to the Quran, *huddood* laws, gang rapes ordered by tribal elders, and other forms of domestic violence all began making banner headlines.[37]

A general drift on the part of pre-Musharraf elected governments spurred many female NGOs and activists to warn prime ministers Nawaz Sharif and Benazir Bhutto of a creeping Talibanization, and some of these women even welcomed Musharraf's coup as a "last resort." Sensitive to a reinvigorated military plus mullah axis due to Musharraf's suspicion of mainstream political parties and the emergence of the Combined Action Forum (MMA) as an Islamist powerbroker, many vocal women became critical of Musharraf.

At the same time, significant differences between Islamist women and their professional and activist counterparts became more acute. Women of Jamia Hafsa, a women's seminary attached to Islamabad's Red Mosque, clad in head-to-toe black burqas, began taking over libraries and brandishing staffs and Kalashnikovs in Islamabad in the early months of 2007. Such actions shocked and angered mainstream Pakistani professionals. Simultaneously, the presence of women at anti-fundamentalism rallies in Islamabad, Lahore, and Karachi inspired Pakistani civil society and for a time even Musharraf seemed to rediscover allies among his former critics. These women, like many middle-class Pakistani men, were apprehensive about the spread of extreme religio-political conservativatism and were reluctant to offer unconditional support to Musharraf, especially following his drastic suspension of the Chief Justice on 9 March 2007. Female activists were also aggrieved by the silence of some female colleagues who made up 33 percent of the assemblies and other elected bodies and yet consistently failed to speak out on democratization and equal rights.

Any general assumptions made about the homogenous nature of Pakistani middle-class women are as problematic as assumptions made about their male counterparts. Recent studies reveal not only that tremendous strides have been made in gender politics, but that the threat of fundamentalism still exists.[38] Similar to the divide between rural/tribal/urban populations, Pakistani women as a group also reflect the ideological divisions with the Indus as a kind of demarcation line.

Class-based divisions remain evident, with urban upper-middle-class women allowed more options than women in the lower-middle-class strata. The women found on billboards, in society magazines, hosting television programs or featuring in music videos are a small minority. According to women's rights activists, women "continue to be abused, beaten, raped and killed—with the tacit consent of the government's functionaries unwilling to take their cause." Many women may turn to more Islamist lifestyles in the hope of finding stronger roles for themselves through a sorority-based solidarity. But despite all the obstacles and gender inequities, there are "thousands of women from middle- and lower-income families across Pakistan today engage[d] with the state and civil society in professional capacities." The IT revolution, revulsion against extremist violence, economic challenges, and a more critical media have all helped women in their quest for improved status and increased opportunities. S.M. Naseem wrote:

> Overcoming traditional constraints and ideologies, the middle-class woman's induction into a life of independence and free choice is all the more encouraging. Tomorrow, they might even form the face of "everywoman." Rather than victims of male crime, or party-animal hedonists, it is these pioneers of feminism in Pakistan who will change the way we see ourselves—and how the world perceives us.[39]

Other than the well-publicized stories of violence against women such as that of Mukhtaran Mai,[40] the higher visibility of women on both sides of the fundamentalism/reformism divide is a recent development that is itself a microcosmic reflection of the Pakistani middle class.

Many writers refuse to view Pakistani Muslim women as imprisoned in an eternal bondage of submission and subordination, and are resentful of any idealized preoccupation with women from the elite. To these critics, the vast majority of Muslim middle-class professional women are constantly ignored, even by otherwise well-meaning scholars who seem unable to move away from the two extremes of eternal victimization and occasional glorification.[41] Media coverage of high-profile Islamist women such as the burqa-clad, staff-brandishing women of Jamia Hafsa further emphasized the apparent ideological fault line between lower-middle-class women. Identified as "ninjas," "chicks with sticks," and "the burqa brigade" by the liberal Pakistani media, these women and their vigilante action attracted a great deal of attention. The activism of these women in early 2007 included the occupation of a children's library and the kidnap of three women accused of prostitution and prompted a debate on the decency of such female activism. Earlier, in 2006 there had been an outcry from men and women from various ideological perspectives against Nilofar Bakhtiar, a paragliding female minister, which had spawned an interesting debate on the role and direction of Pakistani middle-class women. Kamila Shamsie, an award-winning novelist, has alerted people not to lose sight of the parallel ideological strands among these women:

> It's easy to think of the paragliding minister and the burqa-clad militant as opposite poles of Pakistan's complex pictures of womanhood...The more complicated truth is that the real composites are the women who appear on the front pages and those who don't appear anywhere at all, except in small columns tucked away inside, detailing a story of a woman raped, a woman killed for "honor," a woman stoned alive.

Shamsie's argument is a simple but significant one: the debate on the place of women in Pakistani society must include "obscure women" rather than a purely reductionist notion of "progressive" and "retrogressive" women.[42] It is true that some middle-class women may have more in common with middle-class men than they do with women of other classes. Certainly within the last 60 years, Pakistani women have crossed numerous thresholds, unlike previous generations, and are now taking on a more visible and complex array of identities and roles, where change appears triumphant over the forces of a conservative status quo; however, these changes have not made for plain sailing for Pakistani women of this new generation.

Making its mark on society

The middle class in Pakistan continues to be a growing phenomenon, generating hope for greater effectiveness and outspokenness in the near future. Despite its relatively short existence and great plurality, the middle class has already made its mark on Pakistani society, especially when one looks at the growing participation of women in various levels of society, its contributions to the ideological debates on Islam, the military, democracy, foreign policy, militancy, the economy, judiciary, accountability, culture, religion, law, the arts, and education. The middle class is present within all these fields of activity and tends to be self-congratulatory and resistant to change; it is perhaps beginning to show a siege mentality—having acquired many benefits and new rights, it now wishes to protect these against an encroachment from the lower classes, who, in some cases, are reflected in the Pakistani Taliban phenomenon.

The middle class is overwhelmingly centrist or even rightist, and its secular or liberal manifestations often exist at private levels. Given the incessant fundamentalist campaigns, such as the specter of Talibanization in Swat and FATA, the middle class is slowly gearing itself up to claim its own autonomous space. Despite this emerging class's differences, it is fighting the battle for the soul of Pakistan. It remains selfconsciously Muslim, though divided into sects and denominations, yet with the potential advent of fully fledged democracy and a free media, it may transcend these divisions. This class has a serious stake in Pakistan, making it quite nationalistic. It disagrees over the alternative systemic profile of Pakistan but agrees on the need for a strong and coherent institutional framework. Its patriotism may make it slightly suspicious of India, though it envisions peace on a tangible and equal basis; several groups within this class, especially from the intelligentsia and from human rights groups actively seek better relations with India. In 1997, more than 59 percent of Pakistanis aspired to enduring peace with India, while 67 percent rejected restrictive rules against women and minorities. Additionally, 76 percent would prefer the army's role to be strictly professional, and did not yearn for a theocracy.[43]

Ten years after Musharraf's coup, there is increased clarity and unity among the middle class regarding democracy, a tolerant version of Islam, greater institutional accountability, and a vocal criticism of Talibanization and the American militarist interventionism.[44] In other words, despite a level of conservativism, the Pakistani middle class remains quite progressive in areas such as gender equality, minority rights, democracy, education, and relations with India and the West.

In its military incarnation, the Pakistani middle class remains suspicious of both its own politicians and India, while in civil society, the middle class seeks constitutionalism and democracy. These two incarnations have meant that the middle class remains divided in two. In the same vein, many religio-political parties and well-endowed seminaries are led by middle-class clerics who vociferously challenge their liberal and critical counterparts and are sensitive on the issues of gender equality and the uncritiqued absorption of Western norms. As such, it is not surprising that one vocal middle-class section opts for the burqa and gender segregation while demanding Sharia law for Pakistan, whereas the section of well-educated, urban activists aims to mold Pakistan into Jinnah's ideal of a progressive society. Both of these ideological groups may harbor strong suspicions of US foreign policies, while being deeply enamored with Western technology and its standards of living. They all agree on the importance of education, but the liberal component would disagree with the clergy's hold on the country's ideological moorings while the clerics would deride secularism as a form of atheism.

The role of the media The media remains one of the most important and influential middle-class arenas in the country. With the introduction of satellite channels and online forums, the resulting increase in public information and accountability have catapulted the media into being the most powerful mouthpiece of this middle class. Private universities and think tanks also influence the ideologies of this class. The middle class accepts tradition and modernity in varying degrees and can be quite opportunistic in realizing its ambitions. It is participatory, sensitive, well-informed, mobile, flamboyant, oral, charitable, and innovative while it attempts to pursue its own specific interests.

Views on religion Pakistani middle-class opinion remains divided on issues such as the role of religion in political affairs, and the relationship between the sacred and the profane; and it also remains ambivalent about its relationship with India and the West. It seeks a closer relationship with the Muslim world and is in awe of Western economic dominance, though it remains ambivalent about Indian progress. Often, the middle class feels helpless in its ability to assist other Muslims, especially those in India and Kashmir; it is sympathetic toward Afghanistan, but irritated by

Kabul's sustained criticism of Pakistan. Like other similar class structures, it seeks stability, better education, peace, prosperity and the redirection of its national ethos. Its religious elements, like the JI, JUI, and others, resemble the Indian BJP and RSS but unlike India, socialist elements remain quite thin on the ground in Pakistan. Like its Indian counterpart, the Pakistani middle class offers multiple ideological visions and can also be quite chauvinistic. Resembling the American neoconservatives, the middle classes are imbued with a sense of purpose and self-confidence, especially on Islam-related matters.[45] Indian and Pakistani commentators have found a multitude of similarities across South Asia when it comes to class formation and its complex daily interface with state functionaries. Ravian in the *Daily Times* wrote:

> Both India and Pakistan are essentially elitist societies. The middle class is relatively small (in proportion to the population) in both countries with the result that basic governance rules are not user-friendly in either country. Paying a utility bill, getting a license, registering property, access to justice...are considered basic rights in developed societies that have a large middle class. Not so in the sub-continent where the ordinary citizen spends a large chunk of his/her time attending to the minutia of plain living. The sub-continental middle class, therefore, develops a large social network to reduce the hassle factor in complying with the basic governance rules. A friend of a friend ensures that you don't have to queue up with sweaty masses in 40-degree heat.[46]

The Pakistani middle class is still in its embryonic stages, but is growing in number and influence and may yet offer the much-sought-after middle ground to stabilize Pakistan's political situation. The 2008 elections enhanced the profile of this emerging class, which took advantage of this opportunity to make its choices known. By virtue of its links and affinities with Muslims elsewhere, the Pakistani middle class feels secure; however, it does continue to vacillate between optimism and cynicism with regard to India. Like its counterparts elsewhere, this class whinges but then makes quick adjustments and is certainly eager to benefit from Western education, technology, and even an association with the West in professional areas.

Unlike Iran, Saudi Arabia, or even Turkey, the Pakistani middle class is more diverse and vocal, and jealously guards its own space. Due to this class, Pakistan has a unique place among Muslim and other postcolonial nations in retaining an enduring tradition of party politics. As affirmed in the elections of 2008 and since, the Pakistani middle class desires democracy and better economic standards within a stable environment; they blame their leaders for failing the nation time and again, and are willing to send the generals back to their barracks and the mullahs back to the mosques. Cynical about corruption and cronyism, this class welcomes any political change but is becoming exhausted with the nation's predictable cyclical history.[47] They continue to be politicized and recent events such as the suspension of the Chief Justice in March 2007, Musharraf's exit in 2008, and military operations in Swat and FATA in 2009, have inspired high-quality debate, peaceful rallies, and large-scale demonstrations against extremism.

ISLAMIST PARTIES

IN ITS CURRENT STATE, Islam embodies an ambivalent but forceful combination of religion and politics, and its discourse is shared by a number of Muslim regimes and Pakistani Islamist groups who find within it a perfect solution to the country's problems. Islam's significant role in the formation of Pakistan, and the country's use of Islam to justify its domestic and regional policies, gives a kind of credence to this belief. The appeal of Islam as the key solution to the country's ills also reflects widespread dismay over Pakistan's long-term political instability; but it also accords with the anguish felt by Muslims worldwide over Muslim marginalization and loss of life in the pursuit of the war on terror.

The recent resurgence of Political Islam in Pakistan is the result of domestic politico-economic problems and the widely shared sense of dismay, disillusionment, and indifference felt by millions of Muslims all over the world. While there are some Islamist groups that seek to realize their objectives through violent means, Pakistan is unique in fostering a number of religio-political parties that still believe in and practice electoral politics and are not hostile to democracy and dialogue.

It is too easy to characterize Muslim religio-political groups as inherently anti-Western, anti-democratic and anti-reformist by tarring them all with the same brush. However, given the vast diversity of Muslim peoples and societies along ethno-national, class, and doctrinal lines, this generalization is not possible. Averse to the status quo, many Islamist groups desire the radical transformation of national institutions, and while offering Islam as a solution, also hark back to a glorious past when Islam was a force to be reckoned with. Political Islam is both a protest and a formidable opposition, and despite its ambiguities, at its heart it seeks an honorable life for the poor and oppressed masses. Of course, there are Islamist groups that represent totalitarian and anti-Western attitudes both in practice and conviction, but the vast majority of Muslims only seek economic and political empowerment and are eager to obtain better standards of living through peaceful means.

This quest offers positive prospects within global politics, where forward-thinking initiatives can be undertaken in order to secure meaningful peace and interdependence that is respectful to all. A consensus on the politics of the ballot and efforts for the just resolution of conflicts across the Muslim world over and above partisan policies and interests can ensure a more tangible interface among Muslim political and dissident groups. Any substantive and long-term engagement with these sections may also help steer the world towards a more civic and peaceful strategy that would neutralize the polarization that has occurred since 9/11.

Historical and ideological differences: the bigger picture

The relationship between Islam and politics is as old as the classical era; viewed as the ideal of Islamic polity, the early state was created by the Prophet Muhammad in Medina following his migration there in CE 620. Under Muhammad's leadership, the divine laws governed the private and public affairs of this growing Muslim state, which saw its zenith under the Four Caliphs who succeeded the Prophet after his death in 632 and led the community for the next three decades. This intermingling of religion and politics under the dynamic leadership of the caliphs became the ideal for a Muslim utopia in recent centuries when the world's Muslims lost political control to European powers.

Islam has been regularly espoused by both ruling elites and by dissenters, while ordinary, often poor, people have viewed it as a just alternative to an unjust present. During the colonial era, the Muslim elite—themselves often the beneficiaries if not the creators of modernity—used Islam to unite disparate and often segmented societies, over and above any tribal and ethno-sectarian divisions. However, the Westernized elite, also called modernists and reformists, sought a better future by adopting Western ideals of nationalism, statehood, education, urbanization, and industrial development to reach their goals, while the revivalists, known as purists or traditionalists, advocated a back-to-roots approach. In spite of their differences, both ideological groups agreed on the need for change, sovereignty, and greater popular participation in politics.

At present, this duality has created a polarized state, often turning the Westernized modernism into a heavily contested arena of conflicting ideologies and stances. The ongoing political concerns of Palestine, Kashmir, Chechnya, Moroland (the homeland of Muslims in the Philippines), and others are juxtaposed against the collective failure to provide any resolution on debilitating events such as the Iran–Iraq War, the Salman Rushdie affair, ethnic cleansing in Bosnia, the civil war and its aftermath in Afghanistan, and the mayhem in Iraq under Saddam Hussein and after.[1]

The growth of Islamist parties

Increased mobility and education, the salience of diverse groups, and technological developments within an unequal society have sharpened the ideological conflicts between modernity and tradition, and between reformism and revivalism. With the dissolution of the Cold War, these conflicts have become one of the marked realities of our time. However, keeping these statements in mind, one must not stigmatize Muslims as a whole, and careful attention is needed to see that Islam and modernity are not perennial enemies. Political Islam may posit the West as an enemy of "neo-Crusaders," but the West also symbolizes numerous achievements that Muslims idealize. While a monolithic West evokes suspicion as well as envy among Muslims the world over, irrespective of their ethnic and national backgrounds, a similarly monolithic Islam generates images of hordes of angry, hungry people eager to change Western demographies and democracies. Certainly, Western-led interventionism, uneven foreign policies and assaults by neocons, ultra-rightists, Zionists, evangelists, and the *Hindutva* militants have only added to anti-West suspicion, while groups like al-Qaeda, the Taliban, and other disparate militants continue to muddy already murky waters.[2]

Looking at South Asian Islam, one sees this polarization as a persistent reality, though it only dates from the latter half of the 19th century when purists and reformists tried to institutionalize themselves. While the All-India Muslim League, established in 1906, saw redemption for Indian Muslims through sovereign nationhood and selective modernization within the overarching context of Islam, Ulama-led purists, mostly linked with the seminary of Deoband (in present-day India), saw Islam as the only true solution to a pluralist Muslim predicament.[3] The Muslim League led by Muhammad Ali Jinnah, is largely credited with Pakistan's evolution to sovereign state in 1947, whereas many Ulama opposed the idea of a territory-based Muslim nationalism, although some did support the idea of a composite Indian nation.[4] The Jamiat-i-Ulama-i-Hind (JUH), established in 1920 soon after the defeat of the Ottoman Empire in the First World War, worked toward a free India and greater Muslim identity and wrestled with the Muslim League over its demand for a separate Muslim state.[5] The JUH, its clerics and seminaries from all over British India (including present-day Pakistan), allied itself with the Indian National Congress (INC), a party established in 1885 and subsequently led by Mohandas Gandhi (1869–1948) and Jawaharlal Nehru (1889–1964).

While most Muslim revivalists remained concerned with religious and social issues until 1947, one of the most important and organized parties working toward the religio-social regeneration of South Asian Muslims proved to be Jamaat-i-Islami (JI), founded in 1941 by Syed Abulala Mawdudi (1903–79).[6] Mawdudi was a deeply religious journalist who spent most of his life in northern India and the princely state of Hyderabad, until he decided to move to the Muslim-majority province of Punjab in British India. In 1941, Mawdudi established his seminary in Lahore and founded the JI, aimed at the individual and collective Islamization of Muslims. Mawdudi found fault with the West and pro-Western Muslims and strongly advocated a "back-to-roots" approach in his Urdu-language writings, in monthly magazines, and commentaries that were widely available to the growing community of middle-class Muslims. Like other Ulama, Mawdudi was pan-Islamist, but did not believe in militant methods; he decried nationalism, feminism, and total democracy, while considering Islamic Sharia the divine law that could redirect Muslims to a lost glory.

Mawdudi's JI party never sought to become a mass organization overnight, since he felt that an Islamic revolution was to be brought about by preparing a core of morally upright and politically well-integrated Muslims. This gradual approach would ensure the eventual return to an ideal Islamic state that existed at the time of the Prophet and the Pious Caliphs. He blamed past monarchies for the Muslim decline and saw serious problems for contemporary Muslims within Westernization. However, unlike the JUH, he did not support an all-India based nationalism nor did he support the Muslim League's demand for the separate state of Pakistan. His was an evolutionary, gradual, and well-charted strategy for Islamic revolution, framed to create a divine statehood, in which women would be veiled and only a select few men— on the basis of knowledge and piety—would create and explain laws for the rest of society. Quranic and Prophetic traditions would be the mainspring of these Sharia laws, but their interpretation within Mawdudi's ideal Islamic state would be confined to a few and not to the masses. The masses would have no sovereignty in the literal sense, as Allah would be the ultimate sovereign, and ordinary people would simply be His vice-regents through these select few intermediaries. They would be equal and vocal within an Islamic state, but legislation and interpretation of Islamic jurisprudence would not be their prerogative. Mawdudi visualized the JI preparing the masses for this Islamic Utopia with its elite members undertaking the groundwork necessary to transform the society and the state. Issues concerning the boundaries of the states, the role of minorities, and the relationships with the West and the rest of the world remained unclear in Mawdudi's Islamic state, though he fervently believed in the systemic self-sufficiency of Islam.

Many observers have found echos of Mawdudi's teachings in the ideas of Sayyid Qutb (d. 1966), the Egyptian intellectual eventually executed by President Gamal Nasser (1918–70). Qutb had been influenced by the Muslim Brotherhood—an early 20th-century religio-political organization in his native Egypt—but his major inspiration came from Mawdudi's Islamic revolutionism.[7] Like Qutb, Mawdudi had problems with most of the Pakistani regimes and was imprisoned during the state's early years, but his scholarly pursuits and the slowly expanding JI remained unstoppable. Mawdudi wished to see an Islamic state in Pakistan based on the classical era, and saw the transformation of society and state as mutually interconnected. His solution to the Muslim socio-political and economic predicament was in establishing polities akin to the classical caliphate era. The concept of jihad—both for internal purification and for mounting a collective struggle—was to play a crucial role. However, the leadership empowered to declare jihad and transform processes would come only from the select few Islamic elite, rather than from the Muslim laity.[8] Mawdudi was a revivalist, pan-Islamist, and ideologue, and he advocated the concept of an elite-based leadership—though he hated Western definitions of democracy.

The effects of Partition With the Partition of British India in 1947, Muslim religio-political parties such as the JUH, the JI, and even the ML were also divided, and their counterparts and successors soon established themselves within a young Pakistan. Mawdudi was already living and publishing in Lahore, while the JUH had evolved into the Jamiat-i-Ulama-i-Islam (JUI), with its own powerful seminaries across the Indus regions especially among Pushtuns of the NWFP. The Muslim syncretists—unlike the purists—have always viewed Sufi *pirs* as not merely holy men, but as eternal spiritual mentors and intermediaries between God and His disciples. By nature, most South Asian Muslims are Sufi-orientated, whereas the JUH and JI and other such Deoband-related Ulama have tended to view *pirs* as a major source of Muslim fatalism. Here, they certainly resemble their Wahhabi counterparts—who, as the followers of an 18th-century Arab revivalist, advocate a strict return to the early purist and literal interpretations of Islam.

While the seminary of Deoband was emerging as the heart of a revivalist Islam, in the nearby town of Rai Barelli the pro-Sufi movement had also begun to evolve in the late-19th century. These defenders of Sufi

Islam organized themselves in Pakistan as Jamiat-i-Ulama-i-Pakistan (JUP). While the Muslim League and other centrist parties did not show any open resistance to modernity, the JUI, JI, and other revivalists began to focus their efforts on the Islamization of Pakistan. The JUP often raised the flag of Islam but fell short of any organized and transformative campaign for actually implementing Political Islam. What emerged in Pakistan was a tripolar form of contest involving revivalists and modernists on one side and revivalists fighting it out among themselves on the other. The fact remains that the JI and JUI upheld parallel and even hostile politics, in spite of sharing the view that the JUP and parties such as the Pakistan Muslim League (PML) and Zulfikar Ali Bhutto's Pakistan People's Party (PPP) were simply surrogates kowtowing to Western principles. The JUI and JI have always opposed regional and ethnic parties across the NWFP and in urban Sindh, seeing in them a further debilitation of Muslim society.[9]

The power of Political Islam

Due to the ongoing problems of governance marked by intermittent military rule, conflict-laden pluralism, and complex regional geopolitics, Pakistani regimes have viewed Islam as a legitimizing and unifying force in the evolving nation. Pakistan's Western backers have helped the country negotiate its economic and security challenges largely because Pakistan's location suited their Cold War or regional interests, and because the country has mostly been ruled by Westernized elites. General Zia-ul-Haq's (1977–88) military regime was tolerated and assisted by the West because of the Cold War imperatives following the Soviet invasion of Afghanistan in 1979, and with Iran already ruled by Ayatollah Khomeini, Pakistan became even more important. Clerics from the JUI, JI, and JUP were all coopted by Zia during the Afghan resistance, while the CIA, the Pakistani ISI (Inter-Services Intelligence), and other Western intelligence organizations turned Pakistan into a front-line state. The NWFP and Balochistan provinces housed millions of Afghan refugees as well as offering sanctuary to Afghan Mujahideen—the forerunners of today's Taliban.[10] Here, training camps worked in tandem with some madrassas, while the JUI and JI were able to cultivate wider lobbies within Afghan resistance. Mawdudi died in 1979, but his successor Mian Tufail Ahmad lacked the charisma and erudition of his predecessor, though the JI did benefit from closer ties to General Zia-ul-Haq. Succeeding Ahmad, the Pushtun firebrand Qazi Hussain Ahmed turned the JI into a full-time activist organization with its intellectual and ideological work allotted to scholars such as Professor Khurshid Ahmad.

More recently, he has been succeeded by Munawar Hasan, an Urdu-speaking activist-scholar from Karachi.

During the 1990s, as a political vacuum descended in Afghanistan, Islamabad sought "strategic depth" in its neighbor to counter its old enemy of India and began to help train Afghan students at Pakistani madrassas. Since most of these seminaries were run by the JUI, now led by Maulana Fazlur Rahman and Maulana Sami-ul-Haq, who enjoyed links with Pushtuns on both sides of the Pak-Afghan border, the JUI emerged as the focal point in this new phase of activism. The students in these madrassas were called Taliban (meaning "students"), and from 1996 they were catapulted into a political force in Afghanistan through the combined clusters of JUI, ISI, and Pushtun Afghans, all working for their own specific interests. At the same time, the defiance within Indian-controlled Kashmir encouraged young recruits from revivalist groups in Pakistan to stream in and join Kashmiri militants already fighting Indian control. Here, the JUI and JI contributed both men and supplies—often in cahoots with Islamabad—with the JI focusing more on Kashmir Valley, and the JUI mainly helping the Taliban.

With General Musharraf's alignment with the US in warfare and hostilities against Afghanistan following 9/11 and his retreat on Kashmir, the JI and JUI became deeply suspicious and resentful of Musharraf. Perhaps for the first time, both parties were aligned in ruling the NWFP's provincial government while simultaneously forming an opposition group called MMA (Muttahida Majlis-i-Ammal or Combined Action Forum) in Islamabad's central government. During the elections of 2002, this coalition gained several seats in provincial assemblies in the NWFP and Balochistan as well as in the national parliament due to a growing wave of anti-Americanism and Musharraf's stubborn insistence on keeping the mainstream PML and PPP parties at bay.[11]

The MMA, combining the JI, JUI, and other regional groups, hoped to gain electoral clout by continuing their anti-American stance and support for Islamization of Pakistan, Kashmir, and Afghanistan. However, the MMA did not appear to have any deterrent or pre-emptive strategy against the increasing wave of suicide bombings that were rife in 2007, nor was it able to contain the spiralling disorder in FATA and Swat. Pressure on Musharraf continued to grow from within Pakistan and from the US over the growing turmoil in Waziristan and his inability to gain any major concessions from India on the thorny issue of Kashmir.[12] After the storming of the Red Mosque in Islamabad in July 2007 and the wider military operations in the tribal belt, the militants escalated their suicide attacks on military and police targets in the garrison cities of Rawalpindi, Tarbela, Lahore, and Sargodha. The peak of these attacks came with the murder of Benazir Bhutto in December 2007, and to this day, militants continue their attacks on military and police personnel.

The MMA and Musharraf were seen as being completely ineffective in combating disorder and in fact were viewed as causing the increased militancy inside and outside the country. As a result, both were decisively trounced in the elections of 2008. The JI boycotted the elections so as not to be seen endorsing Musharraf's drastic measures, while the JUI lost several constituencies. However, the JUI decided to work with the PPP-led coalition and agreed to cooperate with the ANP in the NWFP. In January 2009, while expanding his cabinet, President Zardari inducted many ministers from the JUI, and it looked like this party, instead of roadblocking the new civilian rule, had staged a comeback by becoming a coalition partner. This kind of pragmatism within a strand of Political Islam was in marked contrast to that displayed by the Pakistani Taliban.

The JI (Jamaat-i-Islami)

The JI is supported by a middle class made up of small-town as well as urban-based Muslims and has similar followings in India and Bangladesh, led by their own autonomous organizations. The JI in Pakistan and Bangladesh has a strong student membership called Islami Jamiat-i-Tulaba (IJT) that brings with it fresh ideas, though the JI itself avoids rushing to become a mass party and is very selective in its membership. Joining the party is a slow and arduous process and there are very few desertions from its ranks. To secularists, it is the most well-organized and well-entrenched party espousing systemic alternatives and has coordinated a voluntary network of men and women. The JI in Pakistan was in opposition against the government for a very long time and its leaders have often suffered imprisonment, although it has had close links with several military regimes as well, playing different roles at different times. For instance, during the civil war of 1971 it supported West Pakistani forces to maintain a united nation when East Pakistan wanted to secede. Later, it accepted the new reality of a divided nation. In 1973, while sitting on opposition benches in government, it cooperated with other legislators in formulating the commonly agreed National Constitution of 1973. The JI was an important component of the Pakistan National Alliance (PNA) in 1977, which demonstrated against Zulfikar Ali Bhutto, and after he was ousted, collaborated with the military regime of General Zia-ul-Haq for the next 11 years. During the 1990s, it participated in all the elections, brought up issues of corruption, raised political and moral issues, and took a vocal stance on Kashmir and Afghanistan. It was initially uncomfortable with Benazir Bhutto's premiership by virtue of her being a woman (and Westernized at that), but it ultimately accepted the reality during her second term.[13]

The JI has never associated itself with the PPP in coalition and was mostly supportive of the Sharif-led PML (Pakistan Muslim League). After General Musharraf's 1999 coup, the JI continued to pursue electoral politics but maintained a populist posture through mass rallies. It participated in the provincial and national elections of 2002 despite serious infighting over Musharraf's alliance with the US and his U-turn on Afghanistan and Kashmir. The JI joined other Islamist groups in organizing anti-US, pro-Taliban rallies but refused to boycott those elections and was at the forefront of opposition at the national level. It supported Musharraf's bid for the presidency in 2002 and was a coalition partner with the JUI in the provincial government of the NWFP. In 2008, it boycotted the elections but agreed to support the new political administration while operating as a major opposition force outside the assemblies.

Since 2007, the JI has actively supported the lawyers' movement in its struggle for the restoration of judicial independence and parliamentary sovereignty. Thus, it is safe to suggest that the JI combines electoral, populist, and pragmatic strategies and is not an obstructionist force that resorts to arms or even refuses to work with national political mechanisms. However, it will never volunteer to forego its own distinct form of Political Islam aimed toward the formation of an Islamic state.

Regarding its views on revolutionary ideals and methods, the JI posits an Islamic system obtained through the gradual transformation of society and state. Periodically throughout the 1990s, some students from its affiliate, the IJT, used violent tactics against other students, but the JI continues to oppose the politics of violence per se. The IJT's single-factor preoccupation with controlling and monopolizing student politics on campuses by relying on small-town supporters has often backfired, for example in Karachi, where it has been vigorously confronted by MQM supporters. In 2007, the IJT roughed up Imran Khan as he came to address an anti-Musharraf rally at Punjab University. A few of its hotheads carried the former cricketer to a waiting van and took him to a police station, causing anger among students and the public at large. The JI often resorts to street agitation on political and economic issues and depends on the unconditional support of its younger members.

The JI has followers among South Asian Muslims settled abroad, especially in the UK where it is engaged in scholarly and seminary pursuits.

The Leicester-based Islamic Foundation was founded by the deputy leader of the JI, Professor Khurshid Ahmad, who had been a senator in Pakistan and had held important offices in Islamabad, especially under General Zia. The JI accepts the plural ethos in the UK and elsewhere in the Muslim world, although it continues to idealize a superordinate Islamic identity. To its credit, the JI does not encourage Shia–Sunni or other sectarian or ethnic violence, though it views Ahmadis as heretical non-Muslims for their refusal to accept the Prophet Muhammad as the final prophet. Thus, while there are some contradictions within the JI's attitudes toward the rights of minorities and women, it believes Islam to be self-sufficient. It views feminism as engendering immoral behavior among younger people, which, in turn, leads to feuds and a weakening of traditional family values. In the same vein, the JI does not allow any kind of sexual liaison outside marriage and abhors homosexuality.

The JUI (Jamiat-i-Ulama-i-Islam)

The second major Islamist group in Pakistan to have regularly engaged in electoral politics is the JUI. Inspired by the Deobandi ideal of Islam as the supreme cure for all Muslim predicaments, the JUI in 1947 (like many other Islamist groups in British India) rejected its former preference for a united, independent India. From Partition on, its Ulama sought to Islamize Pakistan though its major areas of concentration in the NWFP and Balochistan. While on the Frontier, it was able to build links with Afghan purists, as was seen during the 1990s.

The JUI leadership has mainly come from Pushto-speaking clerics, who have followers and colleagues across the Western regions of Pakistan and in Karachi. Through its madrassas, the JUI trains imams (clerics who lead congregational prayers) for mosques in the rural and tribal regions of Pakistan and Afghanistan. In the NWFP, Pushto and Arabic often overtake Urdu as the language of instruction at its all-male seminaries, and the free room and board arrangement allows orphans of the Afghan wars to flock to them. At these madrassas the students are called "Taliban" (students), though this title now causes serious problems. In fact, most of the Afghan Taliban and their Pakistani counterparts have been the former students of madrassas operated by the JUI. Banking on the wave of anti-Americanism and disenchantment with Kabul and Islamabad, the JUI has tried to mobilize its younger groups. The JUI, despite its purist ideas, does not encourage violence against fellow Muslims nor does it allow suicide bombings. However, it has been unable to contain the violent dissent within those regions where it was in power until late 2007.

The seminary of Darululoom at Akora Khattak, by the Grand Trunk Road outside Peshawar, was close to several Afghan refugee camps. Led by Maulana Sami-ul-Haq, it has prepared generations of Pakistani clerics and Taliban.[14] Even Mullah Mohammad Omar, the leader of Afghanistan's Taliban and the Afghan de facto head of state from 1996 to 2001, was reportedly a student here. The two leaders of the JUI, Maulana Sami-ul-Haq and Maulana Fazlur Rahman, are rivals and have led two separate factions of the party since the 1990s. However, Fazlur Rahman has the largest following in Dera Ismail Khan and in the Kohistan district of the NWFP, the tribal regions, Balochistan, and Karachi. Both Rahman and Haq believe in working through the system and have used the ballot box as well as rallies to forward their political objectives.

The JUI's relationship with the army and with Musharraf was, until recently, similar to that of the JI, and as part of the MMA, the JUI was the largest and most formidable element within the alliance. The JUI has been the ruling party twice in the trans-Indus and strategically important provinces of the NWFP and Balochistan and also joined Zardari's PPP-led regime in 2009 by accepting some cabinet positions.

The JUI has been involved in both Kashmir and Afghanistan, though more heavily in Afghanistan, and after 9/11, organized massive anti-US demonstrations. Like the JI, it does not want to reduce Pakistan's borders and views it as an ideological state where systemic and substantial changes are needed in order to return society to the classical era of the early Caliphate. Most JUI clerics and supporters are well versed in traditional Islamic knowledge and less in modern education, though they view Western might with both envy and respect. In terms of membership and education levels, the JUI is behind the JI but ahead of the JUP (Jamiat-i-Ulama-i-Pakistan)—the latter not keeping a formalized electoral and political structure. Both the JI and JUI deride Sufis and shrines and are thus critical of the JUP, who, they feel, lacks purism. The JUI has never advocated violence though it has used jihadi rhetoric; some of its former members have formed their own parties and been involved in the Kashmiri struggle. In the NWFP provincial assembly during the Musharraf years, the JUI led emotional speeches and resolutions to ban music and other "un-Islamic" cultural practices, mainly to appease conservative elements, but banks and other such institutions were allowed to function.

The JUI leader Fazlur Rahman and some of his fellow cleric parliamentarians have been refused visas for some EU countries in the past, something they call a conspiracy against Islam. However, since their visits to India in 2003, their vocal criticism of India has been toned down. Recently, there have been contacts made with the JUH across the border in India.[15] For some Gulf States, the JUI is too radical and Fazlur Rahman was once deported from Dubai soon after his arrival. However, there have been rumors of financial support being given to the group from Arab quarters, though it is difficult to confirm this theory.

The JUI considers Ahmadis to be un-Islamic due to their views on the Prophet and their belief that Muhammad is not the final Prophet; the JUI feels that Islam offers adequate rights to minorities, and that women must stay indoors within the chador (overgarment or cloak) and *chardiwaari* (four walls of the home). Unlike the JI, the JUI is not enthusiastic about women's education beyond basic schooling, although there is a gradual acceptance of college education but not in a coeducational setting. Interestingly, when the PPP and PML-N nominated Fehmida Mirza as the first woman speaker of the Pakistani National Assembly in March 2008, the JUI fully supported her candidacy and in his speech Fazlur Rahman promised to work with her in the larger interests of democracy.[16]

Taking an active political role Both the JI and JUI have tangible organizations and durable networks that ensure their longevity. Their role in the politicization of some sectors of Pakistani society, along with an active participation in ballot-based politics, is seen as positive on the whole, although the nation is sometimes wary of their occasional street agitation. Urdu literature, religious textbooks, commentaries on socioeconomic problems, and a sense of victimhood and resentment among Muslims around the world due to an "arrogant" and "hostile" West keep their seminaries and clerics busy. Even if these two parties fall short of gaining a majority of seats or capturing political power, they are both still crucial coalition partners and vocal opposition forces for any government.

However, the most significant threat to these smaller religio-political parties and and to the civic forces at large comes from extremist elements using resistance and jihad to establish their own authoritarian and gender-specific laws, exacerbating the problems of ordinary people. Applying military power against the extremist elements initially caused a sense of victimization, which resulted in aggrieved Pushtuns willing to join their cadres. However, one saw public opinion turning against these violent and extremist groups in the spring of 2009.

The changing face of Political Islam

While Sufi and syncretic groups remain fragmented into localized shrines, purists such as the JI and JUI have been able to use their educational, organizational, and mobility advantages to transform themselves into enduring political and ideological forces. These groups are the flag-bearers of Political Islam—though not the only ones—as demonstrated by several other groups such as the erstwhile Lashkar-i-Tayyaba (LT), Lashkar-i-Jhangvi (LJ), and Anjuman-i-Sipah-i-Sahaba Pakistan (ASSP), espousing jihadist and sectarian unilateralism that often results in violence. Such groups were banned by Musharraf soon after 9/11. These groups were not enthusiastic about electoral politics and often followed their own agenda underground through all kinds of domestic networks.[17] There exists a serious threat of encroachment by groups such as the Pakistani Taliban in Swat, Dir, Waziristan, and Malakand and their counterparts in other tribal agencies, where a romanticized notion of resistance and a complete disregard for national laws often degenerates into intra-Muslim fratricide.

Of course, Political Islam is not going to disappear from the Pakistani political spectrum, nor is it going to give up its systemic strategy for challenging any given order within the Muslim world. This cauldron of simmering politics found in several Middle Eastern states certainly owes a great deal to the state-led coercion of Political Islam, and this type of policy is fraught with obvious dangers. Democratization, greater dialogue on all sides, and the removal of a sense of victimhood may help channel the violent manifestations of Political Islam into mainstream political processes.

Islamists' role within the political system

Many people in the developing world, including Muslims, view Western attitudes and policies in their regions with suspicion, due to colonial and postcolonial interventions and Western support for authoritarian regimes. They feel that a powerful West subtly controls most of the world's vital resources and international institutions, which are easily molded to serve its own interests. Western rhetoric on human rights, democracy, and good governance is usually translated as a form of double-speak, frequently lacking substance and honesty. Within the Muslim world, Political Islam is seen by some as a force to break this Western dominance. The religious elite, and even urban middle-class groups, see in it a challenge to an almost invincible, irreverent, and ascendant West.

The violence following 9/11 has resulted in a death toll that is predominantly Muslim, causing more and more Muslims to seek solace in their faith. The unrestrained Israeli invasions of southern Lebanon, Syria and, in January 2009, the 23-day-long attack on Gaza in full view of the media intensified Muslim anger at global insensitivity. Anger grew as a consequence of woeful UN inaction over these events; outrage intensified over the stark absence of a Muslim voice in such international developments.

The attacks on the UN facilities and personnel during 2009 in Pakistan and Afghanistan were the violent manifestation of this anger. Even in other countries in the Middle East and North Africa, skepticism about the UN abounds, especially since the 1990s.

It is in these circumstances that Western alliances and regimes need to make bold efforts to transmit balanced and just messages to the Muslim world. For the sake of their own survival, Pakistan's religio-political parties may not go beyond certain limits in challenging the West as they cannot afford to open new conflicts; if they did they would only benefit from anti-Western sentiment in the short-term. That is why parties such as the transnational Muslim Brotherhood (Egypt), Hamas (Palestine), Hizbollah (Lebanon), FIS (Algeria), Nahdatul Ulama (Indonesia), JUH (India), along with JI and JUI (Pakistan), all desire to play a more mainstream role as partners within national and international affairs.

The Pakistani elections of February 2008 spawned several important new developments, including the decisive role of civil society, the primacy of the ballot over the bullet, the rejection of one-man rule, a constructive engagement with activists and militants rather than sheer force, and an undiminished demand for the primacy of constitutional politics. Crucially, the election results dealt a blow to any religio-political parties that failed to deliver on promised reforms in their respective provinces. Moreover, their failure to curb the pervasive violence in FATA and Swat and the inability to offer some ideological retort to suicide bombings loosened their hold on voters. In their place, the mainstream parties regained the center stage, espousing global and secular solutions, preferring dialogue and democracy over violence and intolerance. These elections proved that democratic processes rather than coercion were the best antidote to religious militancy. This is exactly where Western governments as well as the ruling Muslim elite could review their policies on handling Political Islam. William Dalrymple rightly hinted at this urgency for a new interface with Political Islam when he noted:

> There is a clear lesson for US [and other!] policy makers here. The parties of political Islam are like any other democratic parties: they will succeed or fail on what they deliver. The best way of dealing with democratic Islamists, if Pakistan's experience is anything to go by, is to let them be voted into power and then reveal their own incompetence—*mullah*-fatigue will no doubt quickly set in.[18]

This is not to suggest that Political Islam is a temporary and solely reactionary phenomenon, since its own transformation might arise through fuller participation in democratic processes whereas its suppression can only cause more violence. Even for its violent trajectories, perhaps dialogue and development could hold the key to a more peaceful future.

Certainly, an immensely pluralistic Pakistan could not have an Iranian-style revolution, since this would only fragment it along sectarian and ethnic lines, a risk that religio-political groups want to avoid at all costs, excepting the militant factions. The attitudes of these groups toward democracy have already undergone a significant change owing to an increased debate. They would prefer a democracy that sat within the Islamic precept of consultation, but know that they cannot turn the clock back by idealizing any form of dictatorship. They will continue to remain uneasy with terms such as "liberalism" and "secularism," but the phrase "human rights" sits closer to Islamic dictums and is known as *huqooqul ibaad* (rights and duties on humanity). Feminism will not be acceptable, unless couched in some Islamic jargon.

A greater challenge for Pakistani policymakers, Islamists, and Western strategists is how to deliberate together in order to usher in new policies and approaches towards splinter-group Islamists who challenge official authority and block ideological plurality. It is obvious that simply banking on force and disallowing dialogue has not been a constructive solution, nor is the post-9/11 geopolitics a hopeful variable to work with, since it has been anchored in an explicitly anti-Muslim animus.

AWAITING A BREAKTHROUGH

POSTCOLONIAL PAKISTAN with its uneven record of vacillation between military dictatorship and weak civil administration is not so exceptional if compared with a number of other countries including Russia, Nigeria, Thailand, Serbia, Argentina, Chile, and Turkey.[1] Situated within a challen-ging geopolitical location and characterized by enduring political and demographic imbalances, Pakistan continues to wait for a fully participatory system of government that will provide for the peaceful transfer of power as well as representation for its many diverse communities.

Largely run on a modified colonial pattern, Pakistan's highly centralized government has been controlled by the army and civil bureaucracy that have often worked toward state-building at the expense of nation-building. Democratic imperatives, such as constitutionalism, unfettered party politics, and fair and participatory institutional frameworks safeguarded by a free judiciary have been neglected to suit factional and even individual discretion. Every new Pakistani leader, whether military or civilian, has promised a fresh start for the country, only to fall back on the same cronyism that resists long-overdue reforms. So in spite of trans-regional dependence and a shared sense of national identity across the Indus Valley, Pakistan's recurring misgovernance continues to hinder its aspirations towards cohesive nationhood.

Despite Pakistan's nuclear status and impressive economic growth, doubts about the country's ability to survive continue to surface, much to the consternation of concerned Pakistanis. For many, their young country needs more time, honest leadership, and sustained efforts to build institutions in order to enter the cherished realm of cohesive nationhood. Meanwhile the nation's critics feel that a country formed in the name of religion yet crisscrossed by divergent ethnic and sectarian loyalties is untenable. To liberal Pakistanis, the country's redemption rests in its ability to mold itself into Muhammad Ali Jinnah's secular vision, while to religio-political forces, the country requires wholesale Islamization to guarantee its survival and to serve as a role model for other Muslim states. Within these two opinion groups, there are several conflicting strands of thought, where even overarching concepts such as Islam, secularism, and democracy remain contentious. However, the elections of 2008 demonstrated that Pakistanis are ready to make a new, democratic, and forward-looking start, although given the country's previous record of rule by fractious generals and insecure leaders, optimism is qualified with caution.

A third Pakistani opinion group, though appreciative of democratic ideology, seeks a strong, centralized government until the country and its society feel stable enough to enter a democratic phase. They advocate caution, believing that uncontrolled democracy could turn into a free-for-all. Until recently, some of this third group—found in towns and urban areas—were prepared to tolerate a pseudo-democratic facade, anchored by army generals with the purpose of reining in anarchist forces which, considering the lawlessness present in neighboring Afghanistan and a distrustful India, were feared to be waiting in the wings.[2] Many leaders, including Musharraf, have routinely warned against internal "threats to national security" in order to generate a sense of urgency while asserting their own indispensability. Such warnings were periodically followed with news that Pakistan was achieving greater economic growth amidst ever-rising global prestige. This twin-pronged mantra failed to alleviate the national insecurity felt by much of the population, until a more vocal media and civil society began to demand accountable and durable policies in response to the growing turbulence.

Since 9/11, Islamabad's rhetoric has often focused on making the country into a progressive society imbued with what Pervez Musharraf called "enlightened moderation." However, Islamabad's complex and often unexplained alliance with the US over the war on terror had begun to erode enthusiasm for such a euphemism, especially when the chronic problems of governance remained unsolved and Pakistan, instead of being an ally in this war, has begun to look more like a target. It soon became apparent that the General was merely perpetuating his own anomalous rule through a subservient democratic setup.[3]

In addition, despite several radical shifts by Pakistan on the issue of Kashmir, the lack of substantive reciprocity from Delhi began to reinforce the age-old view that Indo–Pakistani discord was intractable. Adding fuel to the fire, India's economic growth and multidimensional relationship with the US and the EU gave the impression that Pakistan had been once again "left high and dry."[4] Bomb blasts on the Lahore-bound Samjotha train in Haryana in February 2007, resulting in 68 deaths and many injuries, did not dampen Pakistan's eagerness for peace with India, but it did raise concerns about the fragility of the process. This atrocity occurred on the fifth anniversary of the Godhra train incident in Gujarat that had also led to significant Muslim loss of life in 2002, and analysts were quick to warn of severe challenges posed by extreme elements on both sides of the border. (Hindu militants fell upon Muslim neighborhoods in Gujarat and killed more than 2,000 people. The genocidal campaign was started with the rumors and propaganda that the fire on the train near Godhra had been started by Muslims and was meant to kill Hindu activists returning from the north.) It is not difficult to detect growing cynicism amidst the pervasive view that powerful global forces are arrayed against Islam, and Muslims have become the victims of an international demonization.[5] Only a few months later Mumbai was the scene of carnage, allegedly at the hands of Pakistani Muslims, bringing Delhi and Islamabad to a dangerous brink.

However, Pakistan's double predicament of misgovernance and the slow pace of national integration are rooted in structural, ideological, and ethno-regional factors, all requiring a redefinition of the concept of security, so far only acknowledged with reference to external threats. Seemingly insurmountable problems at the heart of the dilemma of governability continue to stymie national cohesion despite a widespread desire across the country.

Structural imbalances

While numerous reformist policies have been proposed by independent Pakistani observers, the state itself remains resistant to any major overhaul. The powerful executive office, habitually dismissive of the judiciary and civilian echelons, has often sought its own perpetuation through the politics of patronage, where the landowning elite, religio-political elements and even the emerging middle classes have remained state-dependent while the masses have remained adrift if not totally disempowered. When discussing the debacle of democracy and misgovernance during the country's short history, textbooks written at the behest of military rulers have not been generous to politicians. Several texts and media portrayals were introduced under General Ayub Khan during his 1960s regime and were further employed under General Zia-ul-Haq's dictatorship in the 1980s.[6] Conversely, most Pakistani political leaders (except those obliging politicians who are often coopted by the generals) have laid the blame for all the country's problems on the ambitious generals. The army-controlled authority has not only damaged the political process, tempered democratic institutions, and compromised professionalism within the armed forces, it has transformed Pakistan into a garrison state in which every policy is dependent upon military discretion. Like his predecessors, Musharraf had no qualms in accusing politicians of being adrift and corrupt.

However, in spite of Musharraf's tenure of more than eight years, Pakistan's political uncertainties, economic vulnerability, and ethno-sectarian volatility set against the backdrop of West Asian geopolitics, remained undiminished. Until recently, fatal Sunni–Shia feuds persisted while the restive Baloch and Pushtun tribesmen have kept law-enforcing authorities on tenterhooks since 2005. In Balochistan, authorities routinely accused Baloch chieftains such as the late Akbar Bugti, Ataullah Mengal and Khair Bakhsh Marri, of trying to perpetuate their own feudal hold on the region, blocking developments such as the uplift of Gwadar Port or the construction of new dams in the interior of the province. This discord between Balochistan and Islamabad proved symptomatic of a larger malaise characterized by serious imbalances within the federation, in which some provinces feel marginalized.[7] From the allocation of natural resources to the redistribution of assets and revenue earned from customs, taxes, and natural-gas supplies, the biases at the heart of this centralized polity reflect the absence of a political mechanism based on trust and participatory consensus. Sindh and Balochistan have often been wary of policies pursued by Islamabad, and even with the best of intentions, Islamabad has not commanded confidence among the rural or emerging middle classes. In fact, owing to the proclivities of Pakistan's political economy, the federal government, while seeking alliances and disbursing patronage, has often bypassed the middle classes in order to reach local influentials whose loyalty to Islamabad is based on self-interest rather than the interests of the nation.

A similar situation has also prevailed in FATA and Swat, where these domestic and external differences converged to create an additional security threat to the country. While adhering to its colonial administrative legacies, successive Pakistani regimes have considered the seven tribal agencies within FATA as less than equal to the rest of the country's citizenry. Left to the mercy of a selective system of patronage, Islamabad has ruled millions of people through political agents whose main job is to keep tribal chieftains pacified through bribery and coercion. These bureaucrats use locally recruited militias and operate like semi-monarchs within a region ironically called "no-man's land." The continued disempowerment of these Pushtun tribes, further exacerbated by recent Pakistani military operations, has added to the region's alienation from Islamabad.

The fallout: global war on terror or global war on Muslims?

The Western military campaigns in Afghanistan set in motion in October 2001 are viewed by most locals as offensives against Pushtuns and a war on Islam, while General Musharraf was perceived as aiding these hostile forces. Given the age-old tribal tradition of revenge fueled by strong anti-

Western and anti-Islamabad sentiments, a new era of suicide bombings spread across Pakistan. The killing of several people in a village in Waziristan in January 2007, allegedly by a US Predator drone, was one such event that intensified such retaliatory feelings. Baitullah Mehsud, a leading Pushtun tribal militant in South Waziristan and the founder of Tehreek-i-Taliban Pakistan (TTP), denounced the aerial attack and observed in an interview: "People have seen the injustices of the Americans. They have seen their sons being killed for US dollars. Were we to preach for 100 years, we could not secure the kind of support that is generated by such raids."[8]

Such targeted killings have occured with some regularity without Washington or Islamabad ever accepting any clear responsibility. Even while political parties were pursuing talks to form new central and provincial governments following the elections in February 2008, an American Predator drone targeted a Pushtun house in South Waziristan, killing at least 12 people. Despite protests by Islamabad these attacks continued to cause deaths and resentment in FATA and across Pakistan. Just three days into his presidency, US President Obama approved a similar drone attack on Pakistani soil, resulting in 22 casualties, mostly women and children, though the US military authorities claimed to have been targeting five Arab insurgents in the area. Besides killing hundreds of people, drone attacks and "target killings" led to severe destabilization in Pakistan's "settled" Pushtun districts of Dir, Swat, Kohat, and Dera Ismail Khan. Even Peshawar became unsafe following the kidnaps, selective killings, suicide bombings, and guerrilla-style attacks on NATO convoys traveling through the Khyber Pass, all justified in the name of resisting the Western occupation of Muslim lands.

The fallout from these security operations in FATA and Balochistan led to a radical escalation in suicide bombings against official installations and public institutions in major cities. The years from 2007 to 2009 turned out to be especially violent in Pakistan, with hundreds of people killed in frequent suicide bomb attacks targeting rallies, hotels, public places, military personnel, policemen, and security staff. Only 11 days after the election on 29 February 2008, 40 people were killed and 60 injured when a suicide bomber targeted the funeral of a murdered police officer in Mingora, the capital of Swat. While anger flared over the massive killings in the heart of Swat's safest town, the additional fact of the attack targeting a Muslim funeral deeply angered and saddened Pakistanis from all walks of life, extinguishing any hopes of a possible post-election breakthrough. Two days later, an assembly of tribal elders meeting a few miles outside Peshawar fell victim to a similar suicide attack, resulting in 40 deaths.

These tribal elders had gathered to devise a strategy for countering incursions by the Taliban and al-Qaeda in the Khyber Agency. Meeting in the traditional Pushtun tribal style of openness facilitated a security lapse, which led to the deaths of so many influential pro-Islamabad leaders.

Following a series of small-scale attacks, mostly committed by younger recruits, the next major incident occurred in the town of Dera Ismail Khan on 19 August 2008—a day after Musharraf's resignation speech. A bomb outside the local hospital killed 23 people and wounded 19. The militants appeared unfazed by political changes in the country and seemed hell-bent on destabilizing the country, regardless of its changing political structure, by killing more of their fellow citizens as well as destroying the country's infrastructure. Two days after the attack on the hospital in Dera Ismail Khan, militants carried out another planned explosion, this time at the main entrance of the Pakistan Ordinance Factory in Wah—barely 40 km (25 miles) from Islamabad. The attack on a high-level defense facility—like similar attacks in Rawalpindi on a bus carrying security officials and a more planned attack on a mess hall in Tarbela supposedly under the jurisdiction of the Special Forces Group—highlighted the fact that the militants had developed a network of insiders within the defense establishment.

The installation of the PPP regime in Islamabad led by President Zardari and Prime Minister Gilani, and the formation of a provincial Awami National Party (ANP) government under Amir Haider Khan Hoti, had raised hopes of new strategies for FATA and Swat. Yet, instead of any major breakthrough, the existing policy of applying sporadic force under US persuasion continued. The militants persisted with their suicide attacks and through an undiminished supply of volunteers and resources they were able to continue defying authority and undermining public confidence in the national security apparatus. The frequency of these terrorist attacks in Peshawar, Lahore, Chakwal, Islamabad, and Bannu throughout 2008 and 2009 demonstrated the resourcefulness and commitment of their planners and perpetrators while turning Pakistan into an unsafe place.

The situation in the Kurram Agency within FATA has always been notorious for its frequent Sunni–Shia feuds, and these intensified as many Shias sought refuge across the Durand Line. The Khyber Pass, despite military intervention, often appeared vulnerable to attacks by pro-Taliban elements converging from across FATA.[9] In addition to this volatile backlash against military interventionism, wanton violence occasionally spread far and wide, throughout Pakistan and into the neighboring Sistan region of Iran, where a Sunni militant group was allegedly mounting attacks against civil and military targets.[10] Given the turbulent nature of US–Iran relations and the increased concern over "a rising Shia crescent" between Washington and the Sunni ruling elite in Saudi Arabia, Jordan, Egypt, and the Gulf kingdoms, Pakistan faced heightened sectarian violence.

Al-Qaeda and the Taliban had been able to destabilize FATA and the NWFP at a time when Bush and Musharraf appeared helpless as the results of their disastrous polices pushed one of the largest Muslim states "to the edge."[11] Musharraf's exit and the final days of an immensely unpopular Bush administration provided a golden opportunity for the PPP and ANP to launch new initiatives in the North West Frontier Province. It was necessary for the new Pakistani administration to win the hearts and minds of the silent majority in the area, as well as containing the militants. With Obama continuing Bush's policies and Islamabad remaining tied to the same policies of military interventions and clampdowns, there were few reasons to be hopeful for peace and coexistence in the trans-Indus regions. Schools in Swat continued to be demolished and torched by the Pakistani Taliban, and selective killings continued to be carried out; Maulana Fazlullah (chief of Tehreek-i-Taliban Pakistan/TTP) in Swat and his followers continued issuing threats to anyone cooperating with Islamabad,[12] and in the name of Sharia, Pushtun blood continued to be spilled.

The reality of Pushtun integration

Instead of national integration, tribal Pushtun politics have been left to the whims of local khans, mullahs, and other competing local influences. Official tolerance of unchecked smuggling, the movement of people across borders, the proliferation of arms during the Afghan resistance against the former Soviet Union and the resulting evolution of an idealized jihadi culture had already brought these mountainous regions into the global spotlight.[13] High-profile al-Qaeda figures lurked in the neighborhood and were given shelter by the Taliban regime in Kabul, itself notorious for its archaic laws. The events of 9/11 were the last straw for a vengeful Bush administration and FATA was catapulted into international infamy. Washington, with its failures and frustrations during its eight years in a fragmented Afghanistan, found a convenient scapegoat in Pushtun tribals, especially when some al-Qaeda elements began to seek shelter in Pakistan. Heightened pressure on Pakistan from the US, NATO, the EU, and the Kabul regime to curb Taliban movement across the agencies led to a prolonged Pakistani military campaign against the Wazir and Mehsud tribes, followed by military expansion into the entire so-called autonomous belt.[14]

Renditions and torture Soon after 9/11, Pakistani authorities handed over hundreds of Taliban and other al-Qaeda supporters to the CIA, intensifying resentment against the Musharraf regime, especially amid a rising wave of anti-Americanism in the country and in the Pushtun regions in particular. Many terrorist suspects, irrespective of their nationalities, were bequeathed to the CIA for rendition and torture so that Islamabad would receive a quick reward "totalling millions of dollars."[15] American criticism of Pakistan's inability to curb human and material support for the Afghan Taliban from FATA was a recurring theme running through the relationship. For most Pakistanis, it appeared that their country was being scapegoated for the twin foreign disasters of the Bush administration—namely the wars in Afghanistan and Iraq.

Islamabad signed a peace treaty with Pushtun tribal chieftains in September 2006 guaranteeing their tribal autonomy and peaceful coexistence, both for the security forces and for the tribal people. This treaty was welcomed by the Pakistani population, since a restive FATA threatened to undermine the situation throughout the nation with unnecessary bloodshed of fellow Pakistanis. However, the treaty also exposed the logistical limitations of Pakistani forces in an area where traditional loyalties towards Islam and ethnicity superseded all else.

Despite an almost total news blackout of ongoing military operations in Waziristan, including the mistreatment of local journalists by the authorities, President Musharraf was sensitive to the growing criticism of his policy in the tribal belt.[16] The most serious reservations were expressed by several retired generals who, in a letter to the press in July 2006, strongly rebuked the army's continued political dabbling and instead sought the restoration of empowered political institutions. They warned of an "increasing polarization," which reflected "the dangerous process of exclusion and dominance." The letter proposed a strictly non-interventionist role for the generals as it noted: "Despite the existing legislature and the prospects of the next election, there is a deficit of trust and credibility that marks virtually all political relationships."[17]

In hindsight, it appears that during the last three years of Musharraf's regime, Pakistan's structural problems multiplied due to the subordination of political and civic institutions to his personal whims and those of the generals and external allies. Misgovernance was given further encouragement with the continuing war in Afghanistan and the volatile fallout from the Pakistani Pushtun regions where a vicious cycle of violence began to encroach upon the daily life of tribal, rural, and urban communities. Amid the growing anti-American feeling, Musharraf and Pakistan's armed forces were seen as ineffectual at providing security to ordinary citizens, while the Taliban extended their tentacles through fear, cooption, and the steady erosion of official writ.

Even with daily bomb blasts across Pakistan, many Pakistanis felt that the violence was linked solely to the Western involvement in Afghanistan; they became increasingly despondent over the army's ineffectual handling of the militants. When cosmopolitan and well-placed Swat came under the sway of the Pakistani Taliban in 2009 and the extent of their atrocities became known through the press, the public resolve against the militants became stronger and the armed forces regained the confidence of the populace. With Musharraf gone, the army tried to make a fresh start and its successful military operations in Swat and Waziristan in 2009 earned the backing of a large cross section of society including a vast majority of Pushtuns. Earlier denial was replaced by a realization that the threat to the country was also from within.

However, concerns about Zardari's ambiguous politics and leadership continue. While Prime Minister Gilani gained more ground and clout, Zardari's marginalization appeared to grow with each passing day in late 2009. In the meantime, serious and frequent questions about Pakistan's nuclear warheads and American watchfulness continued to generate controversy, adding to Pakistani complaints of undue American interference. Both Hillary Clinton and US Ambassador Anne Patterson denied the existence of any secret American contingency plan to take over Pakistani weapons.[18] Clinton's visit in November 2009 had been deemed a success but coincided with the bloodiest phase in the country's recent spate of violence. There was disgust with the violence and wanton destruction across the country with people supporting a strong military campaign against these violent elements. The way that Pakistani military, particularly the troops, handled the dislocation and resettlement of more than two million people from Swat and Dir impressed their fellow citizens, especially amidst bombings, food and energy shortages, and threats from within and without.

Sadly, Pakistani political structures have remained weak at a time when internal and external pressures have demanded that these institutions be reformed under dynamic leadership, something which appeared dismally absent. Several new reports on Pakistan, such as "Pakistani Partnership with the United States: An Assessment," [19] and the "Islamist Terrorist Plot in Great Britain: Uncovering the Global Network" raised serious and often critical questions about Pakistan's viability and its position vis-à-vis transnational militancy.[20]

Ideological cracks

Pakistan's simplified rationale as a political entity created in the name of Islam has only complicated the ambiguous interrelationship between politics and religion. It is true that religion played a crucial role in spearheading Muhammad Ali Jinnah's demand for a separate state; however, Islam was seen as an identity marker and a civilizational force to override the ethno-doctrinal differences among South Asian Muslims rather than as a justification for theocracy. This is why Jinnah and many of his followers were denigrated for being secular and were resisted by religio-political parties that in turn either lacked a clear program on the future of Muslims in a post-Raj India or simply advocated a rather ambiguous extraterritorial idealism.[21] Given the open-endedness of both views and the lack of a democratic system after 1958, the official use of Islam for political purposes gained greater ascendancy until the 1980s when General Zia-ul-Haq turned it into the state's main preoccupation. The discretionary use of Islam, particularly in penal matters, not only circumscribed the rights of religious minorities, it also marginalized Pakistani women within an already diminishing public sphere. The acceptance of Islam as the mainstay of governance further exacerbated the divide between antagonistic Sunni and Shia organizations.

The evolution of extremist groups such as Lashkar-i-Jhangvi (LJ) and Sipah-i-Muhammad (SM) was made possible by the lack of any forum to accommodate disparate groups, as well as the emphasis placed on Islam as the major transformative force in Iran and Afghanistan. The focus on a jihadi program to fight the Soviets in Afghanistan was followed by a similar resistance directed towards the Indian control of the disputed Kashmir Valley—supported by both national and international intelligence agencies. This focus and resulting ideological resistance had domestic repercussions, and in the process, even the elected regimes of the 1990s appeared more vulnerable to the competitive and conflicting trajectories of Political Islam. The presence of Afghan refugees in the country and the willingness of many to become Mujahideen due to their own financial needs, zeal, and external encouragement, resulted in a new form of activism on the curricula of some religious seminaries. Eventually some madrassas, especially in the NWFP, turned into recruiting grounds for fighters and the future Taliban. The intractability of the Kashmir dispute, Delhi's political somersaults in the Valley, and a general triumphalism in Southwestern Asia owing to the Soviet retreat helped to strengthen this activism against India.

Up to this point, Musharraf had enjoyed Western support, which saw him as a bulwark against the encroaching forces of radicalism, yet in his own country this closer, costly, and ambiguous interface with the West only heightened local resentment against him and his external allies.[23] The lack of trust in the US leadership and its polices had existed for some time, although Pakistanis never questioned the practical need to maintain a good relationship with Washington through safe and equitable engagement. In spite of this practical understanding, there was grave concern among Pakistanis that some US-led groups were pressurizing Pakistan to undertake increasingly punitive campaigns against Pakistani Pushtuns. Pakistanis' suspicions about undue US pressure were confirmed with Vice President Dick Cheney's unannounced visit to Pakistan in February 2007. The *New York Times*, the *Washington Post,* and the *LA Times* published stories based on "leaked" information from Washington about Cheney arm-twisting Pakistan for its failure to curb Taliban activities on its soil.[24] Even the arrest in Quetta in March 2007 of senior Taliban commander Mullah Obaidullah Akhund was attributed to this American rebuke.[25] Washington and London have viewed the Taliban as a major component of radical Islam and continued to wage war against them because they gave sanctuary to Osama bin Laden and then persisted in carrying out suicide attacks on US and NATO troops. The Taliban were viewed as a militarist threat rather than an ideological challenger.

While it may be true that some young radical Muslims might share al-Qaeda's anti-Westernism, as was the case with the 7/7 bombers in London, the possibility of the Taliban posing any direct threat to the North Atlantic regions is untenable. A weak or Taliban-dominated Afghanistan may possibly provide a haven for all kinds of groups looking to link up with similar organizations across the Middle East and South Asia. According to such a strategic viewpoint, the Taliban were seen as an oppositional force that needed to be broken up through military offensives, while a balanced scholarly analysis may take a contrary view, seeing in the Taliban a model of Political Islam that is predominantly Sunni, puritanical, masculine, and inherently anti-Western.

The process of Talibanization

The Taliban's use of force and their narrow interpretation of Islam are seen as coalescing with the tribal Pushtun tradition of resistance, which could lead to further instability along the Pakistan–Afghanistan border. The process of Talibanization might have been attractive to some Islamists in Pakistan and Central and West Asian Republics, with the exception of Iran, due to age-old differences underlined by Sunni–Shia dissension. In Pakistan, the Taliban model was not seen initially as a military threat to the country since tribal Pushtuns make up only around 7 percent of the population. However, this group did occasionally converge with other

Islamists from the LJ and LT to intensify their bombing campaigns against official facilities. This view of the Taliban is quite prevalent among critical groups within Pakistani civil society, who think the US, Pakistani, and Arab intelligence agencies have been responsible for creating "the Taliban phenomenon."[26] It is seen to be linked with the Mujahideen legacy and the politics of oil, in which Pushtuns were left in the lurch by their former allies with little acknowledgment of their role in the dissolution of the Soviet Union as a result of their defiance in Afghanistan.[27]

Whatever its causes, the Taliban phenomenon is not confined to Afghanistan's Pushtun regions, and by 2005 it had become Pakistan's most debilitating challenge. Despite lacking a united platform, the Taliban were still able to manifest themselves in diverse forms and shades, with many young volunteers ready for self-immolation. Accordingly, by 2009, the Taliban on both sides of the Durand Line and across the Indus Valley were seen as synonymous with al-Qaeda. Like al-Qaeda, the Taliban are decentralized clusters of angry young men and some women motivated by hatred of the West and its Muslim supporters who are viewed as equally pernicious to the cause of idealized pure Islam. Local and personal grievances of such individuals converge into a collective anger towards the perceived common enemy—the West—and, given the context of this extremism, the majority of civilians in areas like Swat and Mohmand initially had no choice but to accept the Taliban's verdict or face dire consequences.

The Taliban model of Islam is strictly purist and does not tolerate either Shia or Sufi traditions, which are usually viewed as misguided innovations. Shia Hazaras, Turis and Bangash in Kurram, and the mainstream Twelvers in Punjab have often been subjected to violence from pro-Taliban elements, including suicide bombings for "straying" from purist Islam. These patterns are similar to the violent anti-Shia backlash in Iraq, which assumed massive proportions following the American invasion of 2003. The lack of sensitivity and prolonged aerial bombardment by Western powers in Southwest Asia triggered old rivalries including the Sunni–Shia divide.

Rehabilitating the ideology of al-Qaeda The Bush administration's destructive and chaotic invasion of two Muslim countries along with Israel's military invasion of Lebanon in 2006 not only rehabilitated the ideology of al-Qaeda, it also weakened pro-West groups across the Muslim world. As a result, the Taliban, Iranians, Hamas, Hizbollah, and Iraqi activists—irrespective of their sectarian allegiances—were soon being idealized as folk heroes standing up to the bullies and their surrogates in the Muslim world.

By early 2009, it was clear that the Western policies pursued in Southwestern Asia had failed miserably, resulting in the rehabilitation of dissident groups. All the states involved, including NATO, Pakistan, and the Kabul regime, seemed to be suffering from exhaustion, confusion, and drift. With Kyrgyzstan's withdrawal of its facility from US use, Pakistan facing its own proverbial "million mutinies" and with Karzai on life support from the West, significant hope for peace in the region seemed to be fading.

During Prime Minister Gilani's first state visit to the United States in July 2008, Pakistan's new political regime had come under pressure from Washington, Kabul, and Delhi to increase its military operations aimed at containing Pushtun militancy on both sides of the Durand Line. The suicide bomb blast in Kabul in the same month targeting the Indian embassy was attributed to the Taliban's closer contacts within the Pakistani ISI, and papers such as the *New York Times* published articles stating that such covert links demonstrated that, in addition to Kashmir, Afghanistan had now become a new arena for Indo–Pakistani hostilities. There is no doubt that the ISI and its Indian rival RAW (Research and Analysis Wing) have often been responsible for clandestine activities across the borders, but following 9/11, the Bush administration began a vigilant watch on ISI, even pressuring Musharraf to replace any Islamist or critical officials. On the other hand, RAW has never been under any such international or American scrutiny, which certainly annoyed many ISI agents, several of whom happened to be Pushtun and viewed the US-led war on terror in Southwest Asia as a war on Pushtuns.

The critique of Pakistan and its intelligence agency was widely reported in the international press and news channels and also attracted some interesting comments.[28] Eric Margolis, a veteran North American journalist with decades-long experience in Afghanistan and Pakistan, viewed the ongoing Pushtun insurgency falling in league with Afghan traditions, and reiterated his early warnings:

"Do not stay in Afghanistan," I had warned in a 2001 article in the *LA Times*. The longer forces remained in Afghanistan, the more the tribes would fight against their continued presence. The Taliban resumed fighting in 2005. Now, as resistance to the US-led occupation of Afghanistan intensifies, the increasingly frustrated Bush administration is venting its anger against Pakistan and its military intelligence agency, Inter-Service[s] Intelligence, better known as the ISI. The White House just leaked claims that the ISI is in cahoots with pro-Taliban groups in Pakistan's tribal agency along the Afghan border and warns them of impending US attacks. The *New York Times*, which allowed the Bush administration to use it as a mouthpiece for Iraq War propaganda, dutifully featured the leaks about the ISI on its front page. Other administration officials have been claiming that the ISI may even be hiding Osama bin Laden and other senior Al-Qaeda leaders.

Margolis had been a vigilant observer of ISI operations during the anti-Soviet resistance in Afghanistan and, before Musharraf's fateful decision following 9/11, viewed it as "the third-world's most efficient, professional intelligence agency." Margolis found a common Pushtun fraternity underlying the resistance, as he observed "ISI, many of whose officers are Pashtun, has every right to warn Pakistani citizens of impending US air attacks that kill large numbers of civilians."

President Musharraf cherished his dictum of enlightenment while rejecting obscurantism, but such ideals could only have been attained through a tolerant and equitable system of democracy. His ignominious exit from power was not followed, as expected, by substantive reforms and changes in structures and policies. Instead, the old legacies were allowed to persist with more wanton bloodshed. The short-lived debate on the redirection and reformation of the educational system, both as a national priority and as the country's major ideological defense, were also dampened amidst the global economic crisis and a stark absence of commitment from the leadership. Pakistan's urgent prerogatives demanded that the ruling elite strictly avoid the use of religion for partisan purposes, and return the country to the reformism that Jinnah and his associates had advocated during the 1940s.[29] For a while, the lawyers and civil society had heightened expectations of such a U-turn, yet Zardari's inexplicable indifference to these civic and constitutional demands only aggravated wider dismay.

Despite reservations about his past activities, Pakistanis were willing to give him a chance to repair the fractured body politic. However, the problems kept mounting up, and Zardari either took to foreign visits or confined himself to the presidential palace. He dragged his feet on the removal of the Seventeenth Amendment—a Musharraf-era legacy—which concentrated all the crucial powers in the president's office over and above parliament and the prime minister; and he showed no interest in the restoration of the senior judges until he faced a mass protest. Zardari's hold on power became more tenuous the longer parliament withheld affirmation of the National Reconciliation Ordinance (NRO) promulgated by Musharraf to commute corruption cases against numerous individuals including Zardari.

It is interesting to note that the day the NRO expired—30 November 2009—Zardari delegated the chair of the National Command Council to

Prime Minister Gilani. Comprising of military chiefs, the prime minister and the defense minister, this powerful body is meant to decide on crucial security matters including the use of nuclear weapons. Zardari's absence gave the image of a solitary man, unsure and vulnerable. His marginalization was noted by the *New York Times* and the *Washington Post*, which began to speculate on the fragility of the PPP-led administration at a time when Obama was streamlining his strategy on Afghanistan with Pakistan as its major security linchpin.[30] Pakistani political commentators began to discuss the possibility of major political changes in the country with Gilani assuming more powers and Zardari eventually becoming a ceremonial head of state, as had been originally envisioned in the constitution of 1973.[31]

Zardari may not have had an easy job, but given the national consensus on education and peace, a demographically youthful society, and the awareness that neighboring India was outdoing its rivals in education and economy, many positive incentives exist for a major transformation. Islamabad did not have to fight Islam; it simply needed to lead the effort in rediscovering its humanity, egalitarianism, elevation of learning, and greater tolerance of debate and differences. Pakistan is not the only country where religion and politics are intertwined, nor is it the only society where the education system presents two class-based extremes of efficiency and waywardness. A systemic overhaul of the education system and other policies could help to achieve economic and political empowerment of the masses, especially women, though the ruling elite will need to be bold to offer such substantive alternatives.

Pluralism and the ethnic divide

For a long time, Pakistan's ethnic pluralism has been a no-go area for real debate, where one encountered only the routine discourse on Islamic unity and the primacy of Pakistani identity. It is only recently, in the wake of a more diverse media and increased openness towards public debate, that commentators and politicians have begun to revisit the subject of ethnic pluralism as not inherently a negative challenge.[32] Studies on the age-old linguistic and regional diversities of Pakistan are appearing more regularly and a vocal middle class, especially from the lower Indus regions, is forcing the Punjab and Pushtun centrist elite to seek cooperation.

Matters such as the construction of new dams and the redistribution of power and resources remain contentious issues, given the existing inter-provincial mistrust, but even the country's military-run systems have not been able to prevent public dissent. It is true that Pakistan's four provinces do not fully reflect four distinct ethnic blocs since they are linguistically and demographically pluralistic, yet there remain areas where ethno-regional commonalities are stronger and easily discernable. General Musharraf's plan of devolution at district and rural levels helped local political forces, yet without a corresponding provincial and nationwide decentralization this scheme was merely seen as a ploy to divert attention and resources from real democratization. Pakistan's limited resources and uneven economy, multiplied by its constant democratic deficit, have added volatility to ethnic dissent. Problems in former East Pakistan, the former demand for Pushtunistan, turbulence in urban Sindh over the past two decades, and the recent simmering of Baloch and Pushtun dissent reveal the incapacity as well as the unwillingness of a narrowly based statehood that continues to overlook the dynamics for a shared nationhood.

Ethnic and religious pluralism must be approached with tolerance in order to guide all Pakistanis through the systemic overhaul and administrative reformism necessary for shared nationhood. Pakistanis, especially in Balochistan, rural Sindh, and the NWFP have to be accorded equal participation in universal citizenship and having become stake-holders, they may then choose to stand by their country during trying times. An empowered judiciary, the restoration of the Constitution without Musharraf's discretionary amendments, a guaranteed parliamentary form of government and substantive devolution at all levels, and a foreign policy of non-interference and constructive engagement could catapult Pakistan into its potential position as an operational and tolerant democracy.

EPILOGUE

BENAZIR BHUTTO'S ASSASSINATION in December 2007, the national elections in February 2008, Musharraf's resignation in August, and Zardari's subsequent ascension to the presidency in September 2008 occurred in quick succession. The restive NWFP, factionalist politics, the food shortages and energy crisis, and the public demand for full-fledged democracy added a sense of urgency to the need for a new system of governance. At first glance, it appeared that democracy in Pakistan was moving full-steam ahead, but in fact the country faced huge challenges and systemic imbalances.

Zardari: savior of democracy or ruler of the status quo?

On 6 September 2008 Asif Ali Zardari, widower of Benazir Bhutto and acting chairman of the PPP, was elected as Pakistan's president following the earlier resignation of a pugnacious Pervez Musharraf. Following the national and provincial elections held earlier in February, Zardari had already emerged as the de facto power broker in his country's labyrinthine political system; and espousing a conciliatory approach to his former foes, Zardari adroitly navigated his path to the presidency. Thanks to Musharraf's Seventeenth Amendment to the constitution, the office of president had acquired discretionary powers over and above those of parliament, the prime minister, and the provincial governments; with Zardari ensconced in office, the prospects for Pakistan seemed simultaneously favorable and ominous. Confronted by the harrowing problems symbolized by the "three Fs" (Frontier, Fuel, and Food crises), Pakistan needed a stable political structure and a new leadership that could steer the country through the prevailing chaos.

Once in office, Zardari's neglect of various promises made at the start of his presidential term—including those to Nawaz Sharif to restore Chief Justice Chaudhry and other deposed senior judges—as well as his procrastination on the annulment of the contentious power-grabbing Seventeenth Admendment distanced him from vital political forces. Additionally, on 25 February 2009 the Supreme Court, presumably under the president's influence, disqualified the Sharif brothers from holding public office, leading to massive protests across the country.[1] Zardari's Uturns on various public commitments contrasted with his conciliatory gestures towards regional parties and his meticulous easing out of Musharraf, while the unnecessary confrontation with the Sharifs and the PML-N spawned questions about the country's political future as well as Zardari's own political survival. For some, Zardari was pursuing a dangerous realpolitik by antagonizing his main challengers such as Nawaz Sharif, while to others he remained beholden to the army and to Western powers.

Despite muffled parliamentary opposition, Zardari began his presidential term more like a tribal chieftain with Punjab as his main testing ground. His decision to contest the presidential elections without consulting Nawaz Sharif as previously agreed, as well as the rushed nature of the elections, dampened hopes for closer cooperation between the two major political forces. Earlier, the two parties had been united in formulating a consensual policy on the primacy of the judiciary and parliamentary democracy. Nawaz Sharif, as late as December 2009, felt despondent about Zardari but refused to create problems for the nascent political system unless and until it fell down of its own accord, paving the way for midterm elections.

Zardari was perhaps relishing his role on the center stage. The generals, the Americans, the British, and a majority of Pakistanis were willing to offer a chance to Pakistan's new strong man, who until a few months prior had lived an anonymous life, in incarceration for some time and under the shadow of his more charismatic wife. Previously known only for financial and personal scandals, Zardari finally attained a lifetime's ambition to disprove his detractors. To some of his allies and critics, his pursuit of power was nothing less than a "degeneration," which had obviated the need for "the strong and united support, needed by the forces fighting security and economic wars on several fronts."[2] To others, it was Zardari's democratic right to become leader, especially since he steered Pakistan's most popular political machine in the aftermath of Benazir's assassination. He had promised to avoid the politics of revenge, but his dismissal of the PML-N government in Punjab ushered in a new crisis and belied his earlier claims. He repaired his relations with the Sharif brothers following the restoration of Chief Justice Chaudhry in April 2009, yet the issues of corruption, earlier commuted by Musharraf through his disputatious National Reconciliation Ordinance (NRO), kept challenging Zardari's political leadership. Zardari's efforts to get Musharraf's NRO through parliament in October 2009 faltered.

New blood: Syed Yousaf Gilani takes the oath

Like other political mavericks, Benazir Bhutto had realized that the road to Islamabad passed through Washington and London; even the commutation of longstanding corruption charges and her own political rehabilitation in 2006–7 needed some assertive British and American arbiters. Musharraf, who had been at the apex of his power just a few months prior, was faced with real political opposition—the familiar fate of President Bush's comrades in the war on terror was soon to claim one more casualty.[3] The weakened and marginalized Musharraf hoped against heavy odds for a miracle to help him sail over the stormy seas,[4] however, his imposition of Emergency rule in November 2007 and the assassination of Benazir Bhutto had failed to stem the tide of political changes already set in motion. Soon a newly elected parliament and a re-energized civilian leadership evolved in Islamabad, raising hopes for a fresh political breakthrough since the civil society desired quick and reformative policies.

On 25 March 2008, Syed Yousaf Raza Gilani (b. 1952–) was sworn in as the 25th prime minister of Pakistan by Pervez Musharraf in an icy five-minute ceremony boycotted by all the major political leaders and parties except for token representation from the PPP and the MQM. The leaders of the PML-N, ANP, and JUI all stayed away and the body language between the president and the new prime minister was stiff and mistrustful. The president, although equipped with his self-engineered unilateral powers and elected from a controversial franchise itself in its dying days, was certainly not sure of his own future.

Gilani, who was the forth politician to hold the prime ministerial office since 2002, had been chosen unanimously in the National Assembly by his fellow PPP legislators and other coalition partners the previous day. Ironically, Musharraf's own political allies were conspicuous by their absence, while diplomats, military chiefs, and senior civil servants sat expressionless during what had become nothing more than a game of musical chairs. Five days later, Gilani received a unanimous vote of confidence from the National Assembly, a rare consensus in an otherwise traditionally polarized political culture. Gilani was present for the presidential oath-taking ceremony of his new cabinet, representing the PPP, PML-N, ANP, and the JUI, with half of them wearing black bands to register their protest against Musharraf's eight-year rule. This occasion was made more somber and ironic as half of the 24 ministers being sworn in by Musharraf had been incarcerated as a result of selective witch hunts by his National Accountability Bureau (NAB) that notoriously targeted only dissenting politicians.

Prime Minister Gilani had himself spent five years in jail for refusing to deny his support for Benazir Bhutto. A bewildered Musharraf could certainly foresee retribution in the pipeline, especially when a re-energized Nawaz Sharif persistently demanded his accountability for constitutional violations. Once again, Musharraf's political supporters were nowhere to be seen, with his former handpicked prime minister Shaukat Aziz already ensconced in the West while others avoided the beleaguered president. Gilani stood next to the man, who, like every other reigning general, had been contemptuous of politicians. However, once again the populace had entrusted politicians to steer the country through the problems of misgovernance, lawlessness, and a precarious economy. Like the generals Ayub Khan, Yahya Khan, and Zia-ul-Haq, General Musharraf was in dire need of his past political allies, but they had already jumped ship.

Musharraf, always confident of his last-minute good fortune, sought reassurance from two areas: firstly, he believed that the politicians currently cooperating with one another would soon revert to their usual cross-party bickering and his office would retrieve its pivotal status. Secondly, he felt that by removing the corruption charges against Bhutto and Zardari and holding elections, he had kept his side of the "deal." His familiar swagger and penchant for long speeches were absent, and he seemed worried about the the fact that the civil society was united in its support of parliamentary primacy, an independent judiciary, a free media and a foreign policy formulated by its elected representatives to serve Pakistan rather than one cobbled together by an individual under the dictates of Washington.

As reported in Pakistan's prestigious newspaper *Dawn*, Musharraf was "startled" when some members in the specially selected audience raised populist slogans remembering the Bhuttos, although they did not include the countrywide refrain, "Go Musharraf, Go," which had resounded in the National Assembly a day earlier. For the second occasion Gilani had restrained his colleagues from brandishing slogans, though parliamentarians belonging to the PML-N and ANP quietly left the hall after the ceremony without staying to socialize with Musharraf.[5]

The advent of the coalition government
Pakistan's new coalition government had begun its tenure amidst widespread public goodwill, yet it was still confronted with major problems including severe threats to the federation itself from the crumbling law-and-order situation in FATA and Swat and a series of

devastating bomb blasts in urban centers. Other than this almost daily loss of life, the number of Pakistani casualties, both military and civilian, since 2006 had already surpassed total NATO losses. Hundreds of Pakistani soldiers had been killed and many more had refused to fight against fellow Muslims; Pakistan's ambassador to Kabul had been kidnapped from the Khyber Pass in February, while fuel convoys to Afghanistan were frequently ambushed with deadly results. Under pressure from the West, the Pakistani army continued its forward policy in the tribal regions and Swat, though it would require further persuasion and serious human rights violations on the part of the Pakistani Taliban for the nation to stand united behind a sustained military operation in the turbulent Frontier regions during May 2009.

Longer power cuts, rising food prices, volatility in Karachi already under the control of the ethnic militant party MQM, and Islamabad's stalemated relations with India over Kashmir combined to pose a serious challenge to the PPP-led coalition government. Amidst high public expectations and support, the challenges of rectifying the structural imbalances within the polity and implementing an alternative foreign policy proved a tall order. Pakistani observers, while appreciative of the election and peaceful transfer of power, were concerned about Pakistan's history of cyclic misgovernance, with the possibility of yet another military takeover in the near future. At the same time, Western policymakers worried about their own interests in the region as their ally Musharraf was visibly weakened with a multitude of forces arrayed against him and intent upon his removal.

Nawaz Sharif and the lawyers prioritized the restoration of the senior judges dismissed by Musharraf, while Zardari dithered in order to gain more time and concessions from the weakened and unpopular president. Zardari seemed reluctant to seek parliamentary or executive reprieve for some of the senior judges, since he held them personally responsible for his own incarceration. Meanwhile, the Pakistani public, suffering from food shortages and power cuts, vacillated between diminished hopes and growing fears. There was widespread uncertainty about the new political state of affairs, and the lawyers resumed their rallies, resentful at the PPP's procrastination over restoring the senior judges and replacing other controversial officials from the Musharraf–Aziz era.

Sharif, the civil society and the critical media found themselves in a Catch-22 situation: while holding their stance on parliamentary and judicial supremacy and Musharraf's replacement, they had to stop short of creating serious difficulties for Zardari and Gilani as that might encourage another military takeover or even Musharraf's rehabilitation. These tensions were exacerbated in February 2009 when the PPP government in Islamabad rushed to replace the PML-N government in Punjab by using a Musharraf-era verdict against the Sharif brothers that had disqualified them from holding any public office. The pro-Musharraf judges in the Supreme Court promptly reissued the verdict on this date and thus the goodwill between the PPP and PML-N nosedived to its lowest level. Pakistan's most significant province became a hotbed of unnecessary rivalry and political instability until the highest court reversed the judgment a few weeks later. Consequently, Shahbaz Sharif resumed his chief ministership, with Governor Salman Taseer reluctantly assuming a lower profile. The country survived this period of instability, but it served to heighten the pervasive dismay with political mavericks.

At the same time Zardari's presidency faced growing unrest in the NWFP. The ANP government in the province had convinced Zardari to hold talks with Maulana Sufi Muhammad, the founder of Tehreek-i-Nafaz-e-Shariat-i-Mohammadi (TNSM), a militant organization seeking the implementation of Sharia law in Pakistan, which had been banned in 2002. Eventually, in February 2009 a five-point plan was agreed upon between the provincial government and Maulana Sufi, who agreed to mutual co-existence in exchange for the implementation of the Sharia penal code in Malakand including Swat. Though opinions were mixed about this agreement, the desire for peace overcame many reservations. However, a triumphant Maulana and his militant son-in-law Fazlullah began to openly defy state authority by creating their own power base within Swat. The arrival of numerous warlords and racketeers, and encroach-ment by them on the neighboring districts of Dir and Buner created a serious threat to state authority and public peace in the region. Imposing discretionary taxes on non-Muslims and eliminating dissenting civil forces only aggravated the situation, until the army and political leaders decided to mount a sustained military campaign to flush out these Taliban militants.

While the army, under pressure from the West, continued with its forward policy in the tribal regions and Swat, the policies of the ruling PPP continued to reflect the whims of Zardari.[6] Both the PML-N and the ANP had been eager to reinstate the deposed judges, to transfer crucial powers from the presidency back to parliament and initiate a policy of dialogue and peace within FATA. Several PPP parliamentarians were equally supportive of these goals so as not to lose the confidence and support of the public, whereas Zardari and some of his closest associates appeared ambivalent on these vital issues. This lack of clarity began to generate widespread speculation and apprehension about the political leadership, which appeared to lack consensus and the will to usher in systemic changes. Backed by a vocal civil society and a probing media, the PPP, PML-N, and ANP had all promised to roll back Musharraf's two Provisional Constitution Orders (PCOs), the Seventeenth Amendment, and the Emergency-rule ordinances, as well as introducing substantial changes to the security policies and economic management. According to many sceptics, "the Musharraf-Bhutto Deal" (power-sharing in exchange for dropping of corruption charges through the NRO), was still dictating political developments from behind the scenes, as Zardari avoided any sort of upfront stance on reform. Instead of streamlining the distorted political setup, Zardari seemed to aspire to be as powerful as Musharraf. The judges were eventually restored, but only once Zardari was left with no choice when faced with a popular campaign of protests and marches by the lawyers supported by Nawaz Sharif. However, the other issues of institutional imbalances and parliamentary sovereignty remained unresolved.

Turning over a new leaf: a four-step plan of action

By 2009–10, Pakistan was eager to turn over a new leaf in its history and to defy its persistent cynics, who every few years readied themselves to pen Pakistan's obituary. The country's concerned citizens and commentators focused their debate on four crucial areas that held the potential to either remake or destroy this Indus nation's new incarnation.

The first challenge—tackling the violence of the insurgency Pakistanis across the board felt that the attacks on security personnel, supply convoys and frequent suicide bombings resulting in massive death and destruction were a fallout from the US-led invasion of Afghanistan, the main brunt of which was suffered by Pushtuns. Washington's own frustration at its inability to apprehend Osama bin Laden, Ayman al-Zawahiri, and Mullah Muhammad Omar, as well as the intensity of guerrilla attacks, gradually began to engulf the entire tribal belt. American policymakers and media had accused Pushtuns of abetting the Afghan Taliban as well as providing sanctuary for al-Qaeda's foreign elements. Pakistan's own military-led intervention dislocated many civilians and fed into the view that the ongoing war on terror was actually a war on Islam being waged through Muslim surrogates. Pakistani troops often found themselves caught in the middle and a few solitary efforts at negotiated settlements were largely bypassed under American pressure, which preferred military force on both sides of the Pakistan–Afghan borders. Frequent aerial bombardment resulting in numerous deaths that were invariably papered over as collateral damage further heightened resentment toward Pakistani security forces.

Emphasizing dialogue with the tribal elders and resisting the military option, the National Assembly and the new ANP-led provincial government in the NWFP evoked some positive responses from FATA, which unnerved Washington. At a time when Pakistani politicians were working to form a new cabinet, the US had already "escalated its unilateral strikes…partly because of anxieties that Pakistan's new leaders will insist on scaling back military operation in that country….The moves followed a tacit understanding with Musharraf and Army Chief General Ashfaq Kayani that allows US strikes on foreign fighters operating in Pakistan, but not against the Pakistani Taliban…" The policy, according to one US official, was called "a shake the tree strategy," though officials on both sides denied the existence of such an agreement. These reports not only further weakened Musharraf, they also added new strains on General Kayani as well as Prime Minister Gilani, who were otherwise expected to offer clear policy alternatives.[7]

The US efforts in 2008 to persuade the new regime in Islamabad through a carrot-and-stick policy could afford to ignore widespread Pakistani public resentment. The NATO summit held in Romania in early April 2008 had deliberated on Afghanistan's deteriorating security situation and reiterated NATO intentions to hold intense negotiations with Islamabad. Positing Pakistan as Afghanistan's "most troubling neighbor, with Taliban forces using its territory as a haven from which to mount attacks," despite its major contributions and the resultant ramifications, did not engender optimism.[8] However, some member states felt that this single-factor focus on security while banking solely on one individual—Musharraf—had insidiously compromised democratic processes in Pakistan. Canadian Prime Minister Stephen Harper was emphatic as he observed: "We were told democracy [in Pakistan] would inflame the radicals. The problem was the previous government in Pakistan was cracking down on the democrats, not the extremists."[9]

Certainly, Pakistani politicians, especially those in the new government, did not subscribe to any inherent anti-Americanism. Instead they were expected to launch negotiations with the tribal chieftains and clerics while also expressing sensitivity to their grievances. A correspondent witnessing the civilian deaths of Pakistani Pushtuns as a result of a botched American aerial operation quoted the US official responsible for this attack, who like his fellow Americans, could "not trust their Pakistani counterparts. 'The Pakistani military is corrupt and lets people come through,' [Captain Chris] Hammond said."[10] It was a serious allegation against an institution that had lost thousands of its troops fighting "America's war in West Asia." This disparaging view held by their powerful Western ally was not unfamiliar to Pakistanis, who had been demanding the reversal of Musharraf's controversial policy.

Prime Minister Gilani's first visit to the US in July 2008 received mixed public and media attention. Not only had it begun in the wake of another CIA missile attack on Waziristan the previous day, causing protests across the country over the violation of Pakistani sovereignty, but Gilani was also subjected to a serious reprimand from President Bush for not restraining covert support for the Taliban emanating from some ISI sections.[11] Preceding Gilani's visit, the Indian embassy in Kabul had been hit by a suicide bomb attack in July resulting in numerous casualties, with both Kabul and Delhi officials accusing Pakistani intelligence of providing support to the perpetrators. While officials in Pakistan rejected these accusations, Islamabad itself seemed to be lacking a coherent policy on controlling its intelligence agencies.[12] Kabul, Washington, and even Delhi took a harsh line toward the newly formed government that only betrayed their own frustrations; they each sought to make scapegoats of Pakistan, the Pushtun Taliban, and the ISI.[13]

Gilani's weak leadership, Zardari's personal control over official policies, and the distancing of Sharif and others from the regime allowed the Pakistani Taliban and NATO troops to mount further operations within Pakistan. Amid the bickering and mutual accusations, Pakistan's political leadership and the ANP administration in the NWFP were in fact still pursuing Musharraf-era policies with regard to the insurgency in Pushtun regions. Like millions of Pakistanis, politicians such as Nawaz Sharif, Imran Khan, and Asfandyar Wali Khan voiced their opposition to this fratricide and led the nation in criticizing Musharraf's policies in FATA. However, they now looked helpless before the rising tide of violence that continued after Musharraf's exit. On 3 September 2008, NATO helicopters violated Pakistani air space and mounted the first ground military operation in Angorada, causing more than 20 deaths of mostly women and children. On the same day, Taliban snipers ambushed Prime Minister Gilani's motorcade on the Islamabad–Rawalpindi Highway, damaging his bullet-proof car and proving that a restive NWFP and a turbulent Afghanistan would continue to threaten even the safe confines of Islamabad.[14]

Two weeks earlier, a suicide attack carried out by two Wazir followers of Baitullah Mehsud (leader of the TTP in Waziristan) outside Pakistan's premier ordnance factories in Wah claimed 70 lives and left hundreds in critical condition. When President Obama's envoy Richard Holbrooke reached Kabul after meeting Pakistani civil and military authorities, a drone attack struck a village in South Waziristan on 13 February, claiming 30 lives. It appeared as if the new administration was planning a military surge in Pak–Afghan border regions, further raising the specter of violence in one of the poorest areas of the world as well as aggravating the Pushtun backlash in the NWFP.[15]

Long before assuming presidential powers, Zardari had been vocal in his denunciation of militarist encroachments and Musharraf's iron-fisted policy, determined to confront the militants in close cooperation with Washington. In an article in the *Washington Post* he noted: "We stand with the United States, Britain, Spain and others who have been attacked. Fundamentally, however, the war we are fighting is our war. The battle is for Pakistan's soul." He found his country "at a crossroad" and the gravity of the situation had compelled him to assume the presidency: "We did not make the decision for me to run lightly. But we know what is at stake. Chief among the challenges that all Pakistanis face is the threat of global terrorism, demonstrated again in this week's assassination attempt against Prime Minister Yousaf Raza Gilani."[16]

By the time President Zardari undertook his first visit to Peshawar in February 2009, the entire province was astir with what he called "an insurgency," combining local Taliban, miscreants, and criminals. While meeting with tribal elders and other officials, Zardari tried to build confidence in Islamabad's policies of reestablishing official authority in the regions, as well as initiating development schemes and the adequate settlement of displaced persons. His visit coincided with a major military offensive near Darra Adam Khel where Pakistani gunship helicopters claimed to have destroyed several structures used by militants in their attacks on traffic through the Khyber Pass.[17] Other than reports of military operations in Swat and the Khyber agency on 7 February, two suicide bombers had struck in the Pass and in Mianwali, again showing that the militants had a sufficient supply of committed volunteers. Ordinary Pakistanis were aghast at the scale of violence, especially when otherwise peaceful places such as Dera Ghazi Khan in southern Punjab suffered a suicide attack in February, killing 35. The deterioration of law and order in Swat was the last straw before the army undertook a well-orchestrated campaign in April 2009 to deal with the militants. However, in the process, nearly three million people were displaced from their homes and compelled to live in tents under a scorching summer sun. The military operations were successfully completed within a few months. Following that, the government undertook a sustained military operation in Southern Waziristan to flush out the Pakistani Taliban.

The second challenge—restoring political institutions The second and perhaps more significant challenge facing Pakistan's new government emanated from the fractured political culture in which the institutions of parliament, the judiciary, and civil society had been grievously infringed. A determination to restore the Constitution of 1973 to its rightful position had been a unifying consensus among most members of the new political administration. This resolve was especially inspired by Clause 58–2 (B), a bill introduced into the Constitution by General Zia in 1985, abolished by Nawaz Sharif in 1998, only to be revived by Musharraf in 2003 as part of his Seventeenth Amendment. It unilaterally allowed a president to dismiss the entire parliamentary structure including the prime minister and assemblies. Musharraf's other major amendments allocated vital powers to the president, including appointments and transfers of senior judges, promotion and selection of all the chiefs of the three defense services and governors of the four provinces, and the nomination of the election commission, leaving very little power for the prime minister. Musharraf's indemnification of all his regulations and measures through the Seventeenth Amendment, PCOs, and Emergency-rule orders had shifted power in favor of the presidency by disempowering parliament and the prime minister.

The new government was expected to ensure a proper and duly empowered parliamentary government as well as reframing equitable relations between the centralized government and federal units. The civil society, PML-N, ANP, JUI, several PPP representatives, Imran Khan, and the JI had provided a consensus on these issues and expected progress on the outstanding structural imbalances, specifically within the initial honeymoon period of Zardari's administration. However, Zardari and some of his colleagues were not emphatic on the restoration of senior judges, constitutional amendments, and fresh initiatives in FATA. Disregard for the restoration of the judiciary, procrastination on 58-2 (B), and confrontations with the PML-N and lawyers proved to be the Achilles heel of the new government, unleashing various assumptions about Zardari's actual intentions as president. His own role as a beneficiary of Musharraf's NRO soon began to haunt him as the public and the vocal media demanded transparency and accountability. The issue, after the NRO was rejected by parliament, turned into a major moral and political dilemma for Zardari.

Once again, the political, judicial, and constitutional issues divided the country's leaders and prolonged Pakistan's agony by keeping its political culture fragmented and unbalanced. Given the public verdict and increased expectations, fear grew that these difficulties would push Pakistan ever closer toward the precipice. Some analysts felt that while Sharif and other political forces inside and outside the assemblies fought for substantive reforms to precede the consolidation of political forces, Zardari prioritized consolidation over reforms in order to ensure his own primacy before confronting Pakistan's problems of governance.[18]

The third challenge—the army's dominance The third major challenge for the new government was the army's ongoing domination of national life. As the army had been responsible for intermittent military takeovers of government, it was held partly to blame for weakening the constitutional and political processes. Imposing a strictly professional role for the army and a nonpolitical profile for its generals without causing new hostilities is crucial to stabilizing constitutional and civic politics. Development of the social sector, strengthening of civil society and, most importantly, substantive efforts towards regional peace and cooperation carry the possibility of reducing the need for military intervention in politics, but will only come about through sustained dialogue, sincere efforts, and untainted reformism. For any civil government in a country such as Pakistan, this progress will always pose a formidable challenge, but resolve and sagacity can help. The politics of mistrust, focusing on the individual while ignoring the strengths and weaknesses of institutions, and procrastination or a misplaced haste to bring about major changes without the support of the civil society and other reform groups, can only increase the malaise. The army, to a great extent, was able to retrieve its prestige by mounting successful operations in Swat and FATA besides reassuring Pakistanis on national security especially in light of the Mumbai attacks in November 2008.

Amidst anger and confusion, the Gilani government has been pulled in many different directions by Zardari, Musharraf, Sharif, Washington, Kabul, Delhi, Pakistan's lawyers, and Pushtun militants. It has been seen as weak, indolent, and indecisive, once again allowing a greater role to the army. In public statements, Washington has supported the Gilani government, yet its "special relationship" with the military forces and its preferential treatment for the formidable defense establishment has been apparent to all.[19] A strong comment in the British *Guardian* newspaper had advised the Pakistani Army

> ...to decide how to save itself and the country it has dominated for so long. In the struggle across the region, it could even be said that decisions made in Rawalpindi, the army's headquarters, may turn out to be more important than those made in Washington, Baghdad, Tehran or Tel Aviv. And this army is highly autonomous. It has been the government, and remains by far the most powerful institution in the country.[20]

The fourth challenge—the economy The fourth major challenge confronting Pakistan's new government is the restoration of the economy through refurbishing the developmental sector and inviting more domestic and foreign investments. Improvements in fiscal management, including broadening the tax base by offering incentives to landlords and businessmen, investment in the education and social sectors, stringent rules regarding financial probity and, above all, a sustained peace, could certainly offer relief to ordinary Pakistanis. Power cuts, poverty, provincial grievances over the distribution of assets, resource allocations, and the lack of transparency and trust in government have proved to be enduring problems requiring bold and substantive reforms. How far post-Musharraf leaders are able to further these aims will only become apparent in the future. While these issues remain urgent, it is important to redirect local and international energies towards a better understanding of domestic and regional problems. Despite the current situation, democracy still offers the only tangible breakthrough for Pakistan, as was opined by the British *Independent* soon after the historic elections on 18 February 2008: "If the past decade in Pakistan has taught anything, it is that dictatorship does not stifle extremism, but nourishes it."[21]

Facing the future

The nation had entrusted its politicians once again, and by sending these representatives to the assemblies with a solid mandate, it has made its verdict clear. Now, amid fears and hopes, the nation anxiously awaits a better dawn. Over the months following the elections, the persistent lack of clarity, decisiveness, or even commitment to alternative policies and systemic overhaul are beginning to take their toll as Pakistanis continue to wait amidst bewildering domestic and regional challenges.

In a nationwide survey based on randomly selected samples of adult men and women from 223 rural and 127 urban areas in all four Pakistani provinces, a broad consensus was reflected on issues confronting the sixth-largest nation in the world. The survey, conducted by the US-based International Republican Institute (IRI) in early June 2008, found that 86 percent of respondents held the view that Pakistan was moving in the wrong direction, while only 12 percent approved of Islamabad's policies. Interestingly, 83 percent of those polled had demanded the removal of Pervez Musharraf, while 82 percent supported Nawaz Sharif, making him the most popular leader in the country, followed by Abdul Qadeer Khan and Chief Justice Iftikhar Chaudhry as the other two most popular individuals. Only 3 percent had anything positive to say about Musharraf, with 75 percent of respondents deeply critical of his policies while in power. Regarding religious extremism, 61 percent viewed it as a serious problem; 45 percent perceived the Taliban and al-Qaeda as a grave concern, whereas 71 percent supported a policy of dialogue rather than military confrontation with them. In the same vein, 61 percent believed economic development and education to be the keys for neutralizing religious extremism, with only 9 percent in favor of military strategy.[22] With such a clear consensus on crucial issues showing an overwhelming rejection of extremism, political vendetta, and military dominance, one could certainly empathize with Pakistanis in their dismay with their leaders. In a country where individual aspirations and insecurities have historically overridden national cohesion, Musharraf's ignominious exit and Zardari's salience certainly offered fresh hopes, as well as new apprehensions. But already both time and patience are running short.

The country, so well endowed with a multitude of natural and human bounties, should be able to achieve cohesive nationhood, pursue egalitarian politics, and establish a balance between the forces of modernity and tradition. This Karakoram country has all the potential to achieve its cherished goals if its leadership is bold and honest, and focuses on creative ideas and enduring institutions rather than pursuing personal agendas. Democracy, dialogue, and distributive justice are the keys to a bright future for Pakistan.

Prologue

1 *Financial Times*, 29 October 2009.
2 In a telephone interview Hakimullah Mehsud, the leader of Tehrik-i-Taliban Pakistan (TTP), disowned the responsibility for the bomb blast in Peshawar. For further details, see www.bbc.co.uk/urdu/pakistan/2009/10/091029_pes_blast_update_rh.shtml.
3 Kamran Khan, "Beleaguered Presidency left with single option," *News International* (Islamabad), 29 October 2009.
4 Declan Walsh, "Market bomb kills at least 100," *Guardian*, 29 October 2009.
5 For a very interesting perspective, see Seymour M. Hersh, "Defending the Arsenal: In an unstable Pakistan, can nuclear warheads be kept safe?" *New Yorker*, 9–16 November 2009.
6 Ansar Abbasi, "Zardari's message to Nawaz has defeat written all over," *News International*, 24 October 2009.
7 Simon Tisdall, "With friends like the US, Pakistan doesn't need enemies," *Guardian*, 15 October 2009.
8 The US tried to assume a less visible role on vital issues and through Holbrooke tried to influence decision-making in the country. For more on the issue of judges, see "Holbrooke expects Pakistan's situation won't get parallel to March 16 crisis," *News International*, 3 November 2009.
9 "The McClatchy Report" portrayed the situation as "very bad, given the serious security problems and the economic crisis with no money, no energy," pushing millions of people into poverty. Jonathan Landay and John Walcott, "Intelligence report: US anti-terror ally Pakistan 'on the edge,'" 14 October 2008, www.mcclatchy.org
10 Historical and political studies focus on Muslim nationalism and the challenges of state building. For a useful selection, see Lawrence Ziring, *Pakistan: At the Crossroad of History*, Oxford, 2003; Ian Talbot, *Pakistan: A Modern History*, London, 2005; and Ayesha Jalal, *The Sole Spokesman: Jinnah, the Muslim League and the Demand for Pakistan*, Cambridge, 1985.
11 Journalists have often dabbled in the newsworthiness of Pakistan. For instance, Christina Lamb, *Waiting for Allah: Pakistan's Struggle for Democracy*, London, 1991; Owen Bennett-Jones, *Pakistan: Eye of the Storm*, New Haven, 2002; and Bernard-Henri Levy, *Who Killed Daniel Pearl?* Translated by James X. Mitchell, London, 2004.

Introduction

1 For a wide variety of cultural manifestations and mores, see Iftikhar H. Malik, *Culture and Customs of Pakistan*, Newport, 2005.
2 For the ecology of this region, see Azra and Peter Meadows (eds.), *The Indus River: Biodiversity, Resources, Humankind*, Karachi, 1999 (reprint).
3 For more on the Kashmir dispute, see Alastair Lamb, *Kashmir: A Disputed Legacy, 1846–1990*, Hertingfordbury, 1991.
4 Hasan Zaheer, *The Separation of East Pakistan*, Karachi, 1994.
5 Olaf Caroe, *The Pathans: 550 BC–AD 1957*, London, 2000 (reprint); James Spain, *The Way of the Pathans*, Karachi, 1972.
6 For more on this, see Philip Mason, *A Matter of Honour: An Account of the Indian Army, Its Officers and Men*, Basingstoke, 1986; and David Omissi, *The Sepoy and the Raj: The Indian Army, 1860–1940*, Basingstoke, 1994.
7 For further details, see Sarah Ansari, *Sufi Saints and State Power: The Pirs of Sind, 1843–1947*, Cambridge, 1992.
8 For further discussion on ethnic politics, see Iftikhar H. Malik, *State and Civil Society in Pakistan: Politics of Authority, Ideology and Ethnicity*, Oxford, 1997.
9 For more details, see Ian Talbot, *Freedom's Cry: The Popular Dimension in the Pakistan Movement and Partition Experience in North-West India*, Karachi, 1996.

10 The rate of literacy and professional mobility remains the highest in Hunza area, due to better organization, less political wrangling, and because of funds and facilities made available by the Aga Khan program. Based on personal visits and field work in the area in summer 2006 in Gilgit and Hunza.

11 Ismail Khan, "Amid rising TTP gains, Army adopts new strategy," *News* (Lahore), 21 January 2009.

12 For a recent survey of religious pluralism, see Iftikhar H. Malik, *Religious Minorities in Pakistan*, London, 2004.

13 For a quick overview of Muslim history, see Karen Armstrong, *Islam: A Short History*, London, 2000.

14 The Aga Khan is a title and not a name. See K. K. Aziz (ed.), *Aga Khan III: Selected Speeches and Writings of Sir Sultan Muhammad Shah*, London, 1998.

15 Ernest Gellner, *Muslim Society*, Cambridge, 1983.

16 Some French scholars have opined a downward trend in such extremist violence, yet it is not fair to assume that Islam has lost its strong relationship with politics. See Gilles Kepel, *Jihad: The Trail of Political Islam*, London, 2006; and Olivier Roy, *The Failure of Political Islam*, Cambridge, Mass., 1994.

17 Some events have a combination of factors behind them. See Robert Fisk, "Once more fear stalks the streets of Kandahar," *Independent*, 20 November 2008.

18 Many observers are using it more often to underline the intensity of violence in the Muslim world. See Paul Berman, *Terror and Liberalism*, London, 2002.

19 Bernard Lewis leads a group of writers, opinion-makers, and propagandists who see everything wrong with the Muslims and their creed.

20 For more lively discussion on ethnicity and languages, see Tariq Rahman, *Language and Politics in Pakistan*, Karachi, 1996.

21 For more on the ancient Indus Valley civilization, see Mark Kenoyer, *Ancient Cities of the Indus Valley Civilization*, Karachi, 1998.

22 A. L. Basham, *The Wonder That Was India: A Survey of the Culture of the Indian Sub-continent before the Coming of the Muslims*, New York, 1954.

23 For a concise work on the Great Mughals, see John F. Richards, *The Mughal Empire*, Cambridge, 1996.

24 See William Dalrymple, *The Last Mughal: The Fall of a Dynasty, Delhi, 1857*, London, 2006.

25 K. K. Aziz, *The Making of Pakistan: A Study in Nationalism*, London, 1967; and Abul Kalam Azad, *India Wins Freedom: The Complete Version*, New Delhi, 1988.

26 For more, see Iftikhar H. Malik, *Islam, Nationalism and the West: Issues of Identity in Pakistan*, Oxford, 1999.

Chapter 1: Return to Democracy?

1 Shaheen Sehbai, "Zardari has forced a confused establishment to decide quickly," *News* (Rawalpindi), 29 August 2008 (available on www.thenews.com).

2 Farhan Bokhari, "Pakistan braced for new wave of violence," *Financial Times*, 22 September 2008.

3 While the Bush administration increased drone attacks on the border areas of FATA, most Pakistanis and analysts felt that these policies were only helping the militants. See Richard Beeston, "The weapon that could backfire," *The Times* (London), 25 November 2008.

4 *The Nation* (Lahore), 22 & 24 January 2009.

5 A vast majority of Pakistanis expected substantive changes under Obama. See Elizabeth Grice's interview with Imran Khan, *Telegraph*, 8 December 2008.

6 *Dawn* (Karachi), 23 & 24 January 2009. Widely reported on Pakistani television, these attacks were defined as a new surge in the offensive under General Petraeus in addition to heralding new political channels with Islamabad and Kabul.

7 "US casualties in Afghanistan to rise, says Biden," *Guardian*, 26 January 2009.

8 Holbrooke observed: "We call this situation Afpak. There will be more focus on Pakistan". Kim Sengupta, "US envoy in Kabul to map out surge," *Independent*, 13

February 2009.

9 Simon Tisdall, "World briefing," *Guardian*, 27 January 2009.

10 David Miliband, "War on terror was wrong," *Guardian*, 15 January 2009.

11 Christina Lamb, "Mission Impossible," *Sunday Times*, 12 October 2008.

12 Interview with BBC Radio 4, "News at One," 20 October 2008.

13 For such works reposing all their early hopes in the Karzai regime, see Ahmed Rashid, *Taliban: Islam, Oil and the New Great Game in Central Asia*, London, 2002; and Christina Lamb, *The Sewing Circles of Herat: My Afghan Years*, London, 2003.

14 Maleeha Lodhi and Anatol Lieven, "Heeding the lessons of another war," *International Herald Tribune*, 6 October 2008.

15 For more on this, Tariq Ali, *The Clash of Fundamentalisms*, London, 2003.

16 "Pakistanis unite to fight extremism," *Guardian*, 10 October 2008; and "Pakistanis sign anti-terror petition," *Dawn* (Karachi), 11 October 2008.

17 *Saturday Telegraph*, 11 October 2008.

18 To many observers, the Mumbai attacks had not only dented Indo–Pakistani confidence-building measures, they also reinstated the generals as the "ultimate guardians" of Pakistan. Based on personal interviews in Islamabad, Rawalpindi, and Faisalabad, 18 December 2008 to 4 January 2009.

19 Declan Walsh, "Pakistan hails progress in Waziristan. But will it stop the suicide bombers?" *Guardian*, 30 October 2009.

20 Pervez Musharraf, *In the Line of Fire*, London, 2006, p. 201. The seven demands by the US were brought in on 13 September 2001 by Wendy Chamberlain, the American ambassador to Islamabad. Some of them were quite extreme and equally couched in threatening language. Ibid., 204–7.

21 "The future begins today," Armitage said [to General Mahmud Ahmad]. "Pass the word to General Musharraf, the Pakistani president – with us or against us." Bob Woodward, *Bush at War*, New York, 2002, p. 47.

22 See Iftikhar H. Malik, "Military Coup in Pakistan: Business as Usual or Democracy on Hold?" *The Round Table* (2001), 360, pp. 357–77.

23 Pankaj Mishra, "The Churchill wannabes destroy any hope of a violence-free life in Pakistan," *Guardian*, 8 January 2008.

24 "US, Nato term situation in Pakistan dysfunctional," *Dawn*, 16 July 2008.

25 Ayesha Jalal, *The State of Martial Rule: The Origins of Pakistan's Political Economy of Defence*, Cambridge, 1990.

26 For further details on Ayub Khan and his reformism, see Altaf Gauhar, *Ayub Khan: Pakistan's First Military Ruler*, Lahore, 1993.

27 For details see Leo E. Rose and Richard Sisson, *War and Secession: Pakistan, India, and the Creation of Bangladesh*, Berkeley, 1990.

28 Pakistan's tripolar forces of authority, ideology, and ethnicity have conflicted largely because of a lack of consensus and proper interface between the respective forces of state and society, though such a problem may not be unique to Pakistan.

29 The speech was delivered to the national convention of Nazims in Islamabad. For details see *Dawn*, 16 August 2001.

30 In his offices in Edgware, London, Hussain has regularly received party leaders from across Pakistan. Imran Khan and a number of British Pakistanis threatened to pursue legal proceedings in the British courts against Hussain and his alleged role in urban violence in Karachi. *Daily Telegraph*, 15 May 2007.

31 For more on the military's control of the country's resources and nomenclature, see Ayesha Siddiqa-Agha, *Military Inc.: Inside Pakistan's Military Economy*, London, 2007.

32 See Seumas Milne, "The war that can bring neither peace nor freedom," *Guardian*, 5 February 2008.

33 Anil Dharker, "In Mumbai's teeming history lies the hope for our recovery," *Independent*, 28 November 2008; and "At war level: India raises security status amid grief," *Guardian*, 1 December 2008.

34 David Miliband, "War on Terror was Wrong," ibid., 15 January 2009.

35 Ibid., 12 February 2008.

36 "Musharraf: Obstacle to Stability," BBC Online, 14 February 2008, http://news.bbc.co.uk/1/hi/world/south_asia/7244018.stm

Chapter 2: Dictators and Dynasties

1 For an account based on secret police reports on the violence, see Patrick French, *Liberty or Death? India's Journey to Independence and Division*, London, 1997.

2 Pervez Musharraf, *In the Line of Fire: A Memoir*, London, 2006, p. 12.

3 A few days later, he was moved to Lahore and finally to Sialkot, "where the famous tank battles of Chawindah were fought. At the end of the war this sector was to become a graveyard of Indian tanks." Musharraf, pp. 45–6.

4 Musharraf, p. 49, 55, 58.

5 While Ali Quli Khan had been superseded by Musharraf, his predecessor General Jahangir Karamat had resigned as the chief of army staff following his suggestion of involving senior defense staff in political decisions through what he called the National Security Council.

6 Musharraf, pp. 86–98.

7 In his interviews, Sharif mentioned Pakistani casualties in the conflict and Musharraf's growing concern about a possible enquiry into the Kargil fiasco, which hastened him and his close colleagues to preempt it with their coup.

8 As late as 2006, Musharraf still held to the myth of universal approval of his takeover, assuming that everyone was fed up with the Sharif government "and impatient to be rid of it." Musharraf, pp. 116, 127.

9 He remained dismissive of Benazir Bhutto, who treated the party and the office like a family property. Musharraf, p. 175.

10 It was one of the main mosques in Islamabad with two seminaries attached to it. Allegedly, its clerics had been involved in gun-running and it was stormed by troops in July 2007, killing many students hiding inside the premises.

11 Mike Marqusee, "Say mullah, and you also say military," *Guardian*, 26 July 2005.

12 Many Pakistanis had been handed over to the CIA, while hundreds were held at different detention centers by the ISI, FIA, IB, and the CID. In 2007 alone, according to a report by the US Department of State, 1,600 Pakistanis remain missing. "US report takes up issue of the missing," *Dawn*, 13 March 2008.

13 It is unclear, even after such a long time, how Mr. Bokhari got hold of millions of email addresses all over the world.

14 These jubilations in Karachi, Lahore, Murree, Rawalpindi, Islamabad, and smaller towns were witnessed by the author between July and August 2007.

15 "Musharraf Obstacle to Stability," BBC Online, 14 February 2008, http://news.bbc.co.uk/1/hi/world/south_asia/7244018.stm

16 Interestingly, this was the second Provisional Constitution Order (PCO) that Musharraf promulgated to concentrate powers in his person and office.

17 In a five-page letter to the president of the US Bar Association, Musharraf put forward a list of allegations against Justice Iftikhar Chaudhry, though he claims to have selected him "strictly on merit, as he was then the senior-most judge of the Supreme Court." Pervez Musharraf to William Neukon, 26 December 2007, available on www.pkpolitics.com, accessed on 13 March 2008.

18 Shyam Bhatia, *Goodbye Shahzadi: A Political Biography of Benazir Bhutto*, New Delhi, 2008, p. 16.

19 His father Altaf Gauhar, a close associate of General Ayub Khan and the latter's powerful secretary of information, had drafted Khan's autobiography *Friends not Masters*, Oxford, 1968.

20 Benazir Bhutto, *Daughter of the East: An Autobiography*, London, 1988, 2007 p. 18.

21 "Many in Pakistan have come to believe that the victimisation of the Bhutto family and our supporters was the Karbala of our generation. The father was not spared. The mother was not spared. The brothers were not spared. The daughter was not spared. The band of followers was not spared. Yet, like the followers of the Prophet's grandson, our resolve never faltered." Benazir Bhutto, p. 299.

22 The son of the US Ambassador John Galbraith, Peter Galbraith was her class fellow and close friend, both in the US and at Oxford. He became the US Ambassador to Croatia in the mid-1990s and helped BB relaunch her career.

23 Bhutto, p. 350.

24 While in London at the time, BB had expressed her readiness to work with Pervez Musharraf. Conversations with mutual friends, London, 13 October 1999.

25 She acknowledged the achievement women had attained over the past 20 years and noted: "I am a woman proud of my cultural and religious heritage." Bhutto, pp. xi–xii.

26 Bhutto, p. 430.

27 Bhutto, *Reconciliation: Islam, Democracy and the West*, London, 2008, p. 8.

28 Bhutto, pp. 1–3.

29 "What is perhaps most remarkable about the Musharraf dictatorship is the disconnect between its rhetoric and its actions concerning the containment of extremism and the pursuit of Al Qaeda, the Taliban, and Osama bin Laden." Bhutto, pp. 158, 215.

30 Bhutto, pp. 48, 68–70.

31 "If democracy is to take hold among the billion Muslims on this planet, the movement must come from our own people standing up to the forces of extremism, fanaticism, and authoritarianism within our own societies." Bhutto, pp. 149, 151.

32 Bhutto, pp. 301, 319.

33 Imran Khan's hospital in Lahore and his books and visual presentations on Pakistan have turned him into a role model for Pakistanis everywhere.

34 Elizabeth Grice, "Imran Khan: Playing for the biggest stakes of his life," *Telegraph*, 8 December 2008.

Chapter 3: Geopolitical Issues

1 For the history of this contested region, see Alastair Lamb, *Birth of a Tragedy: Kashmir*, Hertingfordbury, 1994; and *Kashmir: A Disputed Legacy: 1846–1990*, Hertingfordbury, 1991.

2 In fact, the terrorist attacks on the Indian parliament in 2001 and on several public buildings in Mumbai in 2008 had closer links with Indo–Pakistani acrimony over Kashmir. See William Dalrymple, "Pakistan in Peril," *New York Review of Books*, Vol. 56, No. 2, 2009.

3 Among several studies, one may mention one or two where the community redefinition owing to changes within India under the British control only exacerbated communalist consciousness across the board. See Gyanendra Pandey, *The Construction of Communalism in Colonial North India*, Delhi, 1990.

4 The ultra-right forces demanding India be seen and defined as a Hindu state. *Rashtra* means homeland/country.

5 For a perspective on these lines, see Ayesha Jalal, *Self and Sovereignty: Individual & Community in South Asian Islam since 1850*, London, 2000.

6 For its various explanations, see Ishtiaq H. Qureshi, *The Struggle for Pakistan*, Karachi, 1968.

7 "Mumbai attackers bodies still unburied," BBC Urdu, 20 November 2009, http://bbc.co.uk/Urdu/India/2009/11/091120_bodies_sz.shtml

8 Both India and Pakistan have allegedly been involved in such activities, either directly or through hired agents. Since 2002, both countries have been competing to gain more diplomatic ground in various power centers in Afghanistan.

9 See *Dawn*, 7 December 2008. The Indian Minister for External Affairs, Parnab Mukherjee, disputed making any such call to Zardari and instead attributed it to some Pakistani ploy, while Pakistanis insisted on its origin from Delhi official circles. See *Independent*, 8 December 2008; and also "In Wake of Attacks, India-Pakistan Tensions Grow," *New York Times*, 2 December 2008.

10 "Convoy attacks trigger race to open new Afghan supply line," *Guardian*, 9 December 2008.

11 In addition to Bernard Lewis, Daniel Pipes, Martin Amis, Michael Burleigh on the subject, see Paul Berman, *Terror and Liberalism*, New York, 2003; also John Gray,

Al Qaeda and What It Means to be Modern, London, 2003.

12 For more details on the NWFP, see Stephen Rittenberg, *Ethnicity, Nationalism, and the Pakhtuns: The Independence Movement in India's North-West Frontier Province*, Durham, N.C., 1988.

13 John Keay, *When Men and Mountains Meet: The Explorers of the Western Himalayas, 1820–75*, Karachi, 1993.

14 See Peter Hopkirk, *The Great Game. The Struggle for Empire in Central Asia*, London, 1994; Ahmed Rashid, *Descent into Chaos: How the War against Islamic Extremism is Being Lost in Pakistan, Afghanistan and Central Asia*, London, 2008.

15 For this post-1957 connection with some of the jihadis coming into Buner and other neighboring areas of Swat, see Charles Allen, *God's Terrorists: The Wahhabi Cult and Hidden Roots of Modern Jihad*, London, 2006.

16 Syed Wiqar Ali Shah, *Ethnicity, Islam and Nationalism: Muslim Politics in the North-West Frontier Province, 1937–47*, Karachi, 1999; and M.S. Korejo, *The Frontier Gandhi: His Place in History*, Karachi, 1993.

17 Olivier Roy, *Islam and Resistance in Afghanistan*, Cambridge, 1990.

18 This view was widely shared by Pushtun and non-Pushtun Pakistanis who believed that this was not Pakistan's war and was an engineered fratricide. Many felt that the Pakistani nuclear bomb had led to a consensus among non-Muslim forces to debilitate their country, and this twin-front campaign by NATO in the West and India in the East was meant to bifurcate Pakistan. The truncated maps of a smaller Pakistan, with Pushtun regions going to Afghanistan, were being widely discussed in Pakistan in late 2008, amidst serious criticism of Musharraf's unexplained commitments to Washington. Based on interviews in Pakistan during December 2008 and early January 2009.

19 For early background, see Robert J. MacMahon, *The Cold War on the Periphery: The United States, India and Pakistan*, New York, 1994.

20 See Ian Copley, "Islam and the 'Moral Economy:' The Alwar Revolt," in Asim Roy (ed.) *Islam in History and Politics*, Delhi, 2006.

21 For more on the Tablighi Jamaat and its expansion across South Asia, see Yoginder Sikand, *The Origins and Development of the Tablighi Jama'at (1920–2000): A Cross-Country Comparative Study*, Hyderabad, 2002.

22 Taj ul-Islam Hashmi, *Pakistan as a Peasant Utopia: The Communalization of Class Politics in East Bengal, 1920–1947*, Boulder, 1992.

23 Some of these points have been raised in several studies on Indian Muslims, though it is not uncommon to see Pakistan being singled out as the major reason for the multiple underrepresentation and disempowerment of India's Muslims. For instance, see Mushirul Hasan, *Islam in the Sub-continent: Muslims in a Plural Society*, Delhi, 2002.

24 V.S. Naipaul, *Among the Believers: An Islamic Journey*, London, 2002.

25 V.S. Naipaul, *Beyond Belief: Islamic Excursions Among the Converted*, London, 1999.

26 For a review, see Iftikhar H. Malik, *Crescent between Cross and Star: Muslims and the West after 9/11*, Karachi, 2006, pp. 170–82.

27 While making such claims, one has to be careful, since 1857 usage of the term *"Wahabbis"* has been quite common in official reports. After 9/11, the quest for a single factor explanation of the complex phenomenon of Political Islam has often been reduced to individuals, like Abdullah bin Wahhab, Syed Qutb, and Syed Mawdudi. For instance, see Charles Allen, op. cit.

28 It is true that the fiasco of Islamabad's Red Mosque, resulting in a police siege and more than 100 deaths in July 2007 had more to do with official inefficiency and the unexplained role of different intelligence outfits that had used some of these clerics during the 1980s for mounting jihad in Kashmir and Afghanistan.

29 Zulfikar Ali Bhutto's summit in Lahore in 1974 stemmed from a similar idealism and made Pakistan more West-oriented, with South Asia usually seen only as negative baggage to bring down an otherwise weakened country.

30 Muhammad Iqbal (1875–1938), the famous poet-philosopher, was the architect of such ideas and hoped for universal salvation where Islam would operate as a solution

and not as a problem.

31 For an interesting discourse, see Fazlur Rahman, *Islam and Modernity: Transformation of an Intellectual Tradition*, Chicago, 1982. See Khaled Abou El Fadl, *The Great Theft: Wrestling Islam from the Extremists*, New York, 2007.

32 One may give examples of Muslim Spain, Ottomans, Mughals, and the ruling dynasties in sub-Saharan Africa and Southeast Asia, which protected pluralism, even during their closing years when contemporary North Atlantic pursued hegemonic and racialized politics at the global level. For some recent discussion of this aspect, see Philip Mansel, *Constantinople: City of World's Desire, 1453–1924*, London, 1995; Mark Mazower, *Salonica, City of Ghosts: Christians, Muslims and Jews 1430–1950*, London, 2004; and, Abraham Early, *The Mughal Throne: The Saga of India's Great Emperors*, London, 2000.

33 Pakistani madrassas are routinely defined as Taliban factories, though there is no dearth of analytical works on these subjects. Jessica Stern, *The Ultimate Terrorists*, London, 1999.

Chapter 4: Partition and Punjab

1 At a private meeting in Oxford, a Pakistani academic surprised other guests by identifying India as his favorite place abroad. The academic cherished the cultural commonalities found there, as well as the element of respect that he encountered on his frequent visits across the borders.

2 Such attitudes are not confined to Punjabis, as the Urdu-speaking communities of Indian origin that settled in Pakistan for the last two generations also express similar sentiments. Altaf Hussain, the leader of the MQM, in a speech in India in 2006 dubbed Partition one of the biggest blunders in recent history. Despite raising some controversy, most educated Pakistanis took it as a rhetorical statement by a self-exiled politician settled in London.

3 Not only are visa applications routinely rejected, their processing through the intelligence agencies and the time factor involved in seeking "clearance" is itself quite taxing.

4 For more on Ghadar and its international dimensions, see Harish K. Puri, *Ghadar Movement: Ideology, Organization and Strategy*, Amritsar, 1983; Sohan Singh Josh, *Hindustan Gadar Party: A Short History*, 2 vols, New Delhi, 1977 & 1978.

5 The Unionist Party has attracted scholarly attention in India and abroad, though in Pakistan not enough work has yet been done due to a less developed nature of regional studies. See Ian Talbot, *Punjab and the Raj, 1849–1947*, Delhi, 1988.

6 Under this centralizing scheme, all existing western Pakistani provinces were integrated into a single unit, which created a grudge against the rulers who predominantly came from Punjab.

7 See K. K. Aziz, *The Murder of History: A Critique of History Textbooks Used in Pakistan*, Lahore, 1993.

8 In the case of South Asia, the empowering efforts by Mohandas Gandhi (and Muhammad Ali Jinnah) have been seen as a powerful retort to such Orientalist views. See Ashis Nandy, *The Intimate Enemy: Loss and Recovery of Self Under Colonialism*, Delhi, 1988.

9 See Iftikhar H. Malik, "Identity formation and Muslim Politics in the Punjab, 1897–1936," *Modern Asian Studies*, 29, 2, May 1995.

10 See Ahmed Saeed, *Islamia College Ki Sadd Saala Tarikh*, Vol. 1, Lahore, 1992.

11 For a similar case of population transfer between Greece and Turkey, see Mark Mazower, *Salonica, City of Ghosts: Christians, Muslims and Jews 1430–1950*, London, 2004.

12 Sarah Ansari, *Sufi Saints and State Power: The Pirs of Sind, 1843–1947*, Cambridge, 1992.

13 Claude Markovtis, *The Global World of Indian Merchants, 1750–1947: Traders of Sindh from Bukhara to Panama*, Cambridge, 2000.

14 *Pirs* are the spiritual mentors, whereas *waderas* are the rural landlords in Sindh.

15 Like elsewhere, print material was used to reconnect many Muslims to their religion. *Tabligh* parties undertook weekly visits to Muslim families, inviting them to spend time in the mosques where *pothis* were written in plain Bengali in order to refresh religious knowledge.

16 Rafiuddin Ahmed, *The Bengal Muslims, 1871–1906: A Quest for Identity*, Delhi, 1981.

17 Taj-ul-Islam Hashmi, *Pakistan as a Peasant Utopia: The Communalization of Class Politics in East Bengal, 1920–1947*, Boulder, 1992.

18 The *nawab* of this small principality within Punjab had helped Sikh elders in their early fight against the Mughals and thus his descendants were highly regarded by Sikhs. In 1947 this was the only area where communal violence did not take its toll.

19 For more on the mode and staggered nature of population transfer into and out of Sindh, see Sarah Ansari, *Life After Partition: Migration, Community and Strife in Sindh: 1947–1960*, Karachi, 2005.

20 See Simon Scott Plummer's interview with Christopher Beaumont, *Daily Telegraph*, 24 February 1992. Christopher Beaumont was Cyril Radcliffe's secretary, who left his personal papers to All Souls College, Oxford. Also DO/35-3054, "The Punjab Boundary Award," Public Record Office, London.

21 This certainly happened when Benazir Bhutto, while heading the Pakistan People's Party (PPP) became the Prime Minister in 1988, whereas Mian Nawaz Sharif headed the Punjab government of her opposition party, the Muslim League. Many walls in Lahore carried the graffiti: "*Jaag, Punjabi, Jaag!*" ("Wake up Punjabi, wake up!")

22 Salman Taseer and the Sharif brothers had longstanding personal differences, and Taseer's 2007 appointment by Musharraf as the governor of Punjab was done to neutralize the appeal that the Sharifs enjoyed among businesses and popular opinion. Taseer, by virtue of Musharraf's constitutional amendments, was equipped with discretionary powers, though he lacked any political backing yet continued to pursue confrontational politics with these Muslim Leaguers. His own past associations with the PPP were revived after Zardari's presidential ascendance and led to various suppositions about Zardari's real motives concerning Punjab. While the lawyers re-energized their movement in 2009, the Sharif brothers, without denouncing Zardari, declared to support the vocal judges. In the meantime, the cases lodged against the Sharifs' eligibility went on for months. These cases were based on a petition that, by entering into a written agreement with Musharraf in 2000, the Sharif brothers had foregone their right to actively hold any public office for a decade.

23 *Dawn*, 26 February, 2009; also *Daily Telegraph*, 26 February 2009.

Chapter 5: The Middle Classes

1 See Richard Reeves, *Journey to the Frontier*, New York, 1983; Emma Duncan, *Breaking the Curfew: A Political Journey through Pakistan*, London, 1989; Christina Lamb, *Waiting for Allah: Pakistan's Struggle for Democracy*, London, 1991; and, V.S. Naipaul, *Beyond Belief: Islamic Excursions among the Converted*, London, 1999.

2 There are popular works which acknowledge the basic goodness of ordinary Pakistanis. For instance, see Kathleen Jamie, *Among Muslims: Meetings at the Frontiers of Pakistan*, London, 2002.

3 See Asne Seierstad *The Bookseller of Kabul*, New York, 2002; and Khaled Hosseini *The Kite Runner* (a novel), London, 2003.

4 The views about Political Islam, especially those following the dissolution of the Cold War, have seriously affected such works which seek a single-factor explanation for Muslim disaffection. See Bernard Henri-Levy, *Who Killed Daniel Pearl?* translated by James X. Mitchell, London, 2004.

5 A wide variety of books reveal varying degrees of research and vigor, but, in some cases, even their titles betray a form of sensationalism. See Christophe Jaffrelot, *Pakistan: Nationalism without Nation?* London, 2002.

6 Mark A. LeVine, "Pakistan's Precarious Balance," History News Network.

7 Ibid.

8 Stephen P. Cohen, "Pakistan's Fear of Failure," *Asian Wall Street Journal*, 23 October

2000. Stephen Cohen, *The Idea of Pakistan*, Washington D.C., 2004; and Lawrence Ziring, *Pakistan: At the Crosscurrent of History*, Oxford, 2003.

9 Frederic Grare, *Pakistan: The Myth of an Islamist Peril*, Policy Brief No. 45, Washington, DC, Carnegie Endowment for International Peace, February 2006.

10 Interview with S.R.V. Nasr, "Muslim Democracy," 4 November 2005, http://pewforum.org/events/?eventID=91, accessed on 30 April 2007.

11 Personal notes of President Musharraf's speech at the Oxford Union Society, 16 September 2006; also his *In the Line of Fire: A Memoir*, New York, 2006, pp. 181–94. For speeches by Shaukat Aziz in Beijing on Pakistan's economic performance, see *Dawn*, 17 & 18 April 2007.

12 Adnan Hassan of the World Bank felt that Pakistan ranked higher than many other economies in areas of building business links.

13 The end of the report concurred with this view: "But if the rewards of the boom don't start trickling down, the country's runaway growth could ironically prove to be the government's undoing." Ron Moreau, "Pakistan: A Most Surprising Story, *Newsweek International*, 27 March 2006.

14 William Dalrymple, "A New Deal in Pakistan," *New York Review of Books*, Vol. 55, No. 5, 3 April 2008.

15 Dalrymple, pp. 3–7.

16 William Dalrymple, "Pakistan in Peril," *New York Review of Books*, 56, 2 January 2009.

17 Views based on several informal interviews in India during 1997 and 2006.

18 Yoginder Sikand, "'Progressive Islam' in Pakistan," *Himal Magazine*, May–June 2006.

19 These are ultra-right Hindu parties intent upon changing Indian polity from its secular moorings to a Hindu state.

20 Subhash Kapila, "Pakistan: Do a 'Civil Society' and a 'Peace Constituency' Exist?" South Asia Analysis Group, Paper No. 917, 18 August 2006.

21 Here, explanations by sociologists such as Max Weber, R.H. Tawney, Benedict Anderson, and Ernest Gellner can be referred to as a more modernist view of class formation and identity politics.

22 Sabiha Hafeez, "Social Structure of Pakistan: An Attempt at Developing Some Concepts," *Pakistan Development Review*, XXIV, 3–4, Autumn–Winter 1985, p. 619.

23 Saifur Rahman Sherani, "*Ulema* and *Pir* in the Politics of Pakistan," in Hastings Donnan and Pnina Werbner (eds.) *Economy & Culture in Pakistan: Migrants and Cities in a Muslim Society*, London, 1991.

24 See articles by Faisal Bari and Rasul B. Rais in *Dawn*, 1 August 2004.

25 Abbas Rashid, "Reviewing the state of the middle class," *Daily Times*, 14 August 2004.

26 I have raised this issue in reference to Sufis and Bhagats in early South Asian society. See Iftikhar H. Malik, "Between Identity-Politics and Authoritarianism in Pakistan," in Amyn Sajoo (ed.) *Civil Society in the Muslim World: Contemporary Perspectives*, London, 2002.

27 Akbar Zaidi, "Defining Civil Society," *Dawn*, 18 August 2006, and in *Economic and Political Weekly*, 3 December 2005.

28 Zaidi finds civil society in Pakistan more in tune with liberal but essentially non-democratic forces.

29 S.M. Naseem, "Pakistan's Messy Democracy," *Economic and Political Weekly*, 25 February 2006.

30 *Wakf* meant official land grants to seminaries and shrines by Muslim rulers.

31 Criticism of this argument could be that the serving military and civil officials are status quoists and centrists by profession and disposition. However, on retirement, many of them try to sound liberal and progressive.

32 Abdus Samad, "Our feudal cities are designed only for the rich," www.chowk.com/show_article.cgi?aid=00003968&channel=civi%20center, accessed on 5 May 2007.

33 Zubeida Mustafa, "What Hurts is the Rich-Poor Divide," *Dawn*, 24 April 2007.

34 See Tariq Rahman, *Language and Politics in Pakistan*, Karachi, 1996.

35 For a view reflective of the growing enchantment with the military among middle-class Pakistanis, see Afshan Subohi, "Military and Civilian Welfare Outfits," *Dawn*, 30 April 2007.

36 These terms have been used by Ayesha Siddiqua Agha, a former Pakistani navy officer and now an analyst on security affairs. See "Military, Inc: The Political Economy of Militarization in Pakistan," www.wildsoncenter.org. Also: *Military Inc.: Inside Pakistan"s Military Economy*, London: 2007.

37 Some landowning families in Sindh who lacked sons would not marry their daughters off due to the fear of losing land. Instead, they would arrange their mock marriages to the *Quran* to show that they had performed the ceremony and did not need to find grooms for them. *Huddood* laws introduced under Zia, halved the clout of women's evidence in the courts as well as curtailed rights.

38 Uzma Rizvi, "Working women in Pakistan: Book Review of *Taboo* and *Between Chaddor and the Market*," *Women of Pakistan*, www.jazbah.org/taboo_chaddor.php, accessed on 1 May 2007. This is a well-informed website operated by women and offering extensive information on gender-related issues.

39 Shimaila Matri Dawood, "Will the Real Pakistani Woman Please Stand Up?" *Newsline*, March 2005.

40 Mukhtar Mai, *In the Name of Honour: A Memoir*, with Marie Therese-Cuny and Linda Coverdale, London, 2007.

41 Fawzia Afzal Khan, *No Shame for the Sun: Lives of Professional Pakistani Women* (review), *Comparative Studies of South Asia, Africa and the Middle East*, XXV, No. 1, 2005, pp. 252–3.

42 Kamila Shamsie, "Misguided Women," *New Statesman*, 30 April 2007.

43 For details, see "Fifty Years: Fifty Questions," *Herald* (Karachi), January 1997, pp. 132–92.

44 C. Christine Fair, Clay Ramsay, and Steven Kull, *Pakistani Public Opinion on Democracy, Islamist Militancy, and Relations with the US*, Baltimore/Washington, DC, The United States Institute of Peace and the Program on International Policy Attitudes (PIPA), January 7, 2008, www.WorldPublicOpinion.org. Another opinion survey conducted by the BBC Urdu Service in January 2008 showed pervasive Pakistani resentment against obscurantism and support for democracy. A vast majority of Pakistanis found Musharraf not conducive to democracy. Jill McGivering, "Musharraf 'obstacle to stability,'" BBC Online: http://newsvote.bbc.co.uk/ mpapps/pagetools/print/news.bbc.co.uk/1/hi/world/south_asia, dated 14 February 2008.

45 It imbibes modernity within a traditional mold, as observed by a British journalist in reference to such Muslim ideological groups. See Jason Burke, *On the Road to Kandahar: Travels through Conflict in the Islamic World*, London, 2006.

46 Ravian, "Economy: The Unease about India," *Daily Times*, 15 August 2004.

47 For a more recent discussion on these lives, see Farzana Shaikh, *Making Sense of Pakistan*, London, 2009.

Chapter 6: Islamist Parties

1 The elevation of Islam as the main identity marker among Muslim minority communities across the world may be due to a quest for identity within a pluralist set-up often in conjunction with a secularist ethos.

2 There has been an huge amount of literature on Islam and the West, modernity, fundamentalism, neoconservative clusters and the various forms of Muslim discourses offering diverse perspectives. See Tariq Ali, *The Clash of Fundamentalisms: Crusades, Jihad and Modernity*, London, 2003; also John Gray, "The Atheist Delusion," *Guardian Review*, 18 March 2008.

3 For a good intra-Muslim debate and the politics of Muslim India, see Aziz Ahmad, *Islamic Modernism in India and Pakistan, 1857–1964*, London, 1964.

4 For more on the founder of Pakistan, see Stanley Wolpert, *Jinnah of Pakistan*, Berkeley/Oxford, 2002.

5 For further details on Deobandis and Tablighis, see Barbara Metcalf, *Islamic Revival in British India: Deoband, 1860–1900*, New Delhi, 2002; Yoginder Sikand, *The Origins and Development of the Tabligh Jama'at (1920–2000): A Cross-country Comparative Study*, Hyderabad, 2002; and Muhammad Qasim Zaman, *The Ulama in Contemporary Islam: Custodians of Change*, Princeton, 2007.

6 Syed Mawdudi has attracted enormous scholarship within his own party and from the scholars of contemporary Islam. See Seyyed Vali Reza Nasr, *Mawdudi & The Making of Islamic Revivalism*, New York, 1996.

7 Studies on al-Qaeda and other contemporary groups seek out Qutb as the ideological mentor of their activism. See Paul Berman, *Terrorism and Liberalism*, London, 2002.

8 See Syed Mawdudi, *Al-Jihad fi Sabil Allah* (Jihad in the Path of Islam), Urdu, Lahore, 1989 (reprint). Also Frederic Grare, *Political Islam in the Indian Subcontinent: The Jamaat-i-Islami*, Delhi, 2002.

9 For further background, see Feroz Ahmed, *Ethnicity and Politics in Pakistan*, Karachi, 1998.

10 For an account of the CIA's involvement, see Bob Woodward, *Veil: The Secret Wars of the CIA, 1981–1987*, New York, 1987.

11 It was the ISI's political cell, led by Major-General Ehtesham Zamir, that manipulated the elections at the behest of General Musharraf. The general admitted his guilt during his retirement. *The News*, 24 February 2008.

12 For some analysts, Musharraf was partially sidelined, as was noticed during President Bush's visit to the subcontinent. However, the question being discussed in Washington, London, and elsewhere was: Who next? On the one hand, Musharraf was seen as a reliable asset but the country's governance problems due to the military's position and a continued political instability in the two provinces persuaded some foreign observers for a "smooth" changeover before it was too late. Many voices from within Pakistan also demanded a country-based policy from Western allies instead of merely banking on Musharraf.

13 The JI supported the presidential campaign of Fatima Jinnah in 1964–5 against General Ayub Khan and has exhibited pragmatism.

14 Based on personal visits and interviews in 2002–3.

15 A few years ago, the leaders of the JUH visited Peshawar to commemorate the founding of the JUH, and in May 2006 Maulana Fazlur Rahman was visiting India—which was certainly seen as a major development, given his earlier and longstanding criticism of India over Kashmir. In February 2008, thousands of Ulama gathered for deliberations at Deoband to distance themselves from the violence perpetrated in the name of religion, as well as alerting Muslims to challenges facing the community.

16 The JUI's previous support for Benazir Bhutto, and now its vote for the Speaker from her PPP, showed the JUI's desire to work with other mainstream political forces. The JI did not make the Speaker's gender an issue. Geo TV, live report from Islamabad, 19 March 2008, monitored in Oxford.

17 These groups belong to the Sunni majority in Pakistan, whereas Shias account for 20 percent of the country's population and have their own religio-political organizations. Usually on the receiving end, Shia groups have often retaliated by attacking Sunni rallies and mosques. The Shia militant group Sipah-i-Muhammad (SM) was also banned by Musharraf in 2002, along with these Sunni outfits, though all have now gone underground.

18 William Dalrymple, "A New Deal in Pakistan," *New York Review of Books*, Vol. 55 No.5,3 April 2008.

Chapter 7: Awaiting a Breakthrough

1 Soon after the Cold War, amidst escalating ethno-regional conflicts, some analysts warned of a growing number of failing states. See Robert Cooper, *The Breaking of Nations: Order and Chaos in the Twenty-first Century*, London, 2002 and "Why we still need empires," *Observer*, 7 April 2002.

2 This is not to suggest that the country's problems only emerge due to regional factors and forces, since most challenges to the country's peace and viability accrue from within its own boundaries, a fact recognized by even General Pervez Musharraf. Musharraf's speech to the All-India Muslim League conference, Islamabad, 21 December 2006 (personal notes by the author).

3 For an interesting perspective, see Mohsin Hamid, "General Musharraf: Pakistan's Big Beast Unleashed," *Independent*, 11 February 2007.

4 Based on personal interviews in India, November 2006. See also "India Overheats," *Economist*, 3 February 2007.

5 Such opinions were widely shared by knowledgable Pakistanis during informal meetings in March and December 2006. Even Musharraf, while critical of obscurantism, reminded his Western allies of the ill will created by festering political disputes across the Muslim world, which needed attention to win over Muslim trust. President Musharraf's address to the Oxford Union Society, 26 October 2006 (personal notes by the author).

6 Several writers have raised these issues, while media criticism focused on scarcity of quality teachers, competent texts, and proper research facilities. See Pervez Hoodbhoy (ed.), *Education and the State: 50 Years of Pakistan*, Karachi, 1998.

7 *Dawn*, 26 August 2006.

8 Graham Usher, *The Pakistan Taliban*, (Middle East Report), Washington, MERIP, 13 February 2007. Many Pakistanis felt that Pakistan was being singled out by its allies. Declan Walsh, "Rice puts Musharraf under pressure to rein in Taliban militants," *Guardian*, 19 February 2007.

9 Other than the fallout in the Kurram agency of the militancy engineered by predominantly Sunni Taliban and al-Qaeda elements, the sectarian violence in the settled area of Hangu also worsened, especially in late December 2008. Hangu is a major town within the district of Kohat and is also an area of Shia Pushtuns who often find themselves in conflict with their Sunni neighbours.

10 On 6 February 2009, a Shia procession was struck by a suicide bomber in Dera Ghazi Khan in southern Punjab. *Dawn*, 7 February 2009. The Sunni–Shia feuds and intermittent incidents of violence predate the Taliban and are not merely confined to Pushtun regions. In fact, Punjab and Karachi have often witnessed periods of violent sectarianism.

11 The view on Pakistan's security was posited as "very bad" in a special assessment by the US National Intelligence Estimate. Jonathan Landay and John Walcott, "Intelligence report: US anti-terror ally Pakistan 'on the edge,'" *McClatchy Newspapers*, 14 October 2008.

12 Andrew Buncombe and Omar Waraich, "Taliban broadcast 'Wanted' lists in Swat," *Independent*, 27 January 2009.

13 The autonomous nature of tribal groups, the tradition of building fortress-style houses, and the carrying guns have led to adulation as well as stigmatization. For an interesting perspective, see Robert Kaplan, *Soldiers of God: With Islamic Warriors in Afghanistan and Pakistan*, London, 2001.

14 For background, see Zahid Hussain, *Frontline Pakistan: The Struggle with Militant Islam*, London, 2007.

15 Pervez Musharraf, *In the Line of Fire: A Memoir*, London, 2006, p. 237. For other personal accounts of such illegal transfers, see Moazzam Begg, *Enemy Combatant: A British Muslim's Journey to Guantanamo and Back*, London, 2006; and the *Economist*, 3 February 2007. "EU countries ignored CIA terror suspect flights, report says," *Guardian*, 14 February 2007. For a well-informed monograph on Guantanamo, see David Rose, *Guantanamo: America's War on Human Rights*, London, 2004.

16 In a procession in Kabul on 23 February 2007, following the proposed amnesty for Afghan warlords, participants marched through the streets chanting slogans such as "Death to America." "Afghan warlords in amnesty rally," BBC Online, 23 February 2007, http://news.bbc.co.uk/1/hi/world/south_asia/6389137.stm

"Death to America" and "Death to Karzai" were the slogans raised in Jalalabad in early March 2007 when US troops opened indiscriminate fire on civilians following the suicide bombing of a convoy. In Bajaur agency, 26,000 children were deterred from receiving the polio vaccination by clerics who called it an American conspiracy to sterilize Muslims. While administering the vaccination, the Pushtun doctor Abdul Ghani Khan was killed. *The News*, 23 February 2007.

17 Barbara Plett, "Generals urge Musharraf rethink," BBC Online, 26 July 2006.

18 The News International, 9 November 2009.

19 Daniel Markey, *Pakistani Partnerships with the United States: An Assessment*, Washington, DC, The National Bureau of Asian Research, November 2009.

20 Ted R. Bromund, Morgan L. Roach, "Islamist Terrorist Plots in Great Britain: Uncovering the Global Network," Washington, DC, Heritage Foundation, October 2009.

21 M. Qasim Zaman, *The Ulama in Contemporary Islam: Custodians of Change*, Karachi, 2004.

22 In a speech at the American Enterprise Institute in Washington on 15 February 2007, President George W. Bush reiterated his support for Musharraf, verbally acknowledging his commitment to fighting terrorism. *Dawn*, 16 February 2007.

23 For comment on these parallel policies and pressures on Pakistan, see Khalid Hasan, "Open Season on Pakistan, Hallelujah!," *Daily Times*, 4 March 2007.

24 *Guardian*, 3 March 2007.

25 The military and foreign factors in the evolution of the Taliban remain quite visible in such accounts. See Kamal Matinuddin, *The Taliban Phenomenon*, Karachi, 1999.

26 Ahmed Rashid, *Taliban: Islam, Oil and the New Great Game in Central Asia*, London, 2000.

27 Christina Lamb, "Rogue Pakistan spies aid Taliban in Afghanistan," *Sunday Times*, 3 August 2008.

28 While Pakistani parliamentarians debated a bill to safeguard women's rights against forced marriages, gang rapes, and other customs in some areas, there were reports of women being exchanged in marriage to settle old disputes and in two cases being raped by the aggrieved party on the orders of an assembly of tribal elders. For details, see *Guardian*, 13 February 2007.

29 Peter Baker, David Sanger, and Eric Schmitt, "Obama's Speech on Afghanistan to Envision Exit," *New York Times*, 29 November 2009; Karen DeYoung, "US offers new role for Pakistan," *Washington Post*, 30 November 2009; Pamela Constable, "Pakistan's Zardari holds his political foes – for now," *Washington Post*, 1 Dec 2009.

30 Shaheen Sehbai, "Obama administration fears Zardari collapse," *News International*, 1 Dec 2009.

31 For well-researched data on linguistic and ethnic pluralism, see Tariq Rahman, *Language, Education and Culture*, Karachi, 1999.

Epilogue

1 *Dawn*, 26 February 2009; and the *Daily Telegraph*, 26 February 2009.

2 Shaheen Sehbai, "Zardari has forced a confused establishment to decide quickly," *The News*, 29 August 2008.

3 Tariq Ali, "Musharraf will be gone in days," *Guardian*, 14 August 2008.

4 Prior to the oath-taking ceremony for the cabinet, this protest by ministers had been agreed by Zardari, Nawaz Sharif, and Asfandyar Wali Khan.

5 The ANP government in the NWFP, as well as public pressure convinced Zardari to hold talks with Maulana Sufi Muhammad, as peace was prioritized over every other consideration. Geo TV News, monitored in Oxford 15–16 February 2009.

6 Robin Wright and Joby Warrick, "US Steps up Unilateral Strikes in Pakistan," *Washington Post*, 27 March 2008.

7 *Guardian*, 3 April 2008.

8 Quoted in *Dawn*, 4 April 2008.

9 Ann Scott Tyson, "Border Complicates War in Afghanistan," *Washington Post*, 4 April 2008.

10 "Pakistan to 'weed out' Taliban sympathisers," *Guardian*, 2 August 2008.

11 Christina Lamb, "Rogue Pakistan spies aid Taliban in Afghanistan," *Sunday Times*, 3 August 2008.

12 "Since 9/11, the ISI had been chastised of nationalist and Islamist elements under the American pressure and its 'upper ranks [were] top-heavy with too many yes-men and paper-passers,' though it had its own groups of Pushtun officers who felt it 'right to warn Pakistani citizens of impending US air attacks that kill large number of civilians." Eric S. Margolis, "Can't win in Afghanistan? Blame Pakistan," 4 August 2008, www.ericmargolis.com/archives/2008/08/canat_win_in_af.php, accessed on 5 August 2008.

13 For more details see *Dawn*; and the *Independent*, 4 September 2008.

14 Kim Sengupta, "US envoy in Kabul to map out surge," ibid., 12 February 2009 and *Dawn*, 13 February 2009.

15 Asif Ali Zardari, "Democracy within Our Reach," *Washington Post*, 4 September 2008. He reiterated these views in an interview with ABC TV, praising Pakistani troops for standing in the way of the Talibanization of the entire country. *Dawn*, 14 February 2009.

16 The operation, as shown on television, also claimed to have killed 58 "miscreants." Geo TV, news report, 7 February 2009; also *Dawn*, 8 February 2009.

17 Cyril Almeida, "The president's roadmap," *Dawn*, 3 September 2008.

18 Washington chose to deliver vital military equipment and four F-16s to Pakistani generals at a time when the prime minister was on his first state visit to the United States and ideally should have received the cache himself.

19 It was suggested that other than the precarious situation surrounding Peshawar, supposedly "the number of foreign fighters entering Pakistan is said to be now much higher than those entering Iraq. And they are coming to Pakistan not only to fight in Afghanistan, but in Pakistan itself." Martin Woollacott, "National insecurity. The Pakistani army must change its tactics against the militants, if it is to halt a descent into chaos," *Guardian*, 30 July 2008.

20 "There must be no return to military rule" (editorial), *Independent*, 21 February 2008.

21 Amir Wasim, "86 per cent think Pakistan headed in wrong direction," *Dawn*, 18 July 2008.

POLITICAL PARTIES AND PLAYERS

All-India Muslim League (AIML) was founded in 1906 in Dhaka to voice Indian Muslim concerns to the British Government in view of the coming political reforms of 1909, which allowed some political rights to Indians. It was felt that India's second-largest community needed its own representation, as the Hindu majority had its own representation through the All-India National Congress (AINC). Initially, the AIML and AINC worked in close cooperation, but gradually came to represent two distinct political creeds. Since 1940, the AIML, under the leadership of Muhammad Ali Jinnah, proposed a separate Muslim nation and was credited with obtaining the separate state of Pakistan. After Partition, the AIML became the Pakistan Muslim League and often suffered from factionalist politics.

All-Pakistan Women's Association (APWA) is a body of influential Pakistani women whose aim is better educational and civil rights for women in Pakistan, often led by the wife of the president or the prime minister.

Anjuman-i-Sipah-i-Sahaba Pakistan (ASSP/SSP) was an anti-Shia group of Sunni militants founded in 1980 as a reaction to the Iranian Revolution. During the 1990s, the group was renamed Sipah-i-Sahaba Pakistan. It was eventually banned in 2002.

Awami League (AL) was mainly founded in East Pakistan in 1949, and was known as the Awami Muslim League until 1955. Initially led by the Bengali politician Huseyn Shaheed Suhrawardy, it soon came under the control of Sheikh Mujibur Rahman, especially after Maulana Abdul Hamid Bhashani left to join the Awami National Party in 1957. Rahman made his Six-Point Formula the main agenda during the election of 1970 and sought equal but separate rights for East Pakistan. Following the military operation, East Pakistan emerged as Bangladesh, with the AL often ruling the country. Since Rahman's assassination in 1975, the AL has been led by his daughter Sheikh Hasina Wajid, who is currently the Prime Minister of Bangladesh.

Awami National Party (ANP) is the mainstream Pushtun nationalist party. The group espouses nonsectarian, progressive policies and has ruled the NWFP off and on and during the 1970s, and more recently since 2008. The party was formed under its present name by several former members of the National Awami Party (NAP) and other liberal elements in 1986. Its leaders have included Khan Abdul Wali Khan and Asfandyar Wali Khan, who come from the NWFP and subscribe to the principles of economic and social democracy.

Indian National Congress/All-India National Congress (INC/AINC)
The All-India National Congress was founded in Bombay in 1885 and is the oldest party in South Asia and the former British colonies. At its outset, the group preferred a loyalist policy toward the British control of India. However, after the arrival of Mohandas Gandhi on the political scene and the outbreak of riots in India soon after the First World War, the Congress began to seek complete independence. During the Second World War, the group was led by Maulana Abul Kalam Azad and Pundit Jawaharlal Nehru and mounted the Quit-India Movement. Despite early opposition to the Muslim League's demand for a separate Muslim state, the AINC eventually agreed to partition in 1947. Since independence, the Congress has often ruled India as the majority political party, though in recent years it has been rivalled by regional and communal parties.

Jamaat-i-Islami (JI) is a religio-political party founded in 1941 by Syed Abulala Mawdudi. The party's central aim was the Islamization of state and society through political and religious efforts. At Partition in 1947 the JI was divided, with a small group left in India. In 1971, a part of the JI evolved its own independent course in Bangladesh. One of the most organized parties in the subcontinent, the JI has often depended on support from students and the emerging middle class. Puritanical in its outlook, it is very selective in offering membership and engages in teaching and research. Since Syed Mawdudi's death in 1979, the party has been respectively led by the amirs (leaders) Mian Tufail Ahmed, Qazi Hussain Ahmed, and Munawwar Hasan. Its student wing is known as Islami Jamaat-i-Tulaba (IJT) and is visibly present in the student unions on many university campuses, providing a steady supply of members and workers to the JI.

Jamiat-i-Ulama-i-Hind (JUH) was founded in 1919 in India and led by Maulana Mahmud al-Hasan. This religio-political party advocated a policy of resistance to foreign control and a return to the purist version of Islam among Indian Muslims. In most cases, its founders and members were the alumni of known Muslim seminaries such as Deoband, and used written tracts and mosque-based networks to transform and organize Muslim societies. Most JUH leaders, such as Hussain Ahmed Madni and Abul Kalam Azad, were not in favor of a separate Muslim state and supported the All-India National Congress in its advocacy of a united, independent India. Following Partition in 1947, JUH devoted itself to religious teachings and Islamic education across India and assumed a low-key political role.

Jamiat-i-Ulama-i-Islam (JUI) was created in 1945 by former Deobandi clerics and members of the JUH to support the demand for an independent Pakistan. Its first leader was Maulana Shabbir Ahmed Usmani. The party advocates pan-Islamic politics but also believes in the sovereignty and democratic processes of the country. In the 1970s, it was led by Maulana Mufti Mahmud, an articulate scholar who broadened the party's electoral followings in the NWFP and Balochistan and turned it into a coalition partner with the country's other mainstream parties. After his death, his son Maulana Fazlur Rahman led the JUI, which supported Pervez Musharraf between 2002 and 2007 despite its avowed anti-American stance. Following the 2008 elections, the JUI was once again able to acquire ministerial positions and has avoided open confrontation with the Pakistani state. Its pragmatism is often seen as opportunism, yet the JUI's willingness to participate in electoral politics and avoidance of open support for the Taliban in Pakistan is equally appreciated by many Pakistanis, who may otherwise disagree with its purist and male-centered approaches to Islam.

Jamiat-i-Ulama-i-Pakistan (JUP) Comprised of Sunni Muslims and Sufi saints, the JUP was founded in 1948 at Multan and was led by Syed Muhammad Qadri until charismatic Sufi Maulana Shah Ahmed Noorani became its leader. Often supportive of democratic processes, the party has been opposed to extremist manifestations of Political Islam.

Lashkar-i-Jangvi (LJ) is a sectarian group of Sunni militants, founded in Punjab in 1996. The group was named after Maulana Haq Nawaz Jhangvi, who had been involved in an anti-Shia campaign and was killed in a revenge attack in 1990. The group occasionally worked with the Taliban in Afghanistan and was banned in 2002.

Lashkar-i-Tayyaba (LT) is a puritanical group involved in militancy in Indian-administered Kashmir, and recently has been implicated in the terrorist killings in Mumbai in November 2008. The group was founded in 1991 by Hafiz Mohammad Saeed, a former academic with close ties to the Taliban. It was banned in 2002.

Muhajir/Muttahida Qaumi Party (MQM) is predominantly a party of Urdu-speaking Pakistanis, and it is largely confined to Karachi. It emerged on the political scene in March 1984 to wrest political control of Pakistan's largest city away from parties like the JI and the PPP. In addition, it demanded more jobs and better housing for Urdu-speaking Muhajireen and immigrants. Soon the MQM became involved in ethnic battles with Sindhis, Pathans, and Punjabis to gain control of Karachi's streets and transport. When the Pakistani Army launched a military operation in Karachi in 1992, Altaf Hussain fled to London. During the 1990s, the MQM tried to reach out to other ethnic groups in Pakistan and renamed itself the Muttahida (united) National Party, but its main power base and voting bank remain confined to Karachi. Known for its strong-arm tactics, the MQM has been blamed for factional fighting, as well as killings aimed at other groups, throughout its 25-year political life. The MQM supported Pervez Musharraf until his exit from government in August 2008. MQM has been challenged by another faction called MQM Haqiqi (Real MQM). Karachi has witnessed target killings carried out by each group as they use tough tactics to try and command authority.

Organization of the Islamic Conference (OIC) is the alliance of all Muslim nation-states, and came into existence in 1974. The OIC holds periodic meetings and operates as a pressure group in world politics. Headquarters are in Jeddah, Saudi Arabia.

National Awami Party (NAP), founded in Dhaka in July 1957, is a leftist party that espouses social democracy. NAP leaders have included Maulana Bhashani from East Pakistan and Khan Abdul Wali Khan from West Pakistan. After the separation of East Pakistan in 1971, the NAP was mainly confined to the NWFP and Balochistan, where it established provincial governments and supported Zulfikar Ali Bhutto in formulating the constitution of 1973. But the group soon fell apart, with Bhutto dismissing the NAP's provincial government and jailing many of its leaders, including Abdul Wali Khan. In 1975, the party itself was banned and some of its members joined Sher Baz Mazari's National Democratic Party until the Awami National Party (ANP) evolved in 1986 and became a mainstream Pushtun nationalist party.

Pakistan Muslim League (Convention) was a Muslim League faction promoted by General Ayub Khan. The group became a ruling party, yet it disappeared with the political demise of General Khan in 1969.

Pakistan Muslim League (Council) is a faction of the Muslim League that supported Fatima Jinnah (sister to Muhammad Ali Jinnah) in her opposition to Ayub Khan in the 1965 presidential elections. The group's leaders included Mumtaz Daultana, Khairud Din, and Shaukat Hayat.

Pakistan Muslim League (Functional) is a faction of the Muslim League led by the Pir of Pagaro of Sindh and is known for its steady support of army generals, including Zia-ul-Haq and Pervez Musharraf.

Pakistan Muslim League (Nawaz Sharif Group {N}, PML-N) has been led by Mian Nawaz Sharif since the late 1980s. Mian Nawaz Sharif's younger brother, Shahbaz Sharif, headed the provincial government in Punjab during the 1990s and again following the elections of February 2008. This has proved to be the largest and most popular League group of all. Legal cases against the Sharif brothers by Musharraf were gradually overturned by the Supreme Court, which has added to their following and strengthened their party.

Pakistan Muslim League (Quaid-i-Azam Group {Q}, PML-Q) is the pro-establishment faction of the Muslim League, which General Pervez Musharraf created in the assemblies to provide himself with political support. It became a ruling group led by the Chaudhrys of Punjab and other anti-Nawaz Sharif Muslim Leaguers. With the departure of Shaukat Aziz and Pervez Musharraf from the political scene in 2007–8, the faction became rudderless. Often ridiculed in the press for collaborating with the generals, many in the PML-Q have been routinely embarrassed by criticism in the media.

Pakistan People's Party (PPP) was founded in 1967 by Zulfikar Ali Bhutto and remains one of the country's most popular political organizations. It has mainly revolved around the Bhutto family. In its early years, the party advocated Islamic socialism, and while in power during 1972–7 its government nationalized various banks and manufacturers. The PPP was persecuted by both General Zia-ul-Haq and General Pervez Musharraf until, in 2007, the latter coopted Benazir Bhutto through a power-sharing deal. After Bhutto's assassination in 2007, her widower, Asif Ali Zardari, led the PPP and became president of Pakistan. He continued to prepare their son, Bilawal, to assume PPP leadership. The party continues to pursue centrist policies and remains a populist force across the country. A few of its members became willing partners of Musharraf, but found themselves largely discounted by PPP supporters who remain loyal to the Bhuttos.

Tehreek-i-Nifaz-i-Fiqh-i-Jaafria (TNJF) Led by Shia clerics such as Allama Arif Hussein and Muhammad Musavi, the TNJF organization was founded in 1988 to counteract Sunni sectarianism. Over the past decade it has gradually assumed a quieter position in politics.

Tehreek-i-Nifaz-e-Shariat-i-Mohammadi (TNSM) is an Islamist movement established in 1992 in Dir and Swat by Maulana Sufi Muhammad to spearhead the implementation of Islamic Sharia law in the Malakand region. Following the US-allied invasion of Afghanistan in 2001, Sufi Muhammad sent in thousands of volunteers to fight against Western troops and was put under house arrest by Pakistani authorities. The TNSM was banned in 2002 and its workers disappeared. However, Sufi Muhammad reappeared and revived the TNSM, and in 2007–8 almost took control of vast Pushtun regions in Swat, Dir, Buner, and Malakand before Islamabad undertook a military operation in May 2009. Sufi Muhammad was subsequently arrested and tried, while his firebrand son-in-law, Maulana Fazlullah, remains at large.

Tehreek-i-Taliban Pakistan (TTP) is mainly Pushtun and began in the tribal regions of Pakistan (FATA) around 2005–6. Largely inspired by the Taliban in Afghanistan, the group derives its following from the militant ideology of using force to capture state power in order to Islamize the country. Mostly confined to North and South Waziristan, the TTP soon expanded to other Pushtun regions of the NWFP. Led by various firebrands advocating their own agendas, some Taliban leaders, like Maulana Fazlullah in Swat, came to be disliked for their murder of innocent citizens, flogging of girls, the destruction of schools, and campaigns against non-Muslim Pakistanis. While the Taliban in Afghanistan claim a fight against occupation, the TTP advocates the implementation of their version of Islamic law, which to most concerned Pakistanis smacks of oppressive ideology imposed by force.

Biographical notes on a number of the main protagonists in the political life of Pakistan and the region.

Ahsan, Aitzaz (1946–) Respected barrister, author, and Pakistan People's Party (PPP) leader. Studied at the University of Lahore and the University of Cambridge. Led a movement for the restoration and release of Chief Justice Iftikhar Muhammad Chaudhry in 2008–9.

Aziz, Shaukat (1949–) Born in Karachi and worked as a banker. First served as finance minister under General Musharraf and then as Prime Minister from June 2004 to November 2007. An expatriate who left for London in December 2007.

Bhutto, Benazir (1953–2007) Leader of Pakistan People's Party (PPP), daughter of Zulfikar Ali Bhutto, and twice prime minister of Pakistan (1988–90 and 1993–6). Educated at Harvard and the University of Oxford. Faced investigation and trial for corruption and left Pakistan in 1998, living mostly in Dubai and London. Returned to Pakistan in October 2007 after negotiating a power-sharing deal with General Pervez Musharraf. Published *Daughter of the East* (London, 1988) and *Reconciliation* (London, 2008). Was murdered at a rally in Rawalpindi on 27 December 2007.

Bhutto, Zulfikar Ali (1928–79) Sindhi landowner and lawyer. Studied at the University of California, Berkeley, and the University of Oxford. Served in General Ayub Khan's government as a minister until they parted company in 1966. Founded Pakistan People's Party (PPP) in 1967. After General Khan's exit and the separation of East Pakistan, Bhutto became president of Pakistan in December 1971. After the introduction of the Constitution of 1973, became prime minister. Overthrown by General Zia-ul-Haq in July 1977 and subsequently hanged on 4 April 1979 through a judicial verdict for the murder of a political opponent.

Chaudhry, Iftikhar Muhammad (1948–) Current chief justice of Pakistan. Dismissed by Musharraf on 9 March 2007 but reinstated by the Supreme Court on 20 July 2007 following a campaign by lawyers and civil society. Dismissed again on 3 November 2007 through an Emergency proclamation by Musharraf and put under house arrest. Released along with several other detained judges by the new Prime Minister Yousaf Raza Gilani on 24 March 2008. Galvanized Pakistanis during 2007–9, though Musharraf, Zardari, and some PPP leaders procrastinated on the issue of restoring judges. Reinstated in 2009 by the Zardari–Gilani regime following a mass campaign and protest marches by lawyers and Nawaz Sharif.

Fazlullah, Maulana (1974–) Known as "Mullah Radio," he is the son-in-law of Sufi Muhammad who founded a seminary in rural Swat teaching a narrow version of Islam. Supported by the Tehreek-i-Taliban Pakistan (TTP), he began campaigning against girls' schools, video outlets, and barber shops. His FM radio broadcasts radicalized many young Pushtuns, who soon began to run a parallel state in Swat, based on floggings and beheadings. Responsible for the murders of numerous policemen and other officials, with their brutal deaths graphically shown on the Internet, Fazlullah avoided cameras but used other modern technology including mobile FM transmitters. Following the military operation in April 2009, he went into hiding along with several of his well-known lieutenants.

Fazlur Rahman, Maulana (1953–) Purist leader of the Jamiat-i-Ulama-i-Islam (JUI) and influential parliamentarian. Born in Dera Ismail Khan and son of Maulana Mufti Mahmud, a known politician and Deobandi scholar. Supported Benazir Bhutto, Musharraf, and Zardari by accepting ministerial positions. Pro-Taliban and critical of US policies, he continues to enjoy support in some purist sections in the Trans-Indus regions.

Gilani, Syed Yousaf Raza (1953–) Born into a landed Pir family of Multan, he is a parliamentarian and PPP supporter. Jailed by Musharraf from 2002–7 for refusing to deny his party loyalty. Elected to the National Assembly on 18 February 2008. Won a majority vote to become the prime minister on 24 March 2008.

Haq, General Zia-ul- (1922–88) Educated in Delhi, army chief under Zulfikar Ali Bhutto, he overthrew Prime Minister Bhutto in July 1977 through martial law. Hanged Bhutto on 4 April 1979. Benefited from the Soviet invasion of Afghanistan in 1979 and pushed for Islamization in Pakistan as a military president. Killed on 17 August 1988 in a mysterious plane crash.

Hussain, Altaf (1953–) Born and educated in Karachi. Well known as a student leader and founder of the Muhajir/Muttahida Qaumi Movement

(MQM), he was accused of several human rights violations including murders of political opponents. Hussain fled to London in 1992 and became a British citizen. Through his stronghold on the MQM's central committee, he has effectively controlled the city of Karachi from his office in London. During a speech on a visit to India in 2006, he declared Partition to be the biggest blunder in history.

Iqbal, Sir Muhammad (1875–1938) Most prominent Muslim philosopher and poet of the 20th century, he studied at the universities of Lahore, Cambridge, and Munich. Viewed as the intellectual brains behind Muslim regeneration and as the architect of the idea of Pakistan.

Jinnah, Fatima (1894–1967) Philanthropist and sister of Muhammad Ali Jinnah. Helped her brother during the Pakistan Movement, acted as his official hostess after the death of his second wife, and challenged Ayub Khan in the presidential elections of 1965. Known as *Maadar-i-Millat*, or Mother of the Nation.

Jinnah, Muhammad Ali (1876–1948) Karachi-born lawyer known as *Quaid-i-Azam*, or the Great Leader. He trained at Lincoln's Inn, London, and practiced law in Bombay (present-day Mumbai). Became President of the All-India Muslim League and fought for Muslim interests in India. From 1940 onward he demanded a separate Muslim state— Pakistan—for Indian Muslims and became its founder and first governor-general on 14 August 1947. Known for his honesty and integrity, Jinnah is buried in Karachi, and is survived by a daughter, his only child.

Junejo, Muhammad Khan (1932–93) Sindhi landlord and parliamentarian who led a faction of the Muslim League. Became prime minister of Pakistan in 1985, and was dismissed by General Zia-ul-Haq in 1988.

Karzai, Hamid (1957–) Pushtun leader from the Popalzai tribe in southern Afghanistan. He studied in Delhi and lived in exile in Pakistan. Earlier supported the Mujahideen and the Taliban, but after his father's assassination in the 1990s, Karzai turned against the Taliban. The interim leader of post-9/11 Afghanistan, and formally elected as its president in 2002, he has been widely respected for his moderate and modernist views, although he has come under criticism because of the growing Taliban insurgency and large-scale corruption within his country. Protected by US security, Karzai ran for president in the disputed

August 2009 elections, and came under pressure to fight corruption and establish good governance.

Kayani, General Ashfaq Parvez (1952–) Former Director-General of the Inter-Services Intelligence (ISI), General Kayani became Pakistan's 14th Chief of Army Staff on 27 November 2007 following General Musharraf's retirement. Born in Punjab and trained at military academies in Jhelum, Abbottabad, and Fort Leavenworth, Kayani avoids interviews and in April 2009 was defined by *Newsweek* as the world's 17th most powerful person of the year.

Khan, Abdul Ghaffar (1890–1988) Born in Charsadda, near Peshawar, and known for his pacifism. Participated in the Khilafat Movement and led the Red Shirts Movement in the 1930s and 1940s. Demanded greater rights for Pushtuns in Pakistan, and subsequently founded the National Awami Party (NAP) in 1957.

Khan, Abdul Qadeer (1936–) Respected metallurgist who was trained in Holland during the 1970s. Founded nuclear research laboratories in Kahuta, outside Rawalpindi, and came to be known as the father of the Pakistani nuclear enrichment program. After 9/11, came under serious Western criticism for his alleged links with Iran, Libya, and North Korea and was dismissed by Musharraf following a public apology on national television. A severely ill Khan was released from house arrest in 2008, but was disallowed from traveling abroad.

Khan, Asfandyar Wali (1949–) Born in Charsadda, near Peshawar. The grandson of Abdul Ghaffar Khan and the son of Abdul Wali Khan, he is a Pushtun nationalist. Opposed to the Taliban, he is the leader of the Awami National League (ANP), which is the ruling party in the NWFP. He has been a centrist coalition partner with the Pakistan People's Party regime. Initially in favor of negotiations with Pakistani Taliban, he later supported military operations against them.

Khan, Ghulam Ishaq (1915–2006) Born in Bannu and educated in Lahore. Civil servant from the NWFP. Rose through higher ministerial offices to become the President of Pakistan in 1988. Differences developed between Khan and both Benazir Bhutto and Nawaz Sharif, whose governments he dismissed in the 1990s. Forced out of office in 1993.

Khan, Imran (1952–) Cricketing hero and now politician in Pakistan. Born in Lahore and educated at the University of Oxford. Founder of Shaukat Khanum Memorial Cancer Hospital and leader of Justice Party. He boycotted 2008 elections in protest over Musharraf's state of emergency.

Khan, Liaquat Ali (1895–1951) Muslim landlord from the United Provinces and a leading architect of the Muslim nation. Educated at the University of Oxford and a follower of Muhammad Ali Jinnah, he became secretary-general of the All-India Muslim League and the first prime minister of Pakistan in 1948. He was killed in Rawalpindi while addressing a public meeting. Among various speech collections, he published *Pakistan: The Heart of Asia* (Cambridge, Mass., 1950).

Khan, General Muhammad Ayub (1907–74) Born in the NWFP and studied at Aligarh Muslim University. He joined the British Army before the Second World War and became the first Pakistani to head the country's Army. Took over as chief martial law administrator in October 1958 and then became President through the influence of local bodies. He developed closer relations with the United States and China. Faced a public opposition movement and surrendered powers to General Yahya Khan in March 1969. Published *Friends not Masters* (Oxford, 1968).

Khan, General Muhammad Yahya (1917–80) Served in the British Indian Army and became commander-in-chief of the Pakistan Army under President Ayub Khan. He imposed martial law in the country in March 1969 and pursued a military operation in East Pakistan, which became the sovereign state of Bangladesh following a civil war and hostilities with India.

Khan, Sir Syed Ahmed (1817–98) Muslim intellectual and educationist, born in Delhi. He wrote books on Muslim regeneration in India and established a modern college in Aligarh, which subsequently became Aligarh Muslim University. A preeminent Muslim reformer, he was against the idea of Indian Muslims joining the Indian National Congress.

bin Laden, Osama (1957–) Saudi purist and leader of al-Qaeda. Helped the Afghan Mujahideen against the Soviet Union during the 1980s, but turned against the US during the 1990s and has been involved in high-profile attacks on the US and other Western targets, including the 9/11 attacks.

Amidst diverse reports about his health and safety, he was reported to have been hiding in the tribal territories on the Pakistan– Afghanistan borders.

Leghari, Farooq (1941–) Punjabi landowner and former leader of the Pakistan People's Party (PPP). Became president in 1993 and developed differences with Benazir Bhutto and then Nawaz Sharif. He was forced from office and formed his own party before aligning himself with General Musharraf.

Mawdudi, Syed Abulala (1903–79) Born and educated in Hyderabad, India. Muslim intellectual and founder of Jamaat-i-Islami (JI) in 1941. He opposed the military regime of Ayub Khan and sought the Islamization of Pakistan. The author of several books and commentaries on the Quran and one of the leading influences on Islamist movements in the contemporary world.

Mehsud, Baitullah (1974–2009) Born in the Bannu district of Pakistan, he emerged as the most powerful and feared leader of the Pakistani Taliban, especially after the death of another leader, Nek Muhammad, in 2004. In 2005, he struck a short-lived peace deal with the Musharraf regime—in exchange for money and the release of his detained followers, he released hundreds of Pakistani soldiers. Implicated in the murder of Benazir Bhutto though denied it. On 14 December 2007 formally founded the Tehreek-i-Taliban Pakistan (TTP) and emerged as the most powerful warlord confronting both NATO and Pakistani troops. Camera-shy like Mullah Omar and several other Islamists, Mehsud had been implicated in several suicide bombings across Pakistan. He was killed in a drone attack on 3 August 2009.

Mirza, Fehmida (1956–) PPP parliamentarian from Sindh, she is also a medical doctor and close associate of the Bhutto family. She was elected as speaker of the National Assembly in 2008, the first woman speaker of any Muslim state.

Mirza, Iskander (1899–1969) Powerful civil servant. Rose to become the governor-general of Pakistan and then president, before being exiled by General Ayub Khan in 1958. He died in London in 1969.

Musharraf, General Pervez (1943–) born in Delhi, grew up in Karachi and Ankara, Turkey. He joined the Pakistani Army's elite group, and

Nawaz Sharif appointed him as Army Chief. He led the Kargil campaign in Kashmir in 1999 and then overthrew Sharif on 12 October 1999. After 9/11, Musharraf benefited from a close alliance with the US and faced serious political and constitutional opposition in 2007. He imposed Emergency rule on 3 November 2007 and radically curbed civil liberties, the judiciary, and the media. Resigned as Army Chief on 28 November 2007, he was sworn in for another presidential term on 29 November 2007 amidst growing controversy and was forced to hold elections on 18 February 2008. He became very unpopular due to the war on terror and his domestic policies. Resigned on 18 August 2008 and moved to London.

Omar, Mullah Mohammad (1959–) Born into a peasant family near Kandahar, he is a Pushtun leader and founder of the Taliban in Afghanistan in 1994. Fought the Soviets during the 1980s. In 1996, he emerged as the Amir (leader) of the Taliban regime, though never accepted any official position; he went into hiding after the fall of the Taliban in 2001.

Qureshi, Moeen (1930–) International banker and expatriate Pakistani who lives in the US. He became caretaker Prime Minister for three months in 1993 and held elections in the country. He returned to the US to resume his banking career.

Rahman, Sheikh Mujibur (1920–75) Former student leader from Bengal. He followed H.S. Suhrawardy in his Awami League and demanded complete autonomy for East Pakistan. His party carried an absolute majority in East Pakistan and faced a military operation which led to his arrest. Became the founder-president of Bangladesh in 1972. Killed by military officials along with his family members in Dhaka in 1975.

Sami-ul-Haq, Maulana (1937–) Son of well-known Deobandi Pushtun scholar, he leads the well-known Darul Uloom Haqqania in Akora Khattak, outside Peshawar. He has tutored many Afghan and Pakistani ulama at his seminary, including Mullah Omar and Maulana Fazlur Rahman. A senator in the 1990s, he parted ways with Fazlur Rahman.

Sharif, Mian Nawaz (1949–) Born into a business family and educated in Lahore, he became chief minister of Punjab province under General Zia-ul-Haq; and was twice elected prime minister (1990–3 and 1996–9). Faced a coup on 12 October 1999 led by General Musharraf, and sought exile in Saudi Arabia in 2000. Returned to Pakistan on 10 September 2007, but was sent back to Saudi Arabia from the airport. He led the Muslim League (PML-N) and was blocked from participating in elections on 18 February 2008, but his party won the second-largest number of seats in the National Assembly and in Punjab. After Benazir Bhutto's murder, he emerged as the most popular leader in the country. The Supreme Court, controversially, disqualified him from holding any public office on 25 February 2009, during Asif Ali Zardari's reign. On a subsequent appeal, the Supreme Court overturned that decision, and other similar cases against him dating from the Musharraf era were thrown out by the court. A vocal supporter of the lawyers' campaign to reinstate Justice Chaudhry and other senior judges, he has become one of the most powerful leaders in the country.

Sharif, Mian Shahbaz (1950–) Younger brother of Nawaz Sharif. He was chief minister of Punjab from 1997–9, exiled by Musharraf in 2000, and lived in Saudi Arabia and London with his brother until 2007. In 2008, he was elected to chief ministership of Punjab, though the Pakistan People's Party (PPP) centrist regime disqualified his parliamentary seat as well as his chief ministership on 25 February 2009. The Supreme Court overruled the verdict on 31 March 2009, and he was restored to his former position. A loyalist to his brother, Sharif enjoys his own following among several sections of Punjabis.

Sufi Muhammad, Maulana (1942–) Pushtun cleric born in lower Dir, he was initially a Jamaat-i-Islami worker. During the 1990s, he founded the Tehreek-i-Nafaz-e-Shariat-i-Mohammadi (TNSM), demanding the complete systemic Islamization of the Pushtun regions of Malakand. Instigated thousands of volunteers to fight against Western troops in Afghanistan after 9/11, was interned by Musharraf regime, and his TNSM was banned. Released in 2008, he resumed his demand for Sharia law more forcefully. Entered an agreement with the Awami National Party (ANP)–Pakistan People's Party (PPP) regime for implementation of an Islamic judicial system in Swat on 13 April 2009, but soon began to issue decrees against democracy, parliament, and other official structures, calling them un-Islamic. His challenges to state authority led to the cancellation of the agreement and a military operation in Swat, Buner, Dir, and Malakand in late April 2009, resulting in the exodus of three million displaced people from these areas. Was arrested in Peshawar and has been under house arrest.

Tarrar, Rafiq (1929–) Lawyer and judge, educated in Lahore. With Sharif's support, he became President in 1997. Eased out by Musharraf in 2000.

Zardari, Asif Ali (1954–) Born into a Sindhi landowning family, he married Benazir Bhutto in 1987 and held a ministerial position in her government. Spent many years in jail on corruption charges and was released in 2004. Following Benazir Bhutto's power-sharing deal with Musharraf, these cases were withdrawn through the National Reconciliation Ordinance issued by Musharraf. Zardari became the co-chair of the Pakistan People's Party (PPP) after Bhutto's murder and emerged as the most powerful politician following the elections of 18 February 2008. He assumed the presidency on 20 September 2008. He has undertaken several international trips to seek financial and military support for Pakistan amidst a growing Taliban threat. His procrastination on the annulment of the Seventeenth Amendment, as well as other crucial powers enjoyed by the presidency, greatly diminished his public support. By late 2009 was struggling to survive in office, given the criticism of corruption and a weak administration.

Zardari, Bilawal (1988–) Son of Benazir Bhutto and Asif Ali Zardari, born in Karachi. Studied in Dubai and at the University of Oxford. After his mother's assassination, he became the co-chair of the PPP (with his father) and was renamed Bilawal Bhutto-Zardari.

al-Zawahiri, Ayman (1951–) Egyptian Islamist who rose to the higher echelons of Islamic Jihad and al-Qaeda. Originally an eye surgeon, al-Zawahiri has been viewed as a lieutenant of Osama bin Laden who, following the Western invasion of Afghanistan and the fall of the Taliban regime, was rumored to have been hiding in Pakistan's tribal regions.

BIBLIOGRAPHY

Abbas, Hassan. *Pakistan's Drift into Extremism: Allah, the Army and America's War on Terror*. Armonk, NY: M.E. Sharpe, 2004.

Ahmad, Aziz. *Studies in Islamic Culture in the Indian Environment*. Delhi: OUP, 1999.

Ahmad, Feroz. *Ethnicity and Politics in Pakistan*. Karachi: OUP, 1998.

Ahsan, Aitzaz. *The Indus Saga and the Making of Pakistan*. Karachi: OUP, 1996.

Ali, Tariq. *The Clash of Fundamentalisms: Crusades, Jihad and Modernity*. London: Verso, 2003.

Allen, Charles. *God's Terrorists: The Wahhabi Cult and the Hidden Roots of Modern Jihad*. London: Abacus, 2007.

Ansari, Sarah. *Life after Partition. Migration, Community and Strife in Sindh: 1947–1960*. Karachi: OUP, 2005.

Aziz, K.K. *The Murder of History: A Critique of History Textbooks Used in Pakistan*. Lahore: Vanguard, 1993.

Begg, Moazzam. *Enemy Combatant: A British Muslim's Journey to Guantanamo and Back*. London: Free Press, 2006.

Berman, Paul. *Terror and Liberalism*. New York: W.W. Norton, 2003.

Bhatia, Shyam. *Goodbye Shahzadi: A Political Biography of Benazir Bhutto*. New Delhi: Roli Books, 2008.

Bhutto, Benazir. *Reconciliation: Islam, Democracy and the West*. London: Simon & Schuster, 2008.

———. *Daughter of the East: An Autobiography*. London: Hamish Hamilton, 1988; Pocket Books, 2007.

Bhutto, Zulfikar Ali. *The Myth of Independence*. London: OUP, 1969.

Burke, Jason. *On the Road to Kandahar: Travels through Conflict in the Islamic World*. London: Penguin, 2007.

———. *Al-Qaeda: The True Story of Radical Islam*. London: Penguin, 2007.

Burki, Shahid Javed. *Changing Perceptions, Altered Reality. Pakistan's Economy under Musharraf, 1969–2006*. Karachi: OUP, 2007.

Butalia, Urvashi. *The Other Side of Silence: Voices from the Partition of India*. London: C. Hurst, 2000.

Caroe, Olaf. *The Pathans: 550 BC–AD 1957*. London: Kegan Paul International, 2000.

Cloughley, Brian. *A History of the Pakistan Army: Wars and Insurrections*. Karachi: OUP, 2006.

Cohen, Stephen P. *The Idea of Pakistan*. Washington, DC: Brookings Institution, 2004.

Corera, Gordon. *Shopping for Bombs: Nuclear Proliferation, Global Insecurity, and the Rise and Fall of the A.Q. Khan Network*. London: C. Hurst, 2006.

Crile, George. *My Enemy's Enemy: The Story of the Largest Covert Operation in*

History: The Arming of the Mujahideen by the CIA. London: Atlantic
Books, 2003.

Dalrymple, William. "Pakistan in Peril." *New York Review of Books* January
2009 (Vol. 56, No. 2).

_____. "A New Deal in Pakistan." *New York Review of Books* April 2008
(Vol. 55, No. 3).

_____. *The Last Mughal: The Fall of a Dynasty: Delhi, 1857*. London:
Bloomsbury, 2006.

French, Patrick. *The World is What It Is*. London: Macmillan, 2008.

_____. *Liberty or Death? India's Journey to Independence*. London:
HarperCollins, 1997.

Gauhar, Altaf. *Ayub Khan: Pakistan's First Military Ruler*. Lahore: Sang-e-Meel
Publications, 1993.

Gilmartin, David. *Empire and Islam: Punjab and the Making of Pakistan*.
London: I.B. Tauris, 1988.

Grare, Frederic. *Pakistan: The Myth of an Islamist Peril*. Washington, DC:
Carnegie Endowment for International Peace, 2006.

Gray, John. *Al-Qaeda and What it Means to be Modern*. London: Faber & Faber, 2003.

Haeri, Shahla. *No Shame for the Sun: Lives of Pakistani Professional Women*.
Syracuse: Syracuse University Press, 2002.

Hafeez, Sabiha. "Social Structures of Pakistan: An Attempt at Developing
Some Concepts." *Pakistan Development Review* (XXIV) 1985, pp. 3–4.

Haqqani, Husain. *Pakistan: Between Mosque and Military*. Lahore: Vanguard
Books, 2005.

Hasan, Mushirul. *Legacy of a Divided Nation: India's Muslims since Independence*.
London: C. Hurst, 1997.

Hurd, Douglas. *Memoirs*. London: Little, Brown, 2003.

Hussain, Zahid. *Frontline Pakistan: The Struggle with Militant Islam*. London:
I.B. Tauris, 2007.

Iqbal, Muhammad. *The Reconstruction of Religious Thought in Islam*. London:
OUP, 1934.

Jaffrelot, Christophe, ed. *Nationalism without a Nation?* London: Zed Books, 2002.

Jalal, Ayesha. *Self and Sovereignty: Individual & Community in South Asian Islam
since 1850*. London: Routledge, 2000.

_____. *The State of Martial Rule: The Origins of Political Economy of Pakistan's
Defence*. Cambridge: CUP, 1990.

_____. *The Sole Spokesman: Jinnah, the Muslim League and the Demand for
Pakistan*. Cambridge: CUP, 1985.

Jamie, Kathleen. *Among Muslims: Meeting at the Frontiers of Pakistan*. London:
Sort of Books, 2002.

Jones, Owen B. *Pakistan: Eye of the Storm*. London/New Haven: Yale
University Press, 2002.

Jones, Philip E. *The Pakistan People's Party: Rise to Power*. Karachi: OUP, 2003.

Kaplan, Robert D. *Soldiers of God: With Islamic Warriors in Afghanistan and Pakistan*. London: Vintage, 2001.

Kennedy, Charles H., ed. *Pakistan at the Millennium*. Karachi: OUP, 2003.

Khan, Muhammad Ayub. *Friends not Masters*. London: OUP, 1967.

Lamb, Christina. *The Sewing Circles of Heart: My Afghan Years*. London: Flamingo, 2003.

———. *Waiting for Allah: Pakistan's Struggle for Democracy*. London: Hamish Hamilton, 1991.

Levy, Bernard-Henri. *Who Killed Daniel Pearl?* Translated by James X. Mitchell. London: Duckworth, 2004.

Mai, Mukhtar. *In the Name of Honour: A Memoir*. With Marie Therese-Cuny and Linda Coverdale. London: Virago, 2007.

Malik, Iftikhar H. *The History of Pakistan*. Westport: Greenwood Press, 2008.

———. *Crescent Between Cross and Star: Islam and the West after 9/11*. Karachi: OUP, 2007.

———. *Jihad, Hindutva and the Taliban: South Asia at a Crossroads*. Karachi: OUP, 2005.

———. *Islam, Nationalism and the West: Issues of Identity in Pakistan*. Oxford: St. Antony's Series, 1999.

———. *State and Civil Society in Pakistan: Politics of Authority, Ideology and Ethnicity*. Oxford: St. Antony's-Macmillan, 1997.

———. "Military Coup in Pakistan: Business as Usual or Democracy on Hold!" The Round Table 2001: 360.

———. "Pakistan in 2001: The Afghanistan Crisis and the Rediscovery of the Frontline State." *Asian Survey* (42:1) 2002.

Mernissi, Fatima. *Women and Islam: An Historical and Theological Enquiry*. Translated by Mary Jo Lakeland. Oxford: Blackwell, 1991.

Metcalf, Barbara. *Islamic Revival in British India: Deoband, 1860-1900*. Princeton: Princeton University Press, 1988.

Minault, Gail. *The Khilafat Movement: Religious Symbolism and Political Mobilization in India*. New Delhi: OUP, 1999.

Musharraf, Pervez. *In the Line of Fire: A Memoir*. London: Free Press, 2006.

Naipaul, V.S. *Beyond Belief: Islamic Excursions Among the Converted*. London: Abacus, 1999.

———. *Among the Believers: An Islamic Journey*. London: Picador, 2003.

Nasr, Seyyed Vali Reza. *Mawdudi and the Making of Islamic Revolution*. New York: OUP, 1996.

Pandey, Gyanandra. *Remembering Partition: Violence, Nationalism and History in India*. Cambridge: CUP, 2001.

———. *The Construction of Communalism in Colonial North India*. New Delhi: OUP, 1990.

Qureshi, Ishtiaq H. *The Struggle for Pakistan*. Karachi: University of Karachi, 1969.

Rahman, Fazlur. *Islam and Modernity: Transformation of an Intellectual*

Tradition. Chicago: University of Chicago Press, 1982.

Rahman, Tariq. *Language and Politics in Pakistan*. Karachi: OUP, 1996.

Rashid, Ahmed. *Descent into Chaos: How the War against Islamic Extremism is Being Lost in Pakistan, Afghanistan and Central Asia*. London: I.B. Tauris, 2008.

_____. *Taliban: Islam, Oil and the New Great Game in Central Asia*. London: I.B. Tauris, 2002.

Rizvi, Hasan-Askari. *The Military and Politics in Pakistan, 1947–1997*. Lahore: Sang-e-Meel Publications, 2000.

Rose, David. *Guantanamo: America's War on Human Rights*. London: Faber & Faber, 2004.

Rose, Michael. *Fighting for Peace: Lessons from Bosnia*. London: Warner Books, 1998.

Rose, Leo, and Sisson, Richard. *War and Secession: Pakistan, India, and the Creation of Bangladesh*. Berkeley: University of California Press, 1990.

Saeed, Ahmad. *Anjuman-i-Islamia Amritsar, 1873-1947*. (Urdu) Lahore: Research Society, 1986.

Sajoo, Amin, ed. *Civil Society in the Muslim World: Contemporary Perspectives*. London: I.B. Tauris, 2002.

Shaikh, Farzama. *Making Sense of Pakistan*. London, Hurst & Co., 2009

Siddiqa, Ayesha. *Military Inc.: Inside Pakistan's Military Economy*. Karachi: OUP, 2007.

Sikand, Yoginder. *The Origins and Development of the Tablighi Jama'at (1920–2000): A Cross–country Comparative Study*. Hyderabad: Longman, 2002.

Stern, Jessica. *The Ultimate Terrorists*. London: Harvard University Press, 1999.

Talbot, Ian. *Pakistan: A Modern History*. London: C. Hurst, 2005.

Wolpert, Stanley. *Shameful Flight: The Last Years of British Empire in India*. New York: OUP, 2006.

_____. *Zulfi Bhutto of Pakistan: His Life and Times*. Karachi: OUP, 1993.

_____. *Jinnah of Pakistan*. Berkeley: University of California Press, 1984.

Woodward, Bob. *Bush at War*. New York: Simon & Schuster, 2002.

_____. *Veil: The Secret Wars of the CIA, 1981–1987*. London: Headline, 1988.

Zaidi, Akbar. *Issues in Pakistan's Economy*. Karachi: OUP, 1999.

Zaman, Muhammad Qasim. *The Ulama in Contemporary Islam: Custodians of Change*. Karachi: OUP, 2004.

Ziring, Lawrence. *Pakistan: At the Crossroad of History*. Oxford: Oneworld, 2003.

_____. *Pakistan: The Enigma of Political Development*. Boulder: Westview, 1980.

INDEX

ACKNOWLEDGMENTS

This book has benefited from my travels and conversations across Pakistan, India, the Continent, North America and the United Kingdom. My sincere gratitude is owed to a wide variety of authors, academics and fellow Pakistanis who shared their time, their hopes and fears, as well as their generous hospitality to reflect on the many challenges confronting their nation, which is otherwise endowed with immense human and natural potential. They agonize over external interference in the affairs of Pakistan as they grieve over their own domestic institutional chaos, ideological maze and the bleak failure of their leaders.

This study began with a message from editor Aruna Vasudevan, who had kindly remembered me from my earlier publications with Macmillan-Palgrave. Her persuasion led me to undertake this book, which then benefited from the professional care of Kate Parker, and then Marilyn Inglis who was spot-on in sifting through the labyrinths of my manuscript. Their colleagues Peter Crump, Melanie Dowland and Lorraine McGee, have each, in their own distinct ways, contributed to the production of this work.

I owe special thanks to my immediate family, especially Nighat, Farooq, Sidra, Kiran, Taimoor, Maymu, Raheel, Amara and, of course, Imaan, for standing by and ensuring my privacy and resolve. Supportive fellow historians at Bath and Oxford, along with the helpful staff at the Bodleian, the British Library and the National Archives, kept me traversing this path while daily teaching, frequent meetings and periodic conferences monopolized a great deal of my time and energy. Surely, Tariq Rahman's friendship has been a great source of inspiration.

This book is dedicated to my departed friend Ayyub, a creative soul and a warm human being who, from his resting place in Oxford, keeps an eye on an ascetic biker.

—Iftikhar Malik
Oxford